# THE LYTTELT HART-DAVIS LETTERS

# THE LYTTELTON HART-DAVIS LETTERS

Correspondence of George Lyttelton
and Rupert Hart-Davis
Volume Six 1961-62

*Edited and introduced by*
*RUPERT HART-DAVIS*

I rattle on exactly as I'd talk
With anybody in a ride or walk.
BYRON

JOHN MURRAY

Lyttelton letters © 1984 Humphrey Lyttelton
Hart-Davis letters and notes © 1984 Sir Rupert Hart-Davis

First published 1984
by John Murray (Publishers) Ltd
50 Albemarle Street, London W1X 4BD
Printed and bound in Great Britain by
The Pitman Press, Bath

British Library Cataloguing in Publication Data
Lyttelton, George
The Lyttelton Hart-Davis letters.
Vol. 6: 1960-61
1. English letters
I. Title II. Hart-Davis, Rupert
826'.914'08   PR 1347
ISBN 0-7195-4108-5

*This volume is dedicated
by its editor to*
**ROSALIE NUGENT**
*and to the joyful memory
of her beloved husband*
**TIM**
*who between them were
responsible for all this
correspondence*

# INTRODUCTION

When I introduced the first of these six volumes in 1978 I had no great hope that further instalments would be called for, but the dogged, some might say reckless, courage of my publisher has been rewarded with esteem, if not with much ready money.

I know of no other published correspondence that is so completely antiphonal as this one, each letter answered within a week (with a few tiny exceptions) for six years. In most collections of letters one longs to know what the recipient answered, but here the reader knows that he will get the answer on the next page, and this, as many readers have told me, has made for obsessive readability.

My greatest debt of gratitude is to my publisher John Murray, and to his wife Diana, who was the first person to read the edited first volume, and from whom all subsequent blessings have flowed.

Roger Hudson has proved to be the sort of publisher's editor that all authors pray for but seldom get. He has prevented many a howler and has watched over all six volumes with ruthless but benevolent scrutiny.

To the hundreds of satisfied readers, who have written to me from all over the world, I can send only a wave of heartfelt gratitude, and the same is due to the many who have identified quotations and other references for me. In particular I owe a great deal to my dear friends Ernest and Joyce Mehew, who have looked up countless incidents for me in libraries beyond my reach, and in the process have become experts in the misdeeds of clergymen and other anfractuosities of the human mind.

In case anyone is rash enough to start with this volume I should explain that Comfort was my wife; Bridget, Duff, and Adam my children. Ruth Simon had been my beloved prop and stay since 1946.

As before, in the first letters I have retained the opening and signature, which are afterwards omitted, since they are almost always the same: any variation is printed. Similarly I have given our full home addresses in the early letters and then abbreviated them. From Monday to Friday I lived in a flat above my publishing office at 36 Soho Square. At the beginning of this volume George was almost seventy-eight and I was fifty-three.

RUPERT HART-DAVIS

*Marske-in-Swaledale*
*October 1983*

Ruth
by Consuelo Haydon, 1950

R H-D

G W L

My dear Rupert

Now this really *is* a miserable affair—the cold fact being that we are kept pretty hard at work all day, and after dinner there has been a lot of 'Come and have a glass of port' which always dribbles on till near midnight. And one night my colleagues insisted on taking me to the pictures, if you please—a film called *The Man in the Moon* which they assured me was desperately funny, and indeed they laughed like prep-school boys at what seemed to me to be comicalities of marked insipidity. So what will you, as the French say?

Our whole trip to you was, as always, a real and refreshing break. Your welcome (being *vester*, not only *tuus*) is invariably warming to the cockles (whatever they may be) of one's heart. Your Adam is the sort of boy who reassures one about the country's future—a grand eighteen-year-old, and so Pamela thought too.

Yesterday we were among bibliographers and such, who were talking of a publication of yours of immense size and complexity, full of anagrams and other word-puzzles which do sound very baffling. Someone put the point that there could be no money in such a venture, to which another replied to the effect that R.H-D. didn't worry very much about that side of publishing. And subsequent remarks would have added to the tingling of your ears, if not to the pricking of your thumbs. (Would *Sir Richard Roos* be the book's name?)[1]

I go back to-morrow or Saturday and—*more meo*—am sure that the roads will be icy. Pamela picks me up here, she is at present at the Lawrences' house at Great Milton near Oxford. I was there once with friends who had a caravan. The horse was called Aaron and strongly supported my conviction of horse stupidity. It resisted capture every morning with a sort of lumpish skittishness, and playfully bit the

[1] By Ethel Seaton (1961). A study of a fifteenth-century poet.

owner of the caravan in the elbow, not really meaning to hurt, but as the animal weighed about a ton, it *did* hurt a good deal. I was always busied with setting out the breakfast arrangements.

Yours ever<br>G.W.L.

*7 January 1961*                                          *Bromsden Farm*
*Henley-on-Thames*
*Oxon*

My dear George

Knowing the orgiastic nature of all Examiners' Nights at Cambridge, I think it noble of you to write at all, let alone such an admirable letter. Your visit was, as usual, a tremendous success with all ranks, and I'm only sorry you missed Duff, who is now fully recovered and preparing to start his London career on Monday. This afternoon Adam played chess for Bucks v. Surrey in the Slough Community Centre, and I'm sorry to say was beaten in the thirty-fourth move.

I haven't sent you *Sir Richard Roos* because in any ordinary sense it is unreadable. Don't tell your Cambridge friends, but it has been entirely paid for by its author, so its lack of sales leaves my withers comparatively unwrung.

Today I have wasted much time observing the six long-tailed tits on the bird-table. None has ever come there before, but these six seem to have taken to it, and their combined weight deters even the bullying nuthatch. I hate starlings, don't you? Predatory, clumsy and verminous. Here are two of Max's triolets, which he wrote in a copy of Arthur Benson's *Beside Still Waters*:

> I wish I had been Papa,
>     That arresting Archbishop.
> Crozier'd Cantuar!
> I wish I had been Papa,
>     Whenever folk murmur 'Bah!
>         What sermons you dish up,'
> I wish I had been Papa,
>     That arresting Archbishop.[1]

[1] A.C.B's father Edward White Benson was Archbishop of Canterbury.

Nevertheless, it is my bounden duty to drone on;
And, even were it not, on I should drone.
'Tis hard to keep an always Christian tone in Babylon.
Nevertheless, it is my bounden duty to drone on.
The eighteenth-century divines' tone in comparison
With mine was an inebriating tone . . .
Nevertheless, it is my bounden duty to drone on;
And, even were it not, on I should drone.

There were two others, which I stupidly omitted to copy. One day it might be fun to bring out an elegant little volume of Max's poetical works, but now they would take some rounding up.[1]

I have finished *Oxford Apostles*[2], having enjoyed and admired it enormously. But how odious Newman was! A wonderful preacher and writer, no doubt, and of great personal charm—but chock-full of egotism, self-importance, self-pity, self-concern, the most tedious aspects of femininity—a real stinker, I should say.

By way of contrast I have begun Graham Greene's new novel, which is set, suitably enough, in a West African leper-colony![3]

Did you ever get Lady Lytton[4] and Charles Tennyson Turner?[5] They were supposed to go off to you last week, but our packer disappeared with bronchitis and his relief (a Heinemann man) is almost completely blind—he walked through a glass door recently—so that parcels have been going to extraordinary places. I'm delighted to say Lady Lytton is flourishing after her send-off last Sunday, and Raymond Mortimer rang up to say he was going to review Fleming, so the year is starting well.

Somehow soon, dear George, I shall simply have to put a term to my Oscar researches and reach some sort of expedient compromise between perfectionism and practicality. Ruth says, truly, that at this rate I might go on for years (it's five and a half already) and many of

[1] This was done in *Max in Verse* (1963), edited by J.G. Riewald and published by Stephen Greene.

[2] By Geoffrey Faber (1933).

[3] *A Burnt-Out Case* (1961).

[4] *Lady Lytton's Court Diary 1895–1899*, edited by Mary Lutyens (1961).

[5] *A Hundred Sonnets by Charles Tennyson Turner*, selected by John Betjeman and Sir Charles Tennyson (1960).

the lacunae that worry me will never be noticed by anyone. I know that's right, but I hate letting anything go until it's as good as I can get it. And I so seldom get more than a consecutive hour or two. If this were an American venture (like the Boswell papers or Horace Walpole's letters) it would be limitlessly subsidised, with a team of fully-paid full-time research-assistants. English scholarship (I don't mean my nonsense) is badly handicapped, and the British Museum hasn't even got enough money to catalogue its manuscripts.

Did I tell you that E. Blunden is coming home on leave from Hong Kong this year? I'll be delighted to see him, but I'm a trifle apprehensive, since last time he stayed in the flat for six months. This time he speaks of perhaps six *weeks*, starting in June, when we may well be safely on Kisdon. My life is so full and complicated that even the dearest friend on top of one for weeks can become almost intolerable. Also I long for him to remove his 7000 books from the flat, which he originally promised to do in 1961. I could do with the shelf- and cupboard-room.

Yours ever
Rupert


*12 January 1961*                                    *Finndale House*
                                                     *Grundisburgh*
                                                     *Suffolk*

The really annoying thing is that your last letter is in the bag which I left in the train, and I never write to you without your last letter before me, and my memory being what it is—etc! But a genial winking official at Baker Street affirms that the bag will certainly turn up—in fact he was ready to wager five to one in shillings that I should get it back. Surely such optimists are rare. I certainly was in luck, for son-in-law Alexander Hood's pyjamas fitted me very nicely, and he is always abundantly equipped with spare brushes, razors·etc, so I didn't have to sleep in the buff as in the sixteenth century nor come bearded to breakfast. Meanwhile we live in hope.

Tuesday evening was very good. I don't care tuppence whether Flash Harry is the debutante's dread, the taxi-terror etc, but I do find him quite exceptionally good company at dinner. I got some good stuff out of him about Sullivan for my Gilbert paper, and he told me a good, and unprinted, Gilbert repartee. They asked him how some play of his was doing and G.—a very conceited man—told them how good a play it was. A prim listener said 'But Mr Gilbert, you know self-praise is no recommendation'. To which Gilbert replied 'Perhaps self-abuse would be better, though it doesn't seem to have done *you* much good'. I fear that won't quite do for the G. and S. Society, even after *Lady Chatterley*. But it was a good retort in the Garrick Club in 1900.

After dinner I did what I always (rather intrusively?) do, *viz* go and talk to the members I haven't met before (or is that perhaps being the perfect clubman?). Anyway I got some excellent chat with both Sykes and Irving. With the latter, helped by Jonah and Tim, we kept going till 11, and for once Jonah didn't complain of a too early break-up. Laurence Irving seemed to me a particularly delightful chap, and was most interesting about his father, grandfather and Max. I also had a good crack with Tommy who never fails to be good value.

On the way home to-day I expended a book-token on *The Intelligent Heart* by Moore. All about the man D.H. Lawrence. I saw it recently very well reviewed and so fell, probably to your derision. But at least D.H.L. is a cut above *Lucky Jim*. I haven't got far yet, but am struck by the deterioration in D.H.L.'s face in middle-age from his fresh youth. How much was that repellent beard to blame? Diana[1] met the *Lady C.* prosecuting counsel recently and thought him about the dullest man she had met. *Lady C.* was not mentioned. I should have liked to ask him how he managed to make such a mess of it, or how he expected a British jury to decide against a side which produced thirty-five witnesses in favour of one which produced none. The man must be an ass.

Tell me exactly what you think of the new Betjeman poem.[2] The brief verdict at Cambridge was 'It stinks', which is surely a little exaggerated. Dick Routh *per contra* puts it at the very top of all the poems he had read, which again seems to lack balance. It appears to

---

[1] George's daughter, Diana Hood.
[2] *Summoned by Bells* (1960).

5

me to have every merit except the poetic. Amusing, vivid, moving, full of stuff, obviously the work of a delightful, wise and excellent man. And I suppose it *does* gain by being in blank verse rather than prose? If I say that it doesn't do to me what poetry does—or did—you will answer: 'You must remember you are old and gray and full of sleep'. Leavis has not yet pronounced; he probably thinks it beneath his notice. His disciples at Girton, it is said, send to Coventry any girl who likes it.

I hadn't a book at Diana's and re-read with great pleasure in Winston's history of the first war. With not a word of censure he shows that Joffre, Haig, Robertson and even Foch were dreadfully lacking in ideas, and that we were saved only and entirely by Falken-hayn and Ludendorff being equally lacking. The French and our losses were consistently higher than the German, whether in defence or attack. It is a grim story—but very good reading. Do you know what Winston's favourite adjective is? 'Sombre'. He uses it always relevantly but perhaps excessively. How hard it is to avoid such pit-falls and clichés generally. Maugham, in his autobiographical gallop whose name escapes me, purchases a beautiful lucidity at the cost of numberless clichés.


*14 January 1961*                                    *Bromsden Farm*

To leave my letter in a handbag is so Oscarean that I am bound to forgive you. But will the finder now return the bag, or will he hold my letter for ransom and blackmail? I can't remember what was in it, except for the two Max triolets on Arthur Benson's essays. Here is a third, which I have rescued from a bookseller's catalogue:

> You'd think I must be a clergyman,
>     So like one do I write.
> When I break the news about Queen Anne
> You'd think I must be a clergyman.
> No dips in my ample tub of bran
>     Bring ought but bran to light—

You'd think *I must* be a clergyman,
So like one do I write.

All of them, you will have noticed, are aimed at A.C.B.'s essays, not at the man himself. Tommy rang up on Wednesday morning, to say what a good evening it had been, and added: 'Of course, George is a host in himself', to which I heartily agreed. Didn't you think the food exceptionally good? The club had made a mistake in the prices, and when the waitress was ready to collect the money, she asked me whether I realised the dinner had cost 27/6 instead of the usual guinea! I said certainly not, that the demand for such a sum would cause a riot, and she must collect the usual guinea, leaving the balance (£4. 10. 0) to be paid by the club. This we can well afford, since the accounts (which will reach you soon) show a higher surplus than last year.

So glad you had a crack with Laurence Irving, the most charming of men. He is a close friend of Field Marshal Alexander, whom he quoted at dinner as saying: 'The British are warriors, but not militarists', which I thought very shrewd. Eric Linklater was stone-cold sober and very charming. He is writing what he called 'an off-beat novel', and said that if I would travel to the North of Scotland in a month or two, to read it, he might let me publish it. I shall do so.

I too have always found Flash Harry very entertaining, and welcome his attendance. Cuthbert and the loathsome Lockhart are the only flies in our delectable ointment.

I think I told you once what I thought of the Betjeman poem, but I expect you left my letter in a Gladstone bag somewhere. As B. is almost my exact contemporary, and I knew him (and most of his friends) at Oxford, I cannot pretend to be impartial. I read the poem with great interest, sympathy and pleasure, and towards the end I found I was reading it as prose. Clearly it's scarcely poetry, except occasionally and briefly. So you can put me half way between Routh and the intransigent Cambridge critics. When John Wain said that B's huge sales were the measure of the English fear and dislike of true poetry, he spoke more than a little of the truth.

I was most interested in your remarks on Winston's first-war history. If you ever get through the long and full history of the

Franco-Prussian War which I shall soon be sending you, you will see that there the ineptitude of both sides was equally appalling, and the Germans won simply because the *luck* was always on their side. When they marched the wrong way they accidentally split the French army, but when the French went wrong they marched into Switzerland and were interned. I wonder if things are any different today? Did I tell you that Donald Somervell left first choice of his books to the London Library? The Librarian has chosen splendid ones, many of them big art books, worth he thinks perhaps £1000.

My eye has been swollen and aching all the week, and on Wednesday R. and I sought out a rather *louche* Bloomsbury doctor, who operated with needle and cotton-wool, gave me some auromycin ointment and said all would be well in two days. He lied, for the damned thing isn't right yet, reading is as irksome as writing, and Oscar waits reproachfully. No one (except you and Ruth) will ever realise what this book has cost in time and trouble.

I have just read the new Graham Greene novel. In technique and sheer skill there is no one to-day to touch him. The story is gripping despite the interminable arguments on God and love. I think you should read it. Now I shall relapse upon Carlyle and sleep.


*18 January 1961*                                              *Grundisburgh*


All is well. Miss Prism has got her handbag back, letter and all. The letter should not really have been in it. They usually remain in my pocket for re-reading and answering, but it got stuffed into the bag with a handful of other papers.

How right you are about Newman. In the Holmes-Laski letters L. says 'I should have been slightly nauseated by N. had he not been too remote for anything but curiosity' and H. sums him up as 'a tender spirit, and born writer, arguing like a pettifogger'. I remember being rather repelled by him when I read that he had said his *one* thought was 'Shall I be safe if I die to-night?' It doesn't do to think too much about the next world. Old Holmes was always sound about that.

I like Max on A.C.B., especially 'You'd think I must be a clergyman'. A pity they didn't really know each other. M. would have loved him, as Housman did, and no one can suppose *he* thought anything of those *Threads of Gold, Beside Still Waters* etc.

I have finished Moore on D.H.L. Very interesting, and I should think well done, though he handles his (to me) uncivilised and sneery side too gently. L. seems to have hated every place he went to after a few weeks, and every friend after a few months. I find him tremendously rebarbative (if that is the right word). That letter of his to K. Mansfield, beginning 'I loathe you. You revolt me, stewing in your consumption' in 1920 surely touches a new low in sheer caddishness. Was he really sane at such times? And what of the man Leavis calling him 'the finest literary critic of our time'? Was that before or after D.H.L. had put Fenimore Cooper above Tolstoi, Tourgenieff, and Dostoevsky? And to call 'Lead kindly Light' and 'Abide with Me' 'sentimental messes' is just ordinary Philistine, not judgment or criticism at all. The picture in the book of Frieda in the Fifties, with one eye apparently closed suggests that L. occasionally scored a bull's (or should I say a cow's) eye with his plate-throwing. Anyway Medusa would have thrown up the sponge if she had seen this photo.

Betjeman—no he was not in your former letter. I agree with you. I loved the poem. The Cambridge critics can boil their swollen heads. And John Wain's comment is very pertinent. Milton, Wordsworth, Coleridge, Shelley, Keats, Browning were all derided at first, and the only popular poets roughly were Pope, Scott, Byron and Tupper—all you may say not first-class poets. Was Masefield—and is he class I? Leavis of course would say that Milton etc weren't either, but L. on poetry does not ultimately matter.

I look forward enthusiastically to the Franco-Prussian War—one of those topics I can never read enough about. Bismarck fascinates me— a terrifying man. How nice to think that the one person *he* was afraid of was Queen Victoria. What you say of 'luck' in war reminds me that the French (Clemenceau?) sacked scores of generals merely on the grounds that 'they weren't lucky', and the people understanding this brings the corollary to Alexander on the English, e.g. that the French *are* militarists—or were. They certainly understood more about war in 1914 than the English.

Your lovely book-catalogue has arrived. And as you always encourage the horse-leech side of me, let me tell you there are about *ten*—yes, *ten*—books in it which make my mouth water. And obviously that is going rather too far. I see your Oscar is announced. Will it really be ready? How wonderful if it is. Pamela has just finished Lady Lytton—much struck with the editor's cleverness in making so much of material that might often seem dull, and also disliking good Queen Victoria a little more than before. Really to put Scott at the top of all poets, at the same time regretting his occasional *coarseness*(!!). Did she approve of the draping of pianoforte-legs? They really weren't sane in those days. When Gilbert put *Great Expectations* on the stage, the censor deleted 'a lord' in Magwitch's remark 'Here you are in chambers fit for a lord' and substituted 'Heaven'. And Lewis Carroll,whose amiable hobby it was to photograph little girls naked, protested against the female chorus in *Pinafore* singing 'Why damme, it's too bad'—'Those pure innocent-looking girls, those pure young lips sporting with the horrors of hell'. And I suppose you look on my disapproval of *Lady C.* as being as frumpish as the above. I see the *Daily Mirror*, that leader of enlightened thought, hopes the dear Archbishop's successor will be more modern—which means intrinsically that he must disapprove of nothing anyone does or says and never put his foot down.

I do hope that eye is all right now. Was it some species of stye? The sort of thing doctors are usually quite good at. A *very* tiresome clog on your job's work. You must be firm about Ed. Blunden, however nice he is. Even the best can be curiously unimaginative. Did it never occur to him that you might want your own room-space? But I suspect you are hopeless at saying 'No' to any friend's demands—or even acquaintances'.

I am just off to see my doctor. I expect he will give me six months —with luck. In which case I should be writing you some such letter as John Sterling wrote to Carlyle in similar circs. It isn't a very bad letter, 'written', as T.C. says, 'in starfire and immortal tears'. Do look it up.[1] Pamela sends her love. She almost girds at me for my luck in

---

[1] *10 August 1844*                    *Hillside, Ventnor*

My dear Carlyle, For the first time for many months it seems possible to send you a few words: merely, however, for Remembrance and Farewell. On

having a fairy godmother like you. She won't hear of your disclaimer of any special generosity. 'After all what other publisher acts like that?' she says with that thudding feminine commonsense. Ruth knows too, I bet. Please give her my love.

*21 January 1961*                                                    *Bromsden Farm*

So glad you got your bag back without benefit of blackmailers, and that you approve of the Spring List. Naturally you shall have any books in it that you fancy. The advance sales of Peter's book[1] (which is out tomorrow) are more than double those of *The Siege at Peking*, which I take to be a good omen.

Thank goodness your frightful Archbishop is disappearing. Ramsey looked after the Queen so tenderly at the Coronation (just like a nanny) that I'm sure he's all right, and of course he has the great advantage of never having been a headmaster!

My eye recovered after a week, but today the lid has suddenly and painfully swollen up again, curse it, and I am again very self-pitying.

Nowadays most English publishers make an annual pilgrimage to New York to acquire American books—and most do well out of it. I went in 1950 and again in 1952, but have avoided the effort ever since. Now I feel I must go again, so have taken a deep breath and booked a passage on the *Queen Mary* on February 25. I shall be there for most of March, and get back in time for Duff's wedding, which is to be at Builth Wells on Easter Monday (April 3). The all-important thing

higher matters there is nothing to say. I tread the common road into the great darkness, without any thought of fear, and with very much of hope. Certainty indeed I have none. With regard to You and Me I cannot begin to write; having nothing for it but to keep shut the lid of those secrets with all the iron weights that are in my power. Towards me it is still more true than towards England that no man has been and done like you. Heaven bless you! If I can lend a hand when *THERE*, that will not be wanting. It is all very strange, but not one hundredth part so sad as it seems to the standers-by.

Your Wife knows my mind towards her, and will believe it without asseverations.                                      Yours to the last, JOHN STERLING

[1] *Bayonets to Lhasa* (1961).

about the trip is that Ruth is coming too. For propriety's sake we have to book separately (and so pay double), but we shall be together all the time and are hoping to stay with some very nice people called Gleaves, old friends of mine, whose daughter is married to Ruth's son. By saving all the ruinous hotel-expenses I hope to pay R.'s passage out of the firm's money. Having her there will make *all* the difference (and indeed our unwillingness to be separated for so long has played a big part in my nine years' insularity), since she will bear some of the brunt of the manuscripts and the overwhelming hospitality. I shall have to visit some six different people *every day* we're there—think of it! Except for a week-end in Boston and Harvard, I expect we shall stay in New York. Ruth has never before crossed the Atlantic and is wildly excited. It will be my fifth visit, so I shall be able to show her everything. If the sea is tolerable, the two crossings will be blessed interludes, without social obligations or interruptions. You will have to get some of those sixpenny air-letter forms, and I will write by the same means. It sometimes takes as little as two days. I shall miss only the March Lit. Soc.

Meanwhile my sailing-date has also become the deadline by which the Oscar galley-proofs must return to the printer, and there is much to be done. The book may just *possibly* be out this year—it depends on how quick the printers are, and how long the index takes me to compile. I put it in the Spring List to encourage everyone. When I finally parted with the proofs of *Hugh Walpole* I felt exactly, I'm sure, as a woman must feel after giving birth to twins—empty, proud and slightly bewildered—and now I can hardly imagine life without Oscar.

My clothes are all so old and shabby that I thought I simply *must* get a new suit for America, so Ruth and I went to Burton's in Regent Street, and found a Ready-to-Wear Sale going on. I bought two very nice suits for £8. 8. 0. and £11. 11. 0. and came away rejoicing.

Adam has gone back to Eton, Sixth Form and Van Oss. Comfort's term has begun. Duff is enjoying his work on the *Sunday Telegraph* (which starts on February 5) and has found a very nice flat in Lexham Gardens for his married start. Tim is spending the week-end with Peter, and they may come over tomorrow. Stolchy isn't the word for our surroundings, and I spend almost the whole week-end in the library.

I am reading a life of Oscar Browning (in search of material about *my* Oscar) and do not so far find O.B. very congenial. Did you know him?[1] But all the Eton stuff is interesting. How rich the beaks seemed to get, a hundred years ago!

*25 January 1961*                                                   *Grundisburgh*

Just to show how shameless one can become if encouraged, merely look at the books in the enclosed list which I have marked. Clive said he was astonished at his own moderation. I am equally astonished— and indeed horrified—by my own greed. There can rarely have been anything like it.

Peter's book is immensely readable. I am delighted to hear that the orders are plentiful. And Jonah's stories?[2] I look forward to reading the reviews. What would the world of readers do without the Lit. Soc.?

Your U.S.A. trip should be fun—especially with Ruth. With her even the Antarctic would appear warm and welcoming. The really annoying thing is that I shan't see either of you 'till the almond-tree turns pink, The first flush of the spring', because I have to miss the Lit. Soc. in February, and you will in March. A sister is paying us a visit on February 15, and you will miss the March dinner when I shall be there, as I have a school meeting in the afternoon.

Are you happy about the new Archbishop? 'Too much crumb, you know', as Poll Sweedlepipe—or was it Bailey?—said about Mrs Gamp?[3] He won't be as good as dear Geoffrey Fisher.

I read my Gilbert paper two nights ago. The Society was a little sticky at first but all right in the end. I ended up my researches rather liking Gilbert, absurd though his touchiness was. He was not easy to score off. When a prima donna objected to being told exactly where to stand etc she flung out: 'Why should I? I'm not in the chorus.' All she got from G. was 'No, madam, your voice is not strong enough or you would be.'

[1] Oscar Browning (1837–1923). Eton master 1860–1875, Cambridge don 1876–1909. Author of many books, mostly historical.
[2] *The Bishop's Aunt and Other Stories* by L.E. Jones (1961).
[3] It was Mr Bailey, *Martin Chuzzlewit*, chapter xxix.

13

Your Burton suits make my mouth water. I always get mine there but they cost round about £20. Of course they have to be made. There are *no* advantages in being an outsize. My hats cost £4 or over.

Oscar Browning was repulsive and wholly absurd. The Eton affair was badly managed by Hornby, but O.B. was really becoming rather a menace. He was openly idle about all routine work and frankly favoured all the nicest-looking boys. Arthur Benson once told me that O.B. was talking about Oscar Wilde, and said 'I knew a good deal about all that affair' and, added A.C.B., 'his face as he said that was the face of a satyr.' Of course both Hornby and Warre (like Elliott too) were Victorianly suspicious of art and artists, and O.B. did do some good work encouraging such. Old Warre indeed was something of a Philistine, for all his knowledge of Homer.

*29 January 1961*                                          *Bromsden Farm*

Here I am, faint but pursuing, a day late but still hopeful. My eye flared up again last week, and on Friday night some sort of gastric trouble overtook me. Yesterday, in poor shape, I drove to Oxford, lunched sparingly in the Common Room at Magdalen, and spent the afternoon alone in their handsome Old Library going through the matriculation registers and other records for details of Oscar's contemporaries and friends, most of whom seem to have ended long and blameless lives as vicars or country gentlemen.

Then I got caught (without hat or umbrella) in a cloudburst on the short walk to All Souls, where I took tea with Sparrow. By the time I got home I was feeling wretched. However, by sleeping the clock round (11 to 11) I have restored myself to something like health. Did I tell you that Adam has passed his Prelims (ostensibly a test of his first year's work at Oxford) and now has no exam to do until his final Schools? He is delighted with Van Oss, he says.

Today Duff suddenly announced that his wedding-day may be postponed for a week or so: if it is, and we can switch our bookings, I think we may stay a few extra days in New York. Meanwhile we both have to be vaccinated, though not finger-printed, as I was in 1950.

You shall certainly have all the books you marked in the catalogue, and I daresay others too. Fleming is selling well: he sets off on Friday for Outer Mongolia, and I can't say I envy him. He is rather like an old charger sniffing the air of the battlefield.

I'm delighted with the new Archbishop, much preferring a nanny to an unctuous old sadist—so there!

I'm sure your Gilbert lecture had them rolling in the aisles as much as their rheumatism would allow.

I certainly *must* do the Oscar index. No one else is competent to compile the sort of one I want, least of all the electronic indexer which the Americans now extol.

When Duff was in Cardiff he made friends with a chap who has invented a new (and very cheap) method of amplifying and loud-speakering. Adam thinks that some adaptation of this invention might improve the appalling acoustics of School Hall, and this evening he and Duff are staging some sort of demonstration there.

You must forgive the disjointedness of this letter: perhaps you'll get a better one from the *Queen Mary*, where there will be fewer interruptions and more time.

Do you see the *Listener*? If so, do read Jack Priestley's excellent article on Falstaff, which appeared in two parts in the issues of January 19 and 26. It's a splendid counterblast to all that Cambridge flatulence. As I told J.B.P., I wish he would write a few more pieces like this, and publish them together in a book. He said he would whenever he had enough time and ideas.

Did I tell you that I have asked the Pilgrim Trust for a further £15,800 for the Dickens Letters (they gave me £6000 in 1954)? Their meeting is on February 9, so keep your fingers crossed. Unfortunately Tommy has retired from the Chairmanship, and I don't know his successor, Lord Evershed. The other evening I dined some three places away from him at the Garrick, and he looked charming.


1 *February 1961*                                                *Grundisburgh*


Are you going to the *very best* eye-man in London? Because it is all wrong you shouldn't be cured by now. But the gastric revolt on the top makes me wonder whether you are not suffering from overwork and fatigue. There is a lot of general debility about. I have had a nasty sore throat for five days—and I *never* get a s.t. That is what I have said for half a century and more. The winter—what a hateful thing it is! But what luck I am in. Just when I had nothing particular to do, four lovely books arrived from you—only *one*, if you please from my list, and your equally lovely promise of more. One can understand how a man who murders once and gets away with it, can't stop—people like Jack the Ripper, Christie, Tamburlaine etc. So I, having once got a book from you, am now lost to all sense of decency and just go on asking. The night before your letter—and books—came I refreshed myself with Max's *Around Theatres*. He reviewed two plays by Gilbert and put them neatly in their respective places, *viz* at the very opposite pole to *The Bab Ballads qua* wit, neatness, light touch etc. Gilbert's prose really is! M.B. says it is as bad as Pinero's, implying that nothing can be worse than that. I suppose in Victorian times your sentences were expected to be dressed up.

What a globe-trotter Peter is! Give him my love and good wishes and tell him how greatly I enjoyed his Younghusband book. What a mess the Government made of it. Brodrick of course the chief villain. I met him once and thought him curiously stupid, though he shone in comparison with his brother Arthur, who talked one entire evening at Holkham without saying anything. And what about Kitchener of Khartoum? My uncle General Neville L. who served under him in South Africa always not only disliked him but thought nothing of his brains—in that agreeing with Lloyd George who summed him up as 'a good poster'. He certainly had a tremendous presence. I have now, with your books, got from the library Shirer's Nazi history—1200 large pages[1], and one has read all of it pretty well in Bullock.[2] But somehow one—or at least I—can't resist it. The horrid truth is that Adolf was a genius, and so, in that tiresome way such men have, inexhaustible.

Very interesting about Adam and the acoustics. There must be money there for an inventor—as for the man who prevents or cures the common cold. For in both nothing is known but a few alleviations.

---

[1] *The Rise and Fall of the Third Reich* by William L. Shirer (1960).
[2] *Hitler—A Study in Tyranny* by Alan Bullock (1952).

16

He has done fine work about his exams. I wonder in what ways he will blossom at Oxford. I have read Priestley on Falstaff with the greatest pleasure, and am with you in wanting much more stuff like that from him. Why are subtle perception and sanity so rare a combination? The fiddling little sneerers and hole-pickers turn my stomach. Why do so many always think that a change of fashion must be an advance in wisdom? It is his realisation of this—*inter alia*—that makes old Judge Holmes's comments on men and books so good. His grasp of essentials was Johnsonian. Don't you like his remark to Lady Desborough that the Boer war 'would give England a chance to pay for some of its unearned exquisiteness.'

Lord Evershed is a delightful man—he is a cousin of the headmistress of the Abbey, Malvern, where he gave away the prizes some years ago. He will eat out of your hand in any good cause—and all your causes are good.

*4 February 1961*                                        *Bromsden Farm*

It is now 8 p.m., and I have been working on the Oscar galley-proofs since 11 a.m., with briefest intervals for food. The sheer physical labour of transferring several thousand corrections accurately and legibly on to the printer's set of proofs, clipping on hundreds of new typed footnotes at the relevant places, and so on, is appalling, and I have grave doubts of my ability to complete the task before catching the *Queen Mary*. It now looks as though we may stay a little longer in America than we expected, since Duff has put his wedding off from the 3rd to the 22nd of April. This is a relief, for I couldn't see how I was to get everything into three weeks. Now our return will largely depend on what passages we can get. Ruth is always sending you messages, but as she is never (alas) at hand when I'm writing to you, she doesn't get fairly reported—and anyhow, as I've said before, I'm not sure it's good for you.

My eye, touch wood, is now quite recovered, and everything else too. I have temporarily given up bread, starch, sugar and alcohol, and have lost five pounds of weight in a fortnight. When one eats in someone else's house, all this goes by the board to some extent, as yesterday, when I lunched with the Hamish Hamiltons in St John's Wood. The party was in honour of the Duchess of Kent and her sister Princess Olga, but both of them had succumbed to influenza, so we extras gobbled up the stars' excellent fare. The Birkenheads were there, both delightful; she growing steadily larger while he shrinks. He used to drink like anything, but has now completely given it up, and sits looking thin and miserable with a glass of water and a little silver snuffbox full of saccharine tablets. Only when he accepted a big cigar did the ghost of F.E. flicker out.[1]

Desmond Shawe-Taylor, the *Sunday Times* music critic, was also there—an agreeable rattle. The food wouldn't sound much if I described it, but I was hard put to it to confine myself to one moderate helping of each course.

David Cecil looked in on Thursday to gossip about Max: he hopes to finish his book in a year, but as he hasn't yet begun the writing, I have my doubts. He says Leavis has *no* chance of being elected[2], though he may split and confuse the vote a little. Only M.A.'s have a vote, and in practice only those in Oxford exercise it.

Next week Ruth and I are going to see Peggy Ashcroft in *The Duchess of Malfi*, which I've never seen before. I suspect it will make one realise all over again the excellence of Shakespeare.

Duff's paper, the *Sunday Telegraph*, makes its bow tomorrow after weeks of stress and anxiety. Last week they set up a complete 'dummy run' for practice, and were so nervous lest the Beaverbrook press might get a glimpse of it and mock, that every proof was carefully locked up in a safe each night. Now the worst will be known. Shall you ever see it? Not at home, I imagine.

It is now 9 p.m., and the Saturday evening BBC concert is coming from School Hall, Eton! I suppose they can beat the accoustics with microphones: it sounds all right so far. I wonder if Adam is in the audience.

Do you know anything of an organisation called Voluntary Service Overseas? Fred is now strongly advising Adam to spend a year with

---

[1] F.E. Smith, the first Lord Birkenhead.
[2] As Professor of Poetry at Oxford.

it before Oxford, instead of going to a German university, and Adam is rather taken with the idea. He keeps pointing out that it costs nothing, which is very nice but beside the point. *Not* going to Oxford at all would equally cost nothing, and we are concerned only with what is best for him. Your advice would be most welcome. I think Adam is partially influenced by the fact that, whereas Duff has been to West Africa, Yugoslavia, Greece, Russia, Germany and Austria, he (Adam) has never been further than the Pyrenees, and I see his point.

I am reading nothing but Oscariana, and as I devote more and more time to these proofs in the next three weeks, my letters will get, if possible, scrappier and duller.

Peter must be in Moscow by now, battling for a visa to Outer Mongolia, that desolate buffer-state that surely few can visit for pleasure.


*9 February 1961*                            *Grundisburgh*
                                                    *(summer-house)*


Your Oscar labours make me feel like the Queen of Sheba—whom I do not otherwise resemble.[1] You are just like Boswell (not in all ways!) running, as he said, half across London to fix one date.[2] What a magnificent work it will be. Why have *you* given up all carbo-hydrates, and why should you insist on losing weight? If I *look at* a potato, my weight goes up. Perhaps you are preparing to let yourself go, overseas. I look forward to hearing all about it, though I know you won't really have time to tell me. Why shouldn't Ruth tell me all the news—or would *that* be bad for me, in what I can only regard as your over-cautious opinion?

I wonder what you will make of *The Duchess of Malfi*. One gets an impression of a fine grimness and resonance in the reading of it; I suspect it may be like so many Shakespeare plays, much better when

[1] 'And when the queen of Sheba had seen all Solomon's wisdom, and the house that he had built [etc, etc] there was no more spirit in her.'
*I Kings*, x, 5.

[2] Advertisement to the first edition of the *Life of Johnson*.

19

acted. 'Butcherly rant' was all Shaw saw in Marlowe, but his feeling for poetry was far from strong—he really did think blank verse was easier to write than prose. And so of course Dickens found it. And certainly Mrs Siddons in speech: 'You've brought me water, boy; I asked for beer' is richer than many lines in Tennyson's *Idylls*. Also perhaps Anna Seward's[1] 'My inmost soul abhors the bloody French.'

I have just finished Shirer's 1200 pages on the Third Reich. Quite absorbing. Do you realise on how many occasions Hitler had us *absolutely cold*, and, by (obviously) the grace of God, did exactly the wrong thing? It is almost terrifying to see every time how many and how narrow our squeaks were. And where else in human history do you find so tremendous a blend of genius and wickedness? As a human being he simply had not *one* good quality. I hope whenever you meet a German you will impress upon him that only the Germans regard 'brutal' as a eulogistic word, and that only the German language has to have a word meaning 'pleasure in others' misfortune' (*Schadenfreude*) because the trait is so common in the German nature.

So I have had time for no other reading and will talk of Jonah next week. The library lets one have a book for a *fortnight*. I wonder who but G.W.L. in Suffolk will get through these 650,000 words in that time. (A neighbour's gardener read forty pages of *Lady C.* in a week and then left it as being 'not very interesting'.)

What did you think about the 'kiss-case' (trust our penny-a-liners to vulgarise anything). Silly of the young pair to bring the case I imagine, but really! How can what a couple do in a closed car, at dead of night, in a solitary square be construed as 'indecent conduct in a public place'? But of course *all* the jury weren't going to ruin a couple of honest cops. The pair were very badly advised.[2]

I know, alas, nothing about Voluntary Service Overseas, though I

[1] Poet (1747–1809). Known as 'The Swan of Lichfield'.

[2] On 10 April 1959 a young engaged couple were enjoying a 'kiss and cuddle' in their parked car in a London cul-de-sac which they didn't know was a haunt of prostitutes. They were arrested and charged with 'an outrage to public decency' etc. In May they were tried and acquitted at London Sessions. They then claimed damages in the High Court for 'false imprisonment, malicious prosecution' etc. After one jury had disagreed, a second one awarded them damages of £5200 on 8 May 1961.

have some dim memory of it being a good show. Pick Fred's brains shrewdly and find out if he knows who can give you first-hand evidence. John Hills[2] may know all about it, and his advice on such things is worth having. It may easily be an excellent thing, started in response to a strong and sensible demand. Probably a good deal depends on who is in charge. On the other hand a German university is pretty sure to be a good and valuable experience, and at the end he will *know* German thoroughly and the Germans pretty well, both of which acquisitions are perhaps more *solid* than anything he would get from V.S.O. How difficult these balancings are!

*11 February 1961*                                            *Bromsden Farm*

Ever since I wrote last week I have spent some eight hours a day on these infernal galleys—more today, and only my devotion to you is keeping me from them at this moment. I have got (in my fair copy) to number 417 out of 559, and there are only thirteen more correcting days before embarkation. I shall scramble through somehow, so clear your decks for a pile of page-proof-reading in April or thereabouts.

At the same time my dieting has continued: another five pounds off this week, ten so far in three weeks. I feel much better so, and my trousers button with greater ease.

We didn't greatly care for *The Duchess of Malfi*: indeed we were thankful when the last two characters simultaneously stabbed each other and we could escape. Peggy Ashcroft was lovely, and the staging superb (some of the best I've ever seen), but the other performers were moderate, and the play! The idiocy of Shakespeare's plots is masked and redeemed by the poetry, but except for three or four lines, there is nothing here but rhetoric and wind. Bloodshed and horrors get steadily funnier and more absurd as they multiply. I'm quite glad to have seen it once, but please never again.

I think that kiss-in-the-car couple were most ill-advised to bring their case: attacking the police, however justifiably, is always risky.

[2] Eton master. Later Headmaster of Bradfield.

They're bound to close ranks and swear black's white, and it only needs one stubborn juryman to wash everything out. I expect the young couple started by taking counsel's opinion, which is almost always *wrong*.

You have to be vaccinated before you can enter the Land of the Free, so today I drove down to Henley and was 'done' by our doctor. I asked him for the necessary certificate, but he said I should have to get a special one from the Cunard Line, and after he has signed it I shall have to get the Town Clerk to vouch for his (the doctor's) signature. But who vouches for the Town Clerk's? How much red tape can people think up?

Ruth is busy collecting a trousseau for the trip, but I tell her to save up for the New York shops. I am collecting together a few books to read on the ship. Those five days will be a blessing.

Adam is thoroughly enjoying his German and other work with Van Oss, but is wildly excited about his V.S.O. scheme. I tried to pick Fred's brains on the telephone this evening, without much result.

Duff is getting possession of his new flat in Kensington next week-end, and is planning to camp out there and do most of the decoration before the wedding. The first issue of the *Sunday Telegraph* sold out all its *one million* copies, but they can't tell how much of that is due to curiosity. Most of the other papers' remarks have been fairly acid, as one would expect.

Q. What are Chitterlings?

A. Lady Chatterley's children.

16 *February 1961*                                              *Grundisburgh*

You must be getting positively sylph-like, but no doubt you know what you are doing. Lime-juice and a biscuit at the Lit. Soc. puts you with poor old Headlam, who scowls at the first helping he is given—and of course at his neighbour's. I am not sure that poor old Ivor Brown too doesn't reject a good deal. I hope his teeth are all right. Pamela has had tooth-trouble too and had a very tender mouth for ten days. Nature is conspicuously incompetent about teeth, which start decaying practically with birth, or fits the mouth with more teeth than it wants or can comfortably house.

I suspected you wouldn't think much of the blood-boltered Webster. Only Shakespeare can gild those ridiculous plots.

Jonah's stories are subtle and well-written, with plenty of wit and irony, but whether their *interest* is strong enough seems to me a little doubtful. Did you get the impression that one or two of the stories somehow seem too long? The title-story seems to me much the best. But I may be quite wrong about all this. I shall be interested to see the reviews. Peter F. has had some good ones lately—I hope reflected in the book's sale?

How right you are about counsel's opinion. I remember once, when a housemaster asked the Governing Body some question about responsibility in case of fire. They got counsel's opinion (price five guineas) and sent it to me. I rejoined that it was an exact parallel with the old problem and its answer about how to find the sex of a canary. 'Give the bird a lump of sugar; if it is a he, he will eat it, and if it is a she, she will.' This went to the Bursar who read it out to the G.B. and a loud cackle of laughter from Provost Quickswood prevented my being hauled over the coals for impudence.

Good luck to Ruth with her transatlantic trousseau. I bet she will look lovely in it and knock 'em all on board. No doubt you will be taking *How Green* on the trip? Odd that you should so persistently avoid a book I know would delight you!

'Chitterlings' is lovely. Thank you.

I have just written to nephew Charles about a New Zealand village called 'Taumatawakatangihangakoanstameataturipunakapikimaung-ahoronukupohaiwhenuakitanatahn'. It means 'The brow of the hill where Tamatea, the man with the big knee who slid, climbed and swallowed mountains, the discoverer of land, played his flute to his loved one'.

*18 February 1961*                                          *Bromsden Farm*

Last Sunday evening, just over a day after my smallpox vaccination, I suddenly developed a nasty sore throat, which during a miser-

23

able Monday in the office turned into a cold so whoreson-wild that I had to spend two and a half days in bed, missing the Lit. Soc., incapable of Oscarising, allowing my correspondence to pile up as I coughed and sneezed and groaned and cursed. Ruth cherished me superbly, and had scarcely got me on my feet again when her daughter-in-law's labour-pains began. The child (their first, and Ruth's third grandchild) should have appeared today. How we shall ever get off on Friday goodness knows, but somehow we'll manage it, so imagine us boarding the *Queen Mary* at about 6.30 p.m. on Friday, prepared to sail at dawn. Our address from March 2 to 29 will be c/o Mrs Gleaves, 220 East 61 Street, New York City. My first letter will be slow, because of the boat, but if you use an air-letter-form there should be one waiting for me when I arrive. If the weather is tolerable, the five-day crossing will be bliss, without telephones or letters or (I hope) chattering acquaintances. You shall hear all about it.

So glad you enjoyed some of Jonah's stories: so did Eric Linklater, as you will see from the enclosed. I thought the title-story so much the best that I persuaded Jonah to put it first and call the book after it. I also managed to remove three or four stories of what seemed to me excessive sentimentality, and tried to remove the one about the bull-dog, but Jonah insisted on its retention. I do hope the reviewers don't spoil his fun. The book appears on February 27, when I shall be happily on the high seas.

(Ruth has just telephoned to say there is no baby yet: the labour-pains were a false alarm, and the expectant mother has been sent home —a tiresome anticlimax, poor things.)

As you can imagine, my chief concern, far more compelling than American dollars or visas or office affairs, is to get Oscar ready for the printer before we leave. It's touch and go, with many desperate decisions and wily plans for leaving, here and there, sufficient space for small insertions in the page-proofs. For instance, where I know that a three-line footnote is needed and can't be done in the time, I either write 'Leave space for three-line footnote,' or write three idiotic lines, for which the right ones can be exchanged later without too much worry and expense. Most of them will pass unnoticed anyhow.

To add to the confusion, my beloved sister is arriving from Scotland first thing on Tuesday morning, to stay in the flat. That night

Ruth and I are by way of going to Britten's *Midsummer Night's Dream* at Covent Garden, and on Thursday I have to make a speech to 150 people at a luncheon in honour of a retiring publisher's sales manager —oh dear!

Duff has gone to lecture the Marlborough boys on Greece, with the excellent coloured slides he took there. Have you seen the *Sunday Telegraph* yet? It's more like the *Daily T.* than anything else: masses of material but messily arranged, with too many too narrow columns. I daresay that's what people want.

You do realise, don't you, that the letters you will get from America will be nasty, short, brutish etc. We are to spend the week-end of March 10–13 at Boston—or rather Cambridge, Mass, just across the river. Ruth will stay with a charming Harvard professor friend of ours (they have room only for one), and I perhaps with Henry James's nephew, son of the philosopher and a darling old man —a painter. From New York I have already received invitations to lunch, dinner, theatres, operas, Sundays in the country, and God knows what. Their deep feeling of inferiority leads to a crazy excess of hospitality, and if one persists in praising the country and all its ways they are momently reassured. But oh how exhausting it all is! Almost all the food has been refrigerated into tastelessness—only coffee, orange-juice, ice-cream and oysters are always good. And most of the flowing drink is straight whisky or gin with a lot of ice. All my lost weight will, I fear, return 'with advantages'. I'm already looking forward to boarding the *Queen Elizabeth* for home.

Take care of yourself, dear George, and give my love to Pamela. *Ora pro nobis.*

Do write to Jonah about his stories if you feel you can.


*22 February 1961*                                                *Grundisburgh*


I am of course in the summer-house (only just, if you see what I mean) and all books are in the house. Being swathed in a rug, I am un-willing to move. I am only pretending that it is warm enough. What is the point of thick white cloud on a perfectly dry day? I frequently find myself in agreement with Mrs Besant in her fierce days. Genius on your part to send her life.[1] I am greatly enjoying it. Clearly one of those tremendous, admirable, intolerable women like F. Nightingale and B. Webb. Wonderful character and courage and achievement and all that. But uncomfortable for us humdrum folk whom they clearly despise. But Annie B. must have been less one-track than F.N. and B.W., who saw *no* point in talking or thinking of anything but nursing and gas-and-water respectively. I suppose there must be some of this sort; otherwise Mrs Gamp and Mr Bumble would be still with us. Mrs B's biographer is a bit stuffy and longwinded, but I have plenty of time. I look forward to the India part. At present I am at the Bradlaugh period—I remember Mr Gladstone fulminating about him at the dinner-table. But I suppose if you are sure about the Trinity you are fierce about its enemies—or still more perhaps if you are not *quite* sure.

Tell me what you thought of Britten's *Midsummer Night's Dream* (and Shakespeare's too of course). What can B's music do for S's which is often incomparable there? Old Agate always maintained that first-class poetry and ditto music spoilt each other, and that the insipid libretti of the Wagner operas were all right. He hated, too, grand opera in English—as I do—pointing out that '*Voglio la mia colazione*' did not offend one, whereas 'I want my breakfast' does. Tell me also what *you* think of Shakespeare in modern dress. I always feel I couldn't bear it, but some tell me I am wrong. Hamlet in a tail-coat, Rosalind in a skirt and jumper? But as you are beginning to suspect, I am full of Victorian prejudice. *But*, I must tell you, the man Leavis's article in the *Spectator* on *Lady C.* seemed to me excellent—both very intelligent and quite intelligible. And he ties the English language up in fewer knots than usual. Have you seen my old pupil John Bayley's new book—very respectfully reviewed by Pritchett and others?[2] I shan't understand it, but I must read it.

I haven't yet seen the *Sunday Telegraph*, on which, as you say, the other papers are rather sniffy; but it is a brave venture. I imagine Duff's writings in it are not signed; no doubt that will come later. And has Adam polished off that Chess Cup? Perhaps he will get a

[1] *The First Five Lives of Annie Besant* by Arthur H. Nethercot (1961).
[2] *The Characters of Love* (1961).

chess blue, though I believe the standard is very high. The old Ram[1] was one. He lost his match against Oxford, and was still annoyed about the mistake he made with his knight half a century ago. At Eton he sometimes played with Jelly Churchill[2] who was a stubborn but poor player, though unmoved by disaster. Once Ram took his queen and expected him to show some regret, but so unmoved was Jelly that A.B.R. at last pointed out the loss. All he got was 'Yes, I'm glad she's gone; she was rather in the way,' the fact being I imagine that no player dreams of going on after his queen has perished.

*25 February 1961*                    *R.M.S. Queen Mary*

I somehow missed your letter yesterday: I only hope you're not ill. Anyhow this is just a brief interim report, which can be posted at Cherbourg. Despite persistent catarrh and a hacking cough, I managed to get Oscar back to the printer, and everything else more or less straightened out. We are now blissfully ensconced in two comfortable and almost adjacent cabins. Any amount of excellent food, no letters, telephones or papers, and a free cinema show every day. I am reading a proof of the new Ian Fleming—so far well up to standard.[3] During the rest of the voyage I will endeavour to compile a longer letter, in which Ruth promises to join. Apparently President Kennedy is a great one for the girls, and during the election his opponents said that if he got to the White House they only hoped he would do for fornication what Eisenhower did for golf.

*1 March 1961*                        *R.M.S. Queen Mary*

Heavy seas, mountainous meals, a movie each afternoon, ten hours of sleep each night (including the one caused by putting back the clock), an ever-open bar—all these have proved very beneficial. It

[1] A.B. Ramsay, Eton master, later Master of Magdalene College, Cambridge.
[2] My Eton housemaster.
[3] *Thunderball* (1961).

27

took me three days to shake off cough and catarrh, but Ruth proves a stalwart sailor, and we are both thoroughly relishing these unreal days of suspended animation. Little walks on the icy deck, bowls of broth at 11 a.m., tea and light music after the movie, visits to the library (where this is being written) punctuate the steady rhythm of creaking timbers, throbbing floors and rushing waters. Two days were rough: now all is calm and speedy. I have so far read three thrillers, the proofs of Margaret Lane's new book about Africa,[1] Vita Sackville-West's new novel[2], and *The Bachelors* by Muriel Spark. The new Ian Fleming is disappointingly like a feeble parody of the earlier ones.

The food is excellent, and one can order almost anything one fancies. I have kept a typical menu to send you. Last night, for instance, became a Gala Night, by the general issue of gaily coloured miniature hats, and we consumed oysters (melon for R), turtle soup, skipped the fish, excellent tender fillet steaks, and a deliciously light American pudding called Nesselrode Pie. For breakfast one can have bloaters or minced chicken or onion soup, but we generally stick to the excellent bacon-and-eggs. We have a little table to ourselves, where we are waited on by a charming man who escaped from the 'Free City' of Danzig in 1936 and fought with the Royal Engineers in Italy. Now he is married to a Scottish girl and lives at Eastbourne.

Mercifully there is no one on board who knows us, so we rejoice in this trancelike existence, anonymous, overfed and half-asleep. They tell us we shall dock at 11 a.m. tomorrow—and then the rush and racket will begin. I'll try to send you a brief air-letter on Sunday.

----

My first written word to you, dearest George, and very little space for any outpouring of soul. The best thing so far is that R. seems so definitely rested and better and has thrown away ideas of diet and eats and drinks like his old self. Very, very satisfactory. I shall try and send you a separate word in the next days or weeks. My love to you.

Ruth.

----

[1] *A Calabash of Diamonds* (1961).
[2] *No Signposts in the Sea* (1961).

I am at the moment in London, for two meetings. It will be sad no longer to find my dear Geoffrey Fisher chairmaning the G.B.A. Committee, which he always did extremely well. We shall now be dragooned by Sir Griffith Williams, one of those men who looks far more important than anyone can possibly be—knighted for some incredibly dull services in secondary school education, which have for some reason convinced him that he need not cultivate the graces. He has no manners at all, which I find invariably displeasing.

I am staying with my brother and in my bedroom are no books except a novel by Angela Thirkell and two Agatha Christies which I have read.

How I hate London—especially at the rush hour, which mistakenly I thought yesterday was finished by 6.15. My brother's station is Archway where the train completely empties. I suppose everyone lives at Highgate or Hampstead. Lady Summerskill is close by; I shall not call. They tell me the House of Lords doesn't like her manner which is dictatorial. She thinks that if you are a lord you must be lordly.

I am slowly absorbing Mrs Besant, just getting to the theosophy. She is in process of breaking with most of her previous friends, Bradlaugh etc. Conversely I am reading in bed a life of William Cory, whom I don't much like.[1] Too much sentiment, and though very learned, almost always wrong in his judgments, e.g. that Tennyson was far greater than Milton. His leaving Eton and changing his name was very mysterious and no one has ever really spoken out about it—any more than they have about Oscar Browning. Wortham in his life of O.B. merely abused Hornby—quite wrongly.

---

[1] Presumably *William Cory, a Biography* by Faith Compton Mackenzie (1950). William Johnson (1823–1892), poet, Eton master from 1845 till 1872, when he changed his name to Cory.

Nice letter redolent of ozone arrived this morning (with a builder's bill which I had expected to be about £75 and was £184. But I suppose that happens to everybody—though one item on it was more than surprising, *viz* 'holidays etc').

You sound in good case (as Swithin Forsyte used to say) and it is nice to hear from Ruth that you are rested and no longer dieting. I felt in my bones that this last was somehow all wrong for you. But I also feel that you won't find U.S.A. all that restful, so you will soon be again in your natural element.

I am just finishing Annie Besant—almost equally interested by her and infuriated by the over-wordy author. The book is costive with unnecessary details. I congratulated Jonah on his stories, and got a charming letter back. No reviews out yet. The *T.L.S.* continues to parody itself with long articles of steadily increasing dulness, mostly on foreign writers I at least have never heard of. The present editor is naughtier in this way than even Pryce-Jones. I have sent you a card saying I shall attend the Lit. Soc. but presume it won't be forwarded. Jonah is going to be there.

Sorry about Ian Fleming. James Bond has been a caricature for several books now. No one else surely (except Mellors[1] perhaps?) can sleep happily with a woman a day or so after being tortured practically to death.

Please give my very best love to Ruth, with warm thanks for her little P.S. to yours. It is a pleasant thought—you and she happily enjoying sea and sun and wind, wearing gay hatlets, and tucking into Nesselrode Pie. P. and I supped yesterday on boiled eggs, which Percy Lubbock once called 'stuffy little things' but we both enjoy them. I hope my last week's letter awaited you at Mrs Gleaves's.

---

[1] In *Lady Chatterley's Lover*.

I am in London and—probably—your weekly letter is awaiting my return home to-morrow, so I have momentarily nothing from you to stimulate me—except of course the mere thought of you and R., which is in no way narcotic.

The Lit. Soc. last night produced a fine crowd. The uproar was terrific and prevented my hearing anything my neighbour said to me —that is the defect of hearing-aids *pro tem*. They promise to cure it in a year or two. I sat next to Tommy, and Ivor B. was on my other side. Flash Harry was opposite—in cracking form, clearly enjoying himself madly. Alan Moorehead was very friendly and apologetic at coming so rarely. In fact he said he really ought to resign, but I took it upon myself to say that *you* would not at all approve of that. I had five minutes of Lockhart; we spoke of K.G. Macleod. I suppose he *has* some other topic, but I have still to find it.

Best love to Ruth; it must be lovely having her with you. I gathered she has been firm and salutary about your dieting. I once recommended fruit and salad diet to a cousin and only just in time did her doctor snatch her from the jaws of death.

Do not fancy, my dear George, that an intermission of writing is a decay of kindness. No man is always in a disposition to write, nor has any man at all times something to say. I send you this mangled quotation for the same reason that Alice Meynell on her deathbed murmured 'my bluest veins to kiss'[1]—to show that I am still sentient and at least a fragment of my usual self. This is the first letter I have sent you from America, and it may well be the last, such is the pace here, without cease. Your lovely weekly letters are happy glimpses of reality in what otherwise might be the moon. Mostly freezing days with clear blue sky and all these topless towers glittering in the

[1] *Antony and Cleopatra*, act two, scene 5.

31

brightest sunlight. Two appointments in the morning, an enormous lunch at someone's expense, with much liquor. Two or three more appointments, drinks somewhere before a dinner-party or theatre, or both. Home by 12 or 1 to deepest sleep, and then another similar day. We have been to three plays, two revues, one movie and one opera. Last week-end in Boston and Cambridge (Mass) was enjoyable, but without even enough time to write to you.

Baghdad on the Hudson was a pretty good name for this city of fantasy. We have a lovely little flat on the top floor of the Gleaves's house, and only wish we could spend more time in it. My reason is saved by my beloved Ruth's presence, and she so enjoying it all in the savage way one must, though we shall both be *thankful* to embark on the *Queen Elizabeth* on March 29 (arriving home April 5). I shall try to write you an Easter letter on board. We have between us read, perused or sampled several dozen manuscripts and sets of proofs—most of them quite unsuitable for English publication. Have picked up one or two little things, but so far nothing major or important. We learn that the proof-corrections in the Oscar galleys will cost £500!! and that page-proofs should be ready in April—so clear your decks. The compulsive friendliness and hospitality of Americans is both pleasing and exhausting, and seeing so many people in quick succession makes for endless repetitions. Needless to say, all dieting has gone by the board, all my clothes are tight, and Ruth says it's a very good thing. All helpings of food are enough for three, and enough food must be thrown away in this city to feed half the Congo.

---

There is little I can add to this wonderfully descriptive letter, though I wholeheartedly endorse it all. And darling Rupert is a total success (Americanism) and adored by all these open-armed people. Which is, after all, much like being at home. A great deal of it is rewarding and stimulating, but they have no cubby-holes in their nature where one can curl up and rest. It's all outward striving and constant movement, and my heart yearns for the curlews of Kisdon. Keep yourself warm for our return.　　　　Love Ruth.

What a beautiful Johnsonian opening. You call it 'a mangled quotation' and no doubt the old man demolished Boswell's importunity with some such swashing blow.

I wasn't in the least surprised at a fortnight going by with no letter from you, as I have a vague but strong suspicion of how full they are filling your day with business and hospitality. I do hope it will all be reflected in the balance-sheet. I note in your letter a point that I have always had firmly fixed in my mind, *viz* that it is very hard to take Americans *quite* seriously. As more than one of themselves has noticed, 'not so much an accent as a whiffle, a snuffle, a twang' was the contribution of Howells.[1] Many exceptions of course—there are no two human beings I admire more than Lincoln and old Judge Holmes. I wonder if you will come across any traces of him (H). Of course you might easily go off your rocker with all this, but for the presence of Ruth. I don't know what the statistics are, but surely there are far fewer idiot women than men?

Last night dinner with Wells (C.M.)[2] at the United University Club—his ninetieth birthday, and he was one of the least decayed men in the room. John Christie[3] has had jaundice and has gout. No excuse for the former as he drinks *cream* by the pint (literally). Old Gow[4] is vanishing—really frighteningly thin. He told me he now weighed eight stone odd (At Eton he was *twelve*!). I urged him to eat more food and he said that is the trouble—he hates the stuff. Well they know all about that; it is 'anorexia' and unless cured it kills you, because you become vulnerable to any germ that is about. His state partly comes, as he admits, from having lost *all* interest in life. I had a good crack with G.O. Allen who was at his best—and that is very nice. He knows *all* about modern cricket. He corroborated what nephew Charles told me, *viz* that since Hutton's command of 'no

[1] W.D. Howells, American novelist and critic (1837–1920).
[2] Former Eton master.
[3] Eccentric millionaire (1882–1962). For some years an Eton master. Founded the Glynebourne Music Festival on his own estate 1934.
[4] A.S.F. Gow, former Eton master, then Fellow of Trinity College, Cambridge.

fraternisation' the MCC sides in Australia have been very unpopular —and no wonder. And do you know, and can you believe, that D. Sheppard forbade his Cambridge side to fraternise with Oxford in the match? Unbelievable but true—and quite insufferable, as G.O.A. firmly said.

I stayed with my brother-in-law Leconfield yesterday. A niece of his came in, and we chatted away. Afterwards he told me that I had talked him down—was, to put it shortly, intolerable. He is 83½ and I think had a rush of blood to the head—or is what he said true?

*P.S. for Ruth*

Delightful little note from you—every line of it full of *your* flavour (and if that has a horrible air of *Amplex* about it, well I can only trust you to see that it really hasn't—and I do). It is *good* to hear of R. going down so well, as of course he was bound to. Now I want to hear what they think of the other R. and I bet you won't tell me (but *he* may!). Anyway I don't really need to be told, 'they have no cubby-holes in their nature' I like that—and your longing for 'the curlews of Kisdon'.

*27 March 1961*                                          *220 E 61*
                                                        *N.Y.C.*

Your letter arrived faithfully, but once again the week-end, when I planned to answer it, was entirely occupied with social activities, and on Saturday we didn't get to bed till 3 a.m. on Sunday. Now our last two days are chock-a-block with last-minute shopping, telephoning, appointments, parties and goodness knows what. I need not tell you that Ruth is a *succès fou* with the American gentlemen and finds this very stimulating. We are astonishingly well, considering the life we're leading.

That was Monday morning, and now it's Tuesday evening, and we sail after lunch tomorrow. I shall airmail this before we leave, write again on the *Queen Elizabeth* and post that when we land next Tuesday, so you should get it on Wednesday or Thursday. Write next to Bromsden, which I should reach on the evening of Friday, April 7.

Here the pace quickens, and fatigue is catching up with us. After a midwinter day last week, the temperature today is in the 70s and many of the buildings still have their heating on. We find we need more and more liquor—mostly Bourbon whisky, which we love—to keep us going. The best building since I was last here is the Seagram (whisky) building on Park Avenue. It is some sixty storeys high and made of *bronze*. Very beautiful in sunlight and even more so at night when one of its thousands of windows is permanently lit up. On the ground floor is the world's most *chi-chi* restaurant, called The Four Seasons. It has a Picasso mural forty foot square in the entrance hall, and a pool the size of a swimming bath in the middle of the restaurant, with four *trees* at its corners etc etc. Everything is wildly expensive, except cigarettes, but the firm is paying, so to hell with that. Last week we found two new Oscar letters, which a kindly bookseller allowed us to copy and airmail home for last-minute inclusion.

Everything is brash and loud and brutal, but at night very beautiful. Most of the people are very ugly, but friendly and longing for praise. The subway is indescribably awful. There is no climate in New York, but rather a succession of violent extremes. The city is a vast melting-pot of races and colours and creeds which presumably will one day solidify.

*29 March 1961*                                          *Grundisburgh*

No *arrière-pensées*, no suspicions, no dark thoughts. If you miss a week I know it is for impregnable reasons; and you really are a wonderful correspondent and spoil me for anybody else. I am gradually getting used to the fact that nowadays to answer any letter—even one about money—by return is somehow considered what—? non-U, plebeian, rough manners? I simply don't know. But last week I sent two cheques and got acknowledgement of them exactly eight days later. And neither of the people concerned is one tenth as busy as you are. I am at present owed five letters—four at least from charming nieces who *adore* (their word) getting letters but abhor (not their word) writing them. My nephew does well from N.Z. for the rather sad reason that he has got nobody to talk to out there.

I grow old—physically—rather rapidly. Young ladies offer me

35

their seat in buses—not wholly from kindness, partly in self-defence, for they see how a lurch of the bus shoots me into the lap of some unoffending matron slow in escaping. I expect to find myself sued, like the Rev. Thomas, for embracing. His plea that arthritis and copulation in a taxi were an impossible combination was rejected by the Consistory Court. Have you been reading the case? I met the sublime and the ridiculous in juxtaposition last week—*viz* the whitest magnolia in Suffolk and under it a poster announcing 'Mrs Brandy in the Box'.[1]

The Ancient of Days, who has a fine sense of humour, as we know, must be indulging in Olympian chuckles over the circulation of the New English Bible running neck and neck with that of *Lady Chatterley*. Have you seen it? They seem to me to have altered some things quite needlessly, and surely to fiddle about with the Lord's Prayer is hardly forgiveable. So many people do not appear to realise that language *just a bit* above people's heads is right. Wasn't it Mrs Carlyle who, when an old peasant-woman praised a sermon, asked her if she had understood it and got the answer 'Wad I hae the presoomption?' But she continued to praise the sermon. 'Truly and *indifferently*,' 'true and *lively* word' would the change to 'impartially' and 'living' attract those who are now repelled? But I expect introducing lucidity into the crabbed exhortations of St Paul is a wholly good thing, and after all for centuries St Paul's Christianity has really held the field for discussion. Our rector will have none of the *N.E.B.* Indeed if it was still in print I think he would have Wycliffe's on the lectern.

*Good Friday, 31 March 1961*                    *R.M.S. Queen Elizabeth*

First class on this ship is indeed something, and I have decided that luxury is all right, provided you experience it only occasionally and for short periods: otherwise you simply begin to complain about the quality of the caviare.

---

[1] It was not in a taxi but in his own car, outside Wandsworth Common railway station, and in other places, that the Vicar of Balham was accused of persistent adultery with Mrs Brandy, a forty-year-old school-teacher. He was found guilty on 28 March 1961 and subsequently defrocked.

We have two *huge* cabins with an open door between. Each contains two beds, two armchairs, two dressing-tables, a mass of drawers and hanging-cupboards, and its own bathroom and W.C. When we embarked we found three enormous bouquets for Ruth, three bottles of champagne, a bottle of Bourbon whisky, a vast box of chocolates, sundry books and a cable or two. We managed to restrict the seeing-off party to three faithfuls. So far the sea has been glassy, and all yesterday we sat out on the Sun Deck in comfortable chairs, swaddled in rugs, enjoying bright warm sunshine. Today is wet and grey, so we are catching up on our letters. Putting on the clocks an hour each day is a trifle disconcerting—in contrast to the delicious extra hour a day on the outward journey—so that everything tends to be slightly telescoped. We have a delicious breakfast brought to our cabins between 10 and 11—fresh orange-juice, coffee, rolls, butter and marmalade—then get up slowly and sit outside, or walk on the covered deck if it's wet. We try to eat only a small luncheon, though one can have *anything* one wants, and work our way through afternoon tea, a rest with books, a bath and change, cocktails in the bar, and a superb dinner. Last night we had oysters (smoked salmon for Ruth), delicious poached turbot cooked with mussels and shrimps, the breasts of ducklings done with cherries, and a marrons-glacées ice, washed down by some excellent Montrachet. Each evening at 9.30 there is a free movie in the huge theatre. We saw five on the outward journey, and so far two on this—*Tunes of Glory* with Alec Guinness, and a goodish New York one called *The Rat-Race*. Then bed, and it's an hour later than you think.

The passenger-list includes Sir Bernard and Lady Docker, who last night, so our waiter told us, kept the restaurant staff hanging about till past midnight as they argued loudly, her Ladyship getting steadily drunker and more abusive. A.E.R. Gilligan's[1] name also graces the list, but none of these celebrities has yet been glimpsed by us. The only people we know are Mark Longman, the publisher, and his wife, and I think their desire for quiet is as great as ours, for they haven't bothered us, and we are rejoicing in being alone together, after the ceaseless chatter and small-talk of New York. I am reading that new

[1] Former English cricket captain.

life of Lady Gregory[1] with much enjoyment: it's the first book I've really *read* since we left the *Queen Mary* a month ago: all the books, proofs and manuscripts we dashed through in America were read against time—and mostly against the grain too. These five days of luxurious limbo are a fine bridge between the inferno of Manhattan and the paradise of England. There is an extensive ship's library, but we have enough reading-matter in our cabins to last for weeks. We are due to dock at dawn on Tuesday, and the boat-train is supposed to reach Waterloo at 10.15 a.m.

Ruth and I are now so blissfully accustomed to being together that even our brief partings at home loom depressingly. I shall stop this now and write another page or so before the voyage ends. Despite the rigours of New York, we both feel much better in health than we did a month ago: violent change has perhaps its own therapeutic quality.

*Easter Sunday*

Little sun since Friday, but no waves either, so our Lucullan life drifts on. Last night we drank our first bottle of champagne with caviare, *filet mignon*, asparagus, *crêpes suzettes* and an excellent savoury. The last two movies (*The Magnificent Seven* and *The World of Suzie Wong*) weren't up to much, and we left before the end of *S.W.*

Ruth, alas, has caught a cold in the head: no wonder with all the violent changes of temperature we have experienced: otherwise we are fine. The Dockers, we hear, are behaving better. Tonight there is a concert given by the Vienna Boys Choir. What next? We are prepared for anything.

*Easter Monday. Cherbourg.*

We made landfall here at noon in steady rain, and don't leave again till six. We are tied up to a fine modern quay, built since the war, and could have spent three hours exploring the town if we had wanted to. But the weather is still grey and wet, and we preferred to stay cosily on board. Ruth's cold is much better, and she has been very good about it. We shall be sad to leave our luxurious cabins and endless meals, but maybe five days of over-eating are enough. I shall hope to

---

[1] By Elizabeth Coxhead (1961).

find at least one letter from you at Bromsden and will write from there on Saturday.

---

It's nearly over now—isn't it sad. I can't easily imagine life shorn of its leisured elegance after such a week of luxurious ease. But how the second week would pall and longing set in for one's kitchen sink. My hands have not been so lily-white for *years*. And with so much time to do things nothing at all gets done. What an oddity of nature that is.

We have bought a copy of *The Times* so that we can do our first crossword for five weeks. Perhaps we shan't be able to. And a rather tragic little concourse of elderly gentlemen are playing us to our tea with tunes from *The Merry Widow*—so we must go. My love. Ruth.

*7 April 1961*                                                    *Grundisburgh*

I am not going to let my thanks for this *delightful* Cardus book[1] wait over until Tuesday. I am immensely pleased to have it. Your kindness is unceasing—because I remember (with blood to the face) that this book was not on that shameless list I sent you when your spring list came out. And then that unfortunate letter which went to U.S.A. and probably passed you on the way. Will the good Mrs Gleaves send it back, or is it already behind the fire, as the Victorians put it? Cardus will take the place of Behrman and Max,[2] at present by my bedside. Is it a sign of old and/or mental decay that I find Behrman's beer *a little* small—after sixty pages? Is Miss Jungmann the lady Max married? She sounds a good sort. I like Max's suggestion that a volume could and should be made out of the rot that G.B.S. uttered during his ninety-four years, and his implication that the resulting volume would not be at all a small one.

I look forward to finding you stout, rosy, with a slight accent,

---

[1] *The Essential Neville Cardus* (1949). Reissued as *Cardus on Cricket* (1977).
[2] S.N. Behrman, dramatist and author of *Conversation with Max* (1960).

39

bristling with new ideas—and Ruth too, but as regards her it would perhaps be better if she has not changed in the smallest degree. This house is pleasantly a-crawl with children at the moment—and more to come on Tuesday next. Once, about, every two days I sympathise with Herod, but not for long, and on the whole there is very little grizzling and quarrelling.

<br>

*8 April 1961*                                                *Bromsden Farm*

Your sad mistake in sending your last letter to America was balanced by your earlier error of sending the first one here, so I came back to enjoy your words of February 22—and then this morning arrived your note of yesterday. What a feast!

That Cardus book has been out of print for years, and I searching the hedges for a copy for you. On Thursday after lunch Ruth and I strolled round in bright spring sunshine to Moss Bros to hire me a suit for the three weddings I have to attend (the Devlins' daughter's on Monday, my niece's on Saturday, and Duff's on Saturday week), and on the way I spied that rather battered copy in the Charing Cross Road. Those pages I mentioned have not appeared in any other book.

We landed at 7.15 a.m. on Tuesday in dark grey rain. A most officious Customs man disarranged all our luggage and made us pay £3. 12. 0 for sundry nonsenses. Finding an English translation of *Madame Bovary* in my bag, he made sure he was on the trail of dirty books, but a couple of pages of the learned translator's preface calmed his ardour. The office was piled high with this and that, and we longed for the peace of the *Queen Elizabeth*.

Here I found six weeks' worth of bills, letters and periodicals, and have spent all today coping with them. Adam *lost* the Chess Cup—I suspect through idleness and other distractions. I have put back seven and a half of the ten pounds I had previously lost, but am quickly dropping my American accent.

We shall be eagerly awaiting you at 6 on Tuesday. Siegfried has expressed his intention of attending the dinner, but I'll believe it when I see him.

One's first impression of England in the train from Southampton is of incredible *greenness*. All grass in New York, Boston and between is at this time of year a dark brownish-grey.

How very nice it was to see you again—and looking so well after all the obviously unhygienic ways of New York. And Ruth too—lovely! But I suppose to visit a new continent, and have everyone falling in love with you as they obviously did, *is* invigorating. I hope her dinner-party went as well as ours did. Siegfried S. clearly enjoyed himself—as indeed anyone would between Tommy and John Sparrow. To me there are no evenings in the year of quite the same quality. The hors d'oeuvres so to speak—that hour with you and R.—are an essential part of it, as you must know. And but for you this brightening of my old age would never have happened. Can't you hear Cuthbert 'Why should *he* be a member—a dull pedagogue?' Tim had some good acid-drops from the old asp. Would it not be a good notion if *he* were sent up in *our* first space-rocket?

Two families have just left here and two more just come—the larger ones. But happily only two grandchildren are spoilt and therefore unpleasing and they have gone.

Two thousand more members for the MCC! And the only match I ever go up for is the Australian Test Match when the pavilion is cram-full one and a half hours before play begins—and I only got a seat in 1956 because a man (in the best seat of all) died ten minutes before I arrived, and in Housmanly fashion I took it. I say, how tremendously good Cardus at his best is! The account of McDonald in this book you sent really is superb. What a lot of people don't know the difference between fine writing and 'fine' writing!

I am going to spare you the two full quarto sheets this week—after your nasty gibes about four letters in a week. And am now off to saw wood. Bobby Bourne has to do the splitting, and indeed all the really heavy work. My doctor is rather anile about my using an axe or 'beetle'. Last week I lugged a waggon, full of timber, a good deal impeded by several grandchildren, though when Henry (*aetat* three)

41

was asked by his mother where I was, his answer was 'He's just been helping me bring in the wood.'

So goodbye, my dear Rupert—and love (more than ever if poss!) to Ruth. That was a delicious look on her face when she said you were *not* going to do any more banting. It had the finality (but no other similarity) of a decision of Queen Victoria.


*16 April 1961*                                                    *Bromsden Farm*

I'm so sorry this is a day late. Most of yesterday was taken up with my niece's wedding in London—at that beautiful church opposite Lord's, reception at the Savile Club. Duff and Adam were ushers and all went well, including my proposing the health of the young couple. Many old family friends, unseen for twenty years, turned up and had to be identified. Luckily only two challenged me by saying 'I'm sure you don't know who I am,' and I guessed right both times. Duff's wedding next Saturday is at Builth Wells in Wales, and the distance will keep down the size of the congregation. Comfort and I are driving there and back in the day (135 miles each way), so next week's letter will be a day late too, if it ever gets written at all.

I think Siegfried thoroughly enjoyed his first Lit. Soc., and not least your anecdotes of Ranji and co. On Wednesday I dined at Tommy's: just the two of them, Siegfried and me. The poet was in excellent form and talked to me about poetry in the liveliest way while Tommy slumbered by the fire. I must confess that I was somewhat disarmed by Cuthbert's asking whether he should resign, adding that the Lit. Soc. was the only thing that kept him alive. An exaggeration no doubt, but an engaging one.

I entirely agree with your remarks on the New English Bible. A few fragments of mystery are surely an *asset* to religion, and to slaughter one of the greatest glories of our language and literature to make a Sunday-school holiday is monstrous.

The Eichmann trial seems to me all wrong, because one simply can't help feeling a trace of sympathy for the victim in the glass cage, and clearly one *shouldn't*. I should be happier if they had shot him like a mad dog when they found him. But I suppose the Jews don't want the world to forget what they have been through.

Birley has sent me his Clark Lectures, which I shall certainly publish. They are called *Sunk Without Trace* and deal with six works of Eng. Lit. which were tremendously popular in their day and are now unread and almost forgotten. They are Warner's *Albion's England* (Elizabethan), Nathaniel Lee's *The Rival Queens* (Restoration), Young's *Night Thoughts*, Robertson's *History of the Reign of Charles V*, Moore's *Lalla Rookh*, and Bailey's *Festus*. The manuscript is in longhand: the writing is legible, but it takes much longer to read than a typescript. I am finding it very interesting, and it certainly tells one all one could want to know about those forgotten favourites.

Did I tell you that the page-proofs of Oscar are due to begin arriving tomorrow? And are you still game to read a set in search of misprints and editorial solecisms? A few sets are coming in piecemeal between tomorrow and May 5, and about May 7 a larger number of paper-bound complete ones. Which would you prefer? I quail at the thought of compiling the enormous index, which must be ready by the end of May—then heigh-ho for Kisdon! Blessed thought!

I love this greening time of year, with its birdsong and promise of summer, but it makes London seem even more unattractive than usual, and I long for the great hills of the north country.

Ruth has gone to Essex to spend the week-end with her son and grandson. The simple truth is that I miss her every moment she isn't there, and that after fifteen years! It must be the real thing—and how rarely is that found!

*20 April 1961*                                                           *Grundisburgh*

A perfectly noble quartette of books arrived this morning to the unconcealed envy of my daughters and son-in-law. They seemed to think it was grossly unfair that I should have a fairy godmother all to myself (and so it is!). They ask indignantly 'Do all publishers do things like this?' and my answer is easy 'No, no more than all motor-manufacturers do the same as Lord Nuffield.' I shall have great fun with them. *Pro tem* I am reading Daphne du Maurier on Branwell

Brontë, whose appearance was seemingly like the mildest of spectacled curates. No wonder he could not stand up against his terrifying sisters, but I wonder who could have. Some blend of Heathcliff and Rochester, I suppose. Could the Lit. Soc. provide such do you think?

I got yesterday a perfectly charming letter from Ivor B. asking if I would mind(!) his dedicating his forthcoming word-book to me. It was a wonderfully friendly letter. How much I owe you for the Lit. Soc.—as I have said before and shall say again whatever you may say about the stories I tell you which originally came from you (that was humiliating if you like—but it was a great success in the Ipswich Country Club, so there). Was it you, perhaps, who told me of the advertisement which delighted Max B. (not in Behrman, I think) 'Medical man in Cheltenham can accommodate one female resident patient—epileptic Churchwoman preferred'?

I am glad you recognised your old friends at that wedding. I am always being non-plussed, and lack the thick-skinned ungraciousness of old Broadbent[1] whose answer to an old pupil's 'I bet you don't know who I am, Mr Broadbent' was 'You've won yer bet' and moved off. You won't be writing this Saturday—you can't, in view of Duff's wedding. Give him my warmest regards; in spite of his hair being quite a different colour from what I seemed to remember.

Do you get any kick out of the Budget? I hope the surtax cut benefits you. It doesn't me. I find it annoying that after saving what I could through a working life of thirty-seven years, and investing it in gilt-edged (which have steadily depreciated) and living in my old age modestly and mainly on my dividends, I am regarded (and called) a parasite by half the Socialists, my income is called 'unearned', and I continue to be taxed up to the hilt. And hundreds of thousands of retired professional men—doctors, dentists, lawyers, schoolmasters, dons, deans etc—are in the same boat.

Birley's lectures should be good, but I am not 100 per cent certain that they will be. When an assistant beak at Eton, his reports were curiously and conspicuously dull, for all his ability. I once knew a little about Nat Lee, and Moore, and thought Bailey's *Festus* full of good lines. All I (or anybody else) can ever remember of Young's

---

[1] Former Eton master.

*Night Thoughts* is 'Procrastination is the thief of time'. Milton has better lines but few more widely known.

All decks here are stripped for Oscar. I will go through anything you send with a small tooth-comb (whatever a tooth-comb may be). But you remember what James Agate said about proof-reading, *viz* that real efficiency is impossible. He advocated reading upside down, but even so found that as soon as you recognise a word by its first half you take the second half for granted. Anyway I will do the best I can.

I say, Rupert, the blossom! Surely all the last few days have burst all records. Here it is positively heart-breaking in its loveliness. Never have I seen it so thick and rich. The atmosphere of the summer-house is Housmanly as I survey a prunus, a cherry and an almond.


*23 April 1961*                                                   *Bromsden Farm*


Yesterday Duff's wedding entailed a marathon drive for us. We left here at 8.30 a.m. and got back soon after midnight, having covered 305 miles, mostly in heavy rain. Most of the lovely hills and valleys of the Wye were obscured by rainclouds, but all went off gaily and well. The tiny church of St Bridget at Llansantffraed-in-Elfael is as remote as can be imagined, at the dead-end of a tiny valley, so that all the cars had to be left in wet grass four hundred yards away and the ladies' wedding hats and shoes were sorely tried by two muddy walks in steady rain. Every seat in the church was occupied, and we were so packed in the pews that we had to get up one at a time. The young couple looked exceedingly handsome, and it was all most touching and suitable. The registry was a leaking tent adjoining the east end of the church, but by then we were prepared for anything. Afterwards champagne flowed, with Adam as chief pourer, and we shook innumerable hands and complimented everyone. They have gone by air today to Athens, *en route* for Corfu.

On Friday Comfort and I attended the luncheon in Merton Hall for the opening of the Max Room. Considering that Merton is probably the richest of all the Oxford colleges, the food wasn't all that good, but it served. I was happily placed beside Rachel Cecil (wife of

David C. and daughter of Desmond MacCarthy), an old friend. On my other side was a breezy tutor of English called Hugo Dawson, and opposite me the extremely pretty daughter of John Rothenstein (he and his wife were there too). S.C. Roberts made an admirable speech. Jonah and his wife were there, Jock Dent and many other Maximilians. Before lunch we had a drink with Sir William Hayter, the Warden of New College and former Ambassador to Moscow—a very agreeable chap.

So you can see we've been around a bit these last two days!

I get no kick—or good—out of the Budget, since I have only once paid any surtax, and that was years ago. All my tiny income is 'earned', but there isn't enough of it to qualify.

I very much enjoyed Birley's lectures, and think you will too. Eric Linklater has sent me his new novel to publish: it's called *Roll of Honour* and is all about a *retired schoolmaster* in Aberdeen! Some of it is in an irregular sort of verse, unusual but effective. I shall try to bring it out this year.

The first thirty-two pages of Oscar arrived on Tuesday, but next day the second thirty-two disclosed a hideous blunder (not of mine, but of my colleague or the printer), which has necessitated a hold-up for revision. I hope the flow will be resumed next week, and I will send it to you section by section. Get out your finest tooth-comb and your strongest spectacles, and do your damndest.

Adam has been accepted for Voluntary Service Overseas, though he doesn't yet know where he will be sent, or exactly when. In any case we shan't see him for a solid twelve months (that's part of the contract), which is rather sad.

The garden here is lush and green and badly needs mowing. If only we could find even a part-time gardener, but they all say this is too far to come. We've just heard of a firm that goes round mowing people's grass at fifteen shillings an hour (they say they—two men—could do ours in one hour, and a weekly visit from them would be a blessing). Every drainpipe and gutter is blocked with birds' nests, and the lilac is in bloom. The wallflowers are wonderful, but it's always too wet even to look at them. This morning I burned dozens of old newspapers and clipped a few edges before I was driven in by bouncing hailstones. Oh to be in England . . . !

Gosh, your day! It makes me feel tired even to read about. And on a day when Suffolk, bless its heart, had *one* shower lasting for twelve minutes. Last autumn we overflowed with the best, but normally there is no doubt we are outstandingly dry compared with midlands, west, and especially Wales. But I grant we cannot compete with names like Llansantffraed-in-Elfael. Perfectly superb, a poem in itself. I should like to hear you pronounce it. The champagne, poured by Adam, sounds all right, inferior and vulgar wine though it is, though its effects are good, convincing one without much difficulty that the world is in a better state than in fact it is.

Please tell me whether, in the effort to keep up to date, I ought to read the plays of Wesker and Miss Delaney. They cannot surely be as bad as *Lucky Jim* or *Look Back in Anger*. How refreshing it is when the brilliant young make asses of themselves, e.g. that letter from K. Tynan and others about Cuba, which subsequent writers have shown to be entirely wrong both as to facts and inferences drawn from them.

The Australians. Who is to get wickets when Benaud and Davidson are mastered? Who is to get wickets for us? Statham and Trueman cannot go on for ever. I hope they will find someone who takes fewer steps in his run. They both walked from crease to start in *thirty-five* steps. Mold and Brearley took seven, Larwood ten. *Verb sap.* I shall be watching with Gerald Kelly on the middle gallery, where seats are kept for us by a man who, I think, sleeps there all night. I wish my nephew was at Hagley. I saw the Australians at Worcester in 1948. Charles Fry was there. Bradman of course got 200 and C.B.F. watched every ball through a pair of vast field-glasses. In the evening he said he had never expected to see another batsman who saw the ball as quick as Ranji, but Bradman certainly did—and was R's superior in concentration, which C.B.F. said he had never seen remotely equalled. Interesting.

I don't really much *like* champagne either—Belloc once described

47

it as 'wine, yellow and acid, with bubbles in it'—but it's a great morale-booster, don't you agree?

I'm afraid that Jock Dent probably *is* going downhill: he looks awful now—very fat, red and blotchy. His life of Mrs Pat[1] is a shocking mess, full of coy whimsicalities and messily arranged. All the same, it does contain most of the known facts about that unusual woman, and I can't say I was bored. Most of the reviewers, liking Jock, have concentrated on the subject and disregarded the treatment. I certainly should *not* read the plays of Wesker and Miss Delaney. They may some of them be just tolerable in the theatre (*A Taste of Honey* was more than that), but to *read*—no, my dear George!

This morning was so grey and chilly that I fairly easily conquered my desire to drive to Worcester and sit on the wet grass all day. But how nice it will be to have something interesting in the papers again. I agree about bowlers' idiotic runs—Lindwall's seemed endless, but the worst of all was that of Alf Gover of Surrey: the dreariest bowler I remember, though Nigel Haig is a hot candidate.

On Wednesday Marjorie Linklater (Eric's wife and a friend of more than thirty years) paid one of her rare visits to London, and I (in all good faith) took her to the longest and dullest film either of us had ever seen—the Italian *La Dolce Vita*. It lasts for *three hours*, and there is no plot, only a sequence of incidents. The famous 'orgy scene' is pretty tame, and the whole thing seemed to me pretentious and wearisome.

Last week, when Paris was threatened with invasion, with tanks ready at every corner,[2] my Uncle Duff's old secretary wrote to say that they refused to disconnect the telephone in the Paris flat, because it had been installed in Duff's name and they insisted on documentary proof of his death.[3] I wonder the tanks didn't get tangled in red tape.

I think I heard the cuckoo a couple of days before you did, and now I hear nothing else. The wallflowers and lilac are lovely, and the grass seems to grow faster than we can cut it—particularly with both the boys away. We have mice in the larder, and rats in the compost-heap.

---

[1] *Mrs Patrick Campbell* by Alan Dent (1961).

[2] On 22 April 1961 two French generals brought off an anti-Government *coup d'état* in Algiers. In fear of an airborne invasion and an attempt to assassinate De Gaulle, Paris was put on full alert. The revolt collapsed on 26 April.

[3] He died on 1 January 1954.

The walnut tree is only just showing its buds. Some rabbits have re-appeared, and none of the kitchen garden is wired.

On Monday I go to *Rigoletto* at Covent Garden with the Droghedas, on Wednesday Ruth and I dine with the Eliots, and on Thursday there is a dinner at the Reform Club for Ivor B's seventieth birthday. I'm not sure whether his birthday is that day, but it's pretty close, so do send him a note of encouragement.

My old father is eighty-three on Monday, and it's difficult to wish 'many happy returns' to someone who never stops saying he wishes he was dead. Perhaps he means what he says, but I doubt it. Tommy reports that Malcolm Sargent's speech at the R.A. dinner was too long, in poor taste, and spoken too fast. 'What were the other speeches like?' says I. 'Ball-aching', says Tommy, 'including the P.M.'s.' Perhaps you listened on the radio?

I am reading an excellent life of Maupassant by a charming American called Francis Steegmuller, whose future books I am going to publish. He writes with style and learning: it's an excellent book, which you would enjoy. My bedtime reading has for so many years been largely conditioned by Oscar and the search for quotations used by him, that I suddenly feel liberated, and able for a few minutes most days to follow my fancy in an agreeable way. I see, to my horror, an announcement of a *sequel* to *How Green*. Unless you pronounce against it, I shall soon have two unread books on my conscience.


*29 April 1961*                                                    *Grundisburgh*

Assuming that you want them *quam celerrime* I send the mild little results of my tooth-comb now instead of waiting till my Thursday letter. I find no solecisms by R.H-D. and let me say at once, surely no book since Birkbeck Hill's Boswell has been so comprehensively and beautifully annotated. You will laugh at my one suggestion for the alteration of your English. What the split infinitive is to some (on the whole silly) people the double pluperfect has always been to me.

Very many thanks for your note of April 29 and for your extremely valuable comments on the first thirty-two pages. They are just the sort of thing I was hoping for.

I've hastily removed the double pluperfect and will deal with all the other matters. I checked yesterday and the Tripos is now definitely called Moral Sciences in the plural, though perhaps it wasn't in those days. Here is a note from the *Oxford Companion to Music* which will answer your query about the Skye Boat Song:

> 'One half of the tune is a sea-shanty heard in 1879 by Miss Annie MacLeod (later Lady Wilson) when going by boat from Toran to Loch Coruisk; the other half is by Miss MacLeod herself. The words, by Sir Harold Boulton, Bart, (*Speed bonnie boat, like a bird on the wing*) date from 1884. Later some other words were written to the tune by Robert Louis Stevenson, who apparently believed the tune to be a pure folk-tune and in the public domain.'

I sent you another thirty-two pages yesterday and more should follow tomorrow. Keep up the good work.

I was much relieved to find that my observations were not too fiddling and pernickety, and greatly amused at your being right—as I might have expected—about Moral Sciences and the Skye Boat Song. I hope, and think, that my boats were not utterly burnt by my merely querying both and not bluntly altering them. I shall be increasingly wary, and if I find Sydney Smith referred to as 'Smoth' I shall merely append a dubious query. Today I shall tackle the instalment that arrived yesterday. It is exactly the right time of year for such work—the blank period between two G.C.E. exams. Just before the first proofs arrived I was reduced (wrong word) to re-reading *Mansfield Park*. At first my anti-Austen feelings were reinforced by the immensely insipid and trivial conversations in Chapters 6 and 9 (please have a glimpse and tell me if I am really as wrong as all that).

But I frankly confess (who is humble and I am not humble?, as St Paul obscurely put it) I enjoyed it—so much so that I must shortly have another go at my *bête noire*, *Emma*. I fear I dislike *her* too much.

I fear you may be right about the nightingale. Pamela is with you and ascribes all the *Schwärmerei* about him to the poets. And what about this?

'Fat and sweet is the song of the nightingale. A good full singer he is. A good big chest full of breath, him, and a chest to hold it, too, and up with his head and open with his mouth, thinking it no shame to sing with the voice that God gave to him, and singing with fear for none, true on the note, sharp at the edge, loud, fat with tone, with a trill and a tremolo to make you frozen with wonderment to hear. A little bird he is, with no colour to his feathers, and no airs with him, either, but with a voice that a king might envy, and yet he asks for nothing, only room to sing. No bowing, no scrapes, no bending of the knee, or fat fees for Mr Nightingale. A little bough, a couple of leaves, and nightfall, and you shall have your song with no payment other than the moments of your life while you listen. Such voices have the cherubim.' From *How Green* of course. I am delighted to hear there is to be a sequel, though the fate of sequels is grim—apart from *Alice*, *The Jungle Book*, *The Prisoner of Zenda*, *The Newcomes* and no doubt several others which I have forgotten.

My nephew Charles would corroborate all you say of Gover, and more. By the way I am conscious of decided lumpishness about your lovely Cardus volume. I suppose I wrote before I had read your *quite excellent* introduction. All said that should be said with the utmost concinnity (as Max would say). How cleverly you tell us that N.C.'s mother and aunt were both harlots!

I have sent a line to Ivor B., though in actual fact his birthday is on April 25 (*Who's Who*). I recently read a first-rate review by him of *Mrs P.C.* My aunt Edith Lyttelton was very fond of Mrs P.C. and used to have her to meals—rather to the dislike of General Uncle Neville who was *echt*-Victorian. On one occasion Mrs P.C. turned to Oliver when he was about eighteen and demanded an epigram about life, which O. gave without hesitation. I don't know what it was. The story reflects credit on neither.

Sorry about your father's gloom. I shall be saying the same as he does in five years—but not to you or Ruth! When I grouse about aches and pains to my doctor, he unsympathetically says that such are *en règle* at my age, and that he knows no man of seventy-eight fitter than I am. And my only way of scoring off him would be to die suddenly to-morrow, and then I should miss Oscar. So he has me, damn him, in a cleft stick. Do you remember in that admirable second act of *The Truth about Blayds*[1] the old man's answer to the family's wishes of 'many happy returns' on his ninetieth birthday 'Happy I hope; many, I neither expect nor want.' A good answer, and in fact he died that very night.

Oscar. Tooth-comb, magnifying-glass, hearing-aid, etc. all failed to find anything and produced nothing but a grumpy query about 'moly', so that it was really a relief when your printer gave Forbes-Robertson a life of a hundred and two years (p. 87). Archibald Forbes[2] cuts a morose figure. Surely O.W's letter of Friday March 20 cannot justly be called 'obviously offensive' and to call kindly expressions 'irrelevant expressions of cordiality' is the mark of a curmudgeon.


*6 May 1961*                                                      *Bromsden Farm*

Many thanks for your excellent letter, and for the proofs of pp. 63–94. I fear your patience, eyesight and sealing-wax (very impressive) will be exhausted before we're through. The printers have been so dilatory that the other day I made a great row, and they have promised to work overtime with extra men, all through the week-end, so I'm hoping for better things next week. Yes, moly is just what you think, and I'm most grateful to you for spotting Forbes-Robertson's undeserved longevity. 1835 should indeed be 1853, and it's just those simple misprints that are most apt to escape the jaded eye. I've gone so stale on the whole thing that it will be a miracle if I spot anything. I'm now beginning to veer towards Moral Scien*ce*, but will take further expert advice.

Fancy your succumbing to Jane Austen: perhaps you will soon love Emma as much as the heroine of *How Green*! I know you will be

[1] By A.A. Milne (1921).
[2] Preposterous war-correspondent and lecturer (1838–1900).

disgusted and horrified, but the passage you so kindly copied about the nightingale only increases my trepidation about the whole book— and its sequel.

This week has been hellish. Let me detail it for you. Monday wasn't too bad: a peaceful lunch with Ruth, and in the evening *Rigoletto* in the Droghedas' box at Covent Garden—very enjoyable, and a good serial dinner in a private dining-room in the intervals. Also there Sir Patrick and Lady Reilly (former Ambassador in Moscow, Lady Aberconway (remarkably sober), L.P. Hartley, Loelia Duchess of Westminster and the Droghedas' son. Afterwards in pouring rain to a party at the Redfern Gallery in Cork Street, where my cousin John Julius Norwich's wife is having her first exhibition of abstract paintings. The crush totally obscured the pictures, and I got home by midnight.

On Tuesday Ruth and I lunched with the old poet Andrew Young, and I rushed off to a long meeting of my television company, with Slim in the chair. 6–8 drinks with an American publisher, and manuscript-reading-cum-proof-correcting till 11.30. On Wednesday Adam arrived from Scotland at 8 a.m. with his friend Dunglass (Alington's grandson). I took them both to the neighbouring Lyons Corner House, where the breakfast is quick, plentiful and good. Large lunch with a literary agent. 6 p.m. drinks with an American publisher at Claridge's (with Ruth) and on to an excellent dinner with the Eliots.

On Thursday, lunch with James Pope-Hennessy and much literary discussion. Evening Ivor's birthday party at Reform Club. Indifferent food and drink but agreeable company: some thirty men, including the editors of the *Daily Telegraph*, *Economist*, *Daily Mirror* and *Daily Herald*, Jock Dent, Ralph Richardson, Compton Mackenzie, Robert Morley, Gerald Barry, P. Fleming etc. Many speeches, the best by Priestley in the chair. He said he realised his own plays were out of date, and he was meditating a play in the modern manner, for the Royal Court Theatre. 'There's only one character, a tramp. The whole action takes place in a telephone-kiosk. The tramp spends the first act making up his mind to ring up his cousin in Hackney Marshes; the second act is taken up with his search for the necessary fourpence, and in the third act he *slowly* remembers that he never had a cousin.' All beautifully told with his rich Yorkshire accent. I got drenched in a thunderstorm cloudburst on my way to the dinner, but it had cleared afterwards.

Yesterday (Friday) I attended, on behalf of the London Library, a huge and delicious lunch at the East India Club in St James's Square, and in the evening a banquet for three hundred in Stationers' Hall, to celebrate the jubilee of a publisher called Walter Harrap. Cocktails, madeira, white and red wine, port, brandy, cigar, more speeches. Can you wonder that I feel dim-witted and listless today? Nor is next week going to be much better. It's worse than New York, where the air is more stimulating. Also I've made a hideous blunder and arranged to attend Francis Meynell's seventieth birthday dinner on Wednesday, which this month is the Lit. Soc. day—oh dear!

Ruth has gone to Essex to help christen her grandson. We can neither of us believe that blessed Kisdon is only four weeks away. Shall we ever get there? Somehow we *must*. Then you will get brief notes about curlews and baby grouse.

*11 May 1961*                                                                 *Grundisburgh*

The truth is simply that there has never been any suggestion made to you to which you could say 'no' except one—and that is that you should read *How Green*. I was not greatly surprised by your demurrer to the nightingale sentence, for I have long sensed your allergy to the book. We agree in and on so much, but in any two people with minds of their own, sooner or later some huge gap appears as big as that between Abraham and Lazarus. I remember the shock (but I am older now) it was to find that my old friend Tom Cattley, who had plenty of humour and a feeling for words, saw nothing remotely funny in P.G. Wodehouse. Similarly you have to put up with my thinking *Lady C.* a very dull and pretentious book with all its fourth-form defiance of previous standards. The only superiority I claim is that I have read *Lady C.* and you have not read *How Green*! And there we must leave it.

I am greatly enjoying the O.W. stuff, though fully conscious how few and short (like the prayers they said for Sir John Moore) are my suggestions. I will say again how frankly astonishing the fulness, accuracy, and interest of your editing seems to me. On almost every page one detects *weeks* of hard research, and I like to see you sometimes enjoying yourself. E.g. p. 125 the 'American lobbyist, financier, talker and gastronome' and just below after O.W's ecstatic praise of *A Daughter of the Nile*[1] produced on September 6, your laconic statement 'It was withdrawn on 23 Sept.' What an extraordinarily *nice* man O.W. was, so kind and courteous, till pricked. Did his extremely beautiful wife remain loyal to the end, or was her stuffy family too much for her? It was a dreadful business really and need never have come to a head at all. O.W. didn't corrupt anybody, and everyone now knows that the clause in Labby's[2] bill making private behaviour a public offence was passed at the end of the day when all MPs wanted their dinner, and weren't attending. I hope you are as pleased as I am by the outcome of the 'Kiss in the Car' case? I followed it daily and—as so often—was puzzled by the neglect of what seemed to me a very important point, *viz* the absurdity of calling what two people do in a closed car at dead of night, in a dark corner of a dark square, an offence against *public* decency.

Why is T.S.E. not among the 'Companions of Literature,' the new order just started. He is a better man than either old Maugham or E.M. Forester (*sic* in *Daily Telegraph*). Perhaps he didn't want to be.

I have also just got Connolly's *Enemies of Promise* which I remember finding interesting years ago. Do you know him? Shall I write and tell him that he is in error saying the book was banned at Eton? Eton is particularly good at *not* being thin-skinned about hostile opinions (partly, of course because she does, or did, not, like the Duke, care one twopenny damn what hostile critics think). I remember Tuppy Headlam being much pleased by C's eulogy of him as teacher and influence, but I fear it was much too favourable. T.H. never had 'much the best house at Eton', and if as C. says he 'hated idleness' he got over it: for in his last years he was conspicuously idle in school (golf at Swinley *every* Sunday!) partly because he had formed the opinion that history was not a good subject for teaching to the great majority of boys. And he may have been right.

[1] A play by Laura Don.
[2] Henry Du Pré Labouchere (1831–1912). Radical M.P. for Northampton 1880–1905. Founded *Truth* 1876.

Slightly comic Governors' meeting of Woodbridge School yesterday. Next year we are to have tercentenary celebrations. What big noise shall we try to get? The Duke of Edinburgh? Well who do we approach to find if he could or would? The Lord Chamberlain. Who is he? Lord Nugent. Does anyone know him? G.W.L.: 'My first pupil'—but he isn't the Lord Chamberlain. Who is? Eric Penn. Does anyone know him? G.W.L:' He was in my house', but he isn't the man. Some governor 'No, the man to go for is Sir Edward Ford. Does anyone know him?' G.W.L: 'He is my cousin.' Another governor: 'I believe the right man is Sir Michael Adeane; does anyone know him?' G.W.L: 'He is my wife's cousin.' Another: 'Suppose we can't get him. What about the Queen-Mother? Does anyone know her?' G.W.L: 'She was a great friend, before marriage, of my wife's.'

So now I am in the eyes of my fellow-governors either *very* highly connected or the biggest snob in England. *Que voulez-vous?*


13 *May 1961*                                    *Bromsden Farm*


Very many thanks for your letter, and for your comments on pp. 95–222. They are most valuable, and your name will have to be added to the list of my benefactors in the Introduction. You are particularly good at spotting printers' errors in people's dates. I should never have noticed Vernon Lee's 99 years: in fact she died at 78: I must check the exact date. Of your other queries: I've no idea what a 'pen-rog' is or was, but this text is from a catalogue and is probably wrong. I like to think that you have enjoyed Lafite all your life, wrongly believing it to be Lafi*tte*! ' *Je pruse*' and '*Oxonicuris*' are the printer's versions of ' *Je pense*' and *Oxoniensis*'. Doubtless my handwriting was to blame, but such obvious nonsenses are much easier to spot than those plausible but wrong dates. Do try and find the reference for Carlyle on Margaret Fuller: God (or Gad) knows where I took it from.

Your return of the misdirected pp. 223–254 was so cryptic that I'm not sure whether you got two sets, or only this one. I rang up Henry Maas, but he is away till tomorrow morning, when I will try him again. My secretary's wits are clearly going—so sorry.

Peter reports an agreeable Lit. Soc., and I wished I was there, for

Ruth and I had a pretty tedious evening at Francis Meynell's seventieth birthday dinner. There were far more men than women, and I was between Reynolds Stone (Foxy's engraver son—very nice) and a Central European typographer. The food was quite good, but there were *eight* speeches—all poor—and the final one, by F.M. himself, lasted over an hour. I twice almost dropped off.

Earlier in the day I went to Geoffrey Faber's Memorial Service, at which T.S.E. spoke well. He refused that ridiculous award, and I encouraged him to do so. The Royal Society of Literature—a miserable institution—is simply trying to bolster itself by crowning five octogenarians, who were too vain, gaga or polite to refuse. In any case, I told Tom, a stripling like him is far too young for such a questionable *galère*.

You always write as though *Lady C.* was my favourite book, whereas I feel almost exactly as you do about it.

So glad you're enjoying Oscar, though we're barely a third of the way through yet. Your praise of the notes is very comforting. After six years I have lost all sense of proportion, and simply don't know whether the notes are too long or too short, too detailed, too dull, or too frivolous—so you see I'm in need of reassurance. Yes, Constance Wilde behaved well all through, as you will see, though at the end she was quite out of her depth. Hold on—the best is yet to come.

I am reading Tyson's autobiography, which I think he certainly wrote himself. How many professional fast bowlers are capable of quoting from Keats's letters? He has some good stories too. Do you know the one of Bradman, overhearing British criticism of Australian umpires, and interjecting 'That's all nonsense. Mel McInnes played several times for South Australia before his eyes went.' Would it amuse you to read the book when I've finished it?

I had a protracted and pathetic luncheon with my old father at White's on Wednesday. He has to totter with two sticks, seldom recognises anyone, and if he does can't remember their name. He reads all day and night, but enjoys very little, finding his adored Dickens now quite unreadable. Self-pity is surely the least attractive of all faults, and it prevents one's own pity from functioning. He never stops saying he has made a mess of everything and wishes he was dead. What can one answer? He refuses to have TV and seldom switches on the radio—what a life! He has day and night nurses permanently in attendance. Sorry to be so depressing. You could easily be my father—what a difference!


*18 May 1961*                                                          *Grundisburgh*

Rather a moderate harvest this week, I fear. You and your minions are wonderfully accurate on the whole. I am greatly enjoying the job and childishly pleased when I discover an error. The letters are crammed with interest.

I have searched hard but without success for the Fuller-Carlyle episode, though I have the irritating certainty that it must be somewhere in my room. I suggest you might find it in that portentous biography of T.C. by D.A. Wilson, which, though Ipswich has it not, must be in the London Library. It is a very ridiculous book in seven volumes—fattish ones too, with much triviality and irrelevance; what in the world the dear old curmudgeon would have said about it, one just dares not think. But at any rate it does tell us that his tobacco was Bird's Eye, which Froude does not. I am rather glad too that he doesn't put all the blame of Mrs C.'s unhappiness down to C.'s bearish ways. She exaggerated everything, and Froude had no more perception of exaggeration than a boy has of irony. I have a *very strong* feeling that he said 'Gad' and not 'God'. I hope you will find it. I continue my search.

I much enjoy your dislike and contempt for literary societies and—to a great extent—men. Do you remember Henry James's reply to John Bailey when asked to be chairman of the English Association?[1] Edel missed it in his volume of selected letters (published by you) just as he missed another immortal one to Walter Berry who had pre-

[1] '. . . Let me, for some poor comfort's sake, make the immediate rude jump to the one possible truth of my case: it is out of my power to meet your invitation with the least decency of grace. When one declines a beautiful honour, when one simply sits impenetrable to a generous and eloquent appeal, one had best have the horrid act over as soon as possible and not appear to beat about the bush and keep up the fond suspense . . .'
After which he delightfully beats about the bush for several pages.

sented him with a dressing-case.[1] Really a very extraordinary omission, because I have never read letters more packed with character and vivacity and humour, both incomparable in style. Do look them up in Percy Lubbock (unless of course I have said all this before!).

How right you are about the rarity of literary style among fast bowlers. Few of them have put pen to paper. I must read Tyson's book, what a pity he lasted so short a time, he was one of the very few really fast bowlers.

I am sorry about your father—knowing enough of the stresses of senescence to sympathise with him—knowing too how many people wish they were dead but manage to refrain from saying so.

*20 May 1961*                                              *Bromsden Farm*

Your comments continue to be most acute and helpful. I should *never* have noticed that the printers had changed Blackwood's birth-year from 1836 to 1886, thus depriving him of fifty years. I've *got* those portentous seven vols of Carlyle source-book, and sure enough you're right, though the phrase is given as part of a conversation between T.C. and Margaret Fuller: 'I accept the Universe'. 'Gad, you'd better!' I am most grateful. What should I do without you?

[1] '. . . You had done it with your own mailed fist—mailed in glittering gold, speciously glazed in polished, inconceivably and indescribably sublimated, leather, and I had rallied but too superficially from the stroke. It claimed its victim afresh, and I have lain the better part of a week just languidly heaving and groaning as a result *de vos œuvres*—and forced thereby quite to neglect and ignore all letters. I am a little more on my feet again, and if this continues shall presently be able to return to town (Saturday or Monday;) where, however, the monstrous object will again confront me. That is the grand fact of the situation—that is the tawny lion, portentous creature, in my path. I can't get past him, I can't get round him, and on the other hand he stands glaring at me, refusing to give way and practically blocking all my future. I can't live with him, you see; because I can't live *up* to him. His claims, his pretensions, his dimensions, his assumptions and consumptions, above all the manner in which he causes every surrounding object (on my poor premises or within my poor range) to tell a dingy or deplorable tale—all this makes him the very scourge of my life, the very blot on my scutcheon . . .'

By now you could have received up to page 446, which is about half-way through. Can you bear it? Last week I bullied some information out of the printers which makes it quite certain that the book can't appear before January. *Eighteen tons* of paper will be needed, costing almost £3000. The printing, on the biggest machine working day and night, will take fifteen weeks. And *when* am I to compile the enormous index, and fill in all those missing dates? The index I can do on Kisdon, but little else. It looks as though, for January publication, I must finish everything off by mid-July. It is a job for a team of subsidised young experts, not for an ageing publisher in his non-existent spare time.

I do indeed know the James letter to Walter Berry, and in March when I was staying in the James home in Cambridge, Mass, I made Billy James (H.J.'s nephew) read it aloud. He has a barely perceptible and rather attractive hesitation in his speech; and it might have been the Old Master himself—a delicious experience. In justice to Leon Edel, it's fair to remind you that in his introduction to the *Selected Letters* he explains that he has deliberately omitted famous letters already known or printed, in favour of others hitherto unknown.

Last week was pretty exhausting. It began with *two* cocktail parties on Monday, the earlier and more interesting one at the American Embassy in Grosvenor Square. T.S.E. was there, in excellent form, also a lot of poets and littérateurs. All that New York hospitality is coming home to roost, and last week R. and I lunched three separate lots of Americans. On Wednesday evening I went to hear Alistair Cooke give the Annual Discourse at the Royal Institute of British Architects in Portland Place. It was the first time a layman had been invited to speak, and A.C. acquitted himself nobly. Afterwards there was a dinner-party of twenty, including most of the leading architects—Basil Spence, William Holford etc, all very agreeable. And so it went on, day after day, with my Oscar proofs piling up. We plan to drive to Kisdon on June 6 and stay there three weeks. It seems too near and too good to be true.

Duff and his bride are here for Whitsun—very sunburnt and happy. Peter's annual cricket match against the village is on Monday. Duff is playing, but not I fancy Tim, who with Rosalie is staying with the Flemings.

A *most* boring thing has happened. I read your—as always—admirable letter at breakfast yesterday, meaning, *more meo*, to read it again
at least once before answering it when it is always open before me.
And then in the course of yesterday (after one rapid perusal) it
vanished and in my senile decay I remember only a few patches of it.
Damnable. My capacity for losing things grows steadily. I know
exactly where I have put something—but it isn't there half-an-hour
afterwards. Well anyway—

I greatly enjoy this scrutiny of your proof-sheets, but the job grows
lighter owing to your—and really your printers'—outstanding accuracy. The two lots I send herewith are practically flawless, as far as I
can see. As you prophesied, the interest grows with each page. But
the amount of hard labour still before *you* in the way of references is
horrifying. To be done at Kisdon? But surely you need half the
London Library and British Museum to give you any real help.

Have you passed the Strand Theatre recently? outside which the
play is blurbed as 'Delightful, bawdy, wonderful, amoral, indecent.'
A direct result, as it seems to fuddy-duddies like me, of the *Chatterley*
verdict. Words are reversing their old meanings. Whereas 'bawdy' is
now a word of praise, no self-respecting young modern critic will ever
refer without a sneer to writing for which 'beauty' or style is claimed.
I have just read a book (*Mirror for Anglo-Saxons*[1]) in which the author
condemns the English wholesale for being 'gentlemanly'. U.S.A.
writers are praised heartily for their 'brashness'. Have you seen the
book? It says some sensible things but very many silly ones. How
tiresome these young men are who complain of having been 'ruined'
by being sent to Oxford or Cambridge.

Are you hot under the collar about the latest plan for the Oxford
road? A.W. Whitworth[2]—*not* a Christ Church man—says a lot of rot
is talked about the incomparable beauty of Ch. Ch. Meadow. I don't
know it. What would be a real crime would be to spoil the Parks. But I
suppose you all realise that you have literally the loveliest cricket-
ground in the world. It would *not* be improved by a motor-road across

[1] By Martin Green (1961).          [2] Former Eton master.

the pitch. Fenner's on the other hand would. It might also improve their cricket. Annoying your missing the Lord's Test. We could have split a ham sandwich. But I expect you regard the cry of the Swaledale curlew as superior to that of the score-card boy, and the company of Ruth as making all that you miss at St John's Wood of no account. I shall be *chez* my brother at Highgate Village—bus to Golder's Green, change, bus to Swiss Cottage, change (I think), bus to St John's W. (past the home of Jonah).

I am just off to judge a reading competition at Ipswich—the first at which I shall be using my hearing-aid. Old Rendall[1] went on judging when he could hear only treble voices, so all the prizes went to the small boys—which gave rise to the murkiest and most unreasonable theories.

*28 May 1961*                                                    *Bromsden Farm*

Your question about the change in Oscar's attitude to Bosie between May 1895 and May 1896 has probably now been answered by your reading the *De Profundis* Letter. He had had a whole year to think about it all: Bosie had never once even written to him: the attempted publication by B. of O's letters and the suggested dedication of B's poems—all combined to this end.

Yesterday was joyful. Lord's only half-full, and a bitter north-eastern blowing. I had failed to get a Rover for Ruth, so we paid six shillings each and sat in the front row, ground floor, in the middle of the Grand Stand, whence we had a splendid view. The sun shone on us all the morning, but in the afternoon we got colder and colder, and at the Tea Interval went back to Soho Square for a hot bath to stave off *rigor*. We sat next to an amiable young man from Hobart, Tasmania, who repeatedly lent us his superb binoculars. They were Japanese, and he told us he bought them new in Singapore for £9.

After our bath we went to a revue called *Beyond the Fringe*, which is the talk of the town. I expect you have read of it—just four young

[1] Montague John Rendall, 1862–1950. Headmaster of Winchester 1911–1926. In retirement he restored and transformed Butley Priory, near Woodbridge in Suffolk, and was chairman of many committees.

men, who wrote it all—and I must say it was vastly amusing. The best things were a skit on Macmillan speaking on TV, and a mock-sermon.

One day last week R. and I lunched with Sybil Thorndike and Lewis Casson, whom we found enchanting. She is seventy-eight and he eighty-five—a little deaf but right on the spot, and full of plans for future plays.

I hold no brief for Christ Church Meadow—a dreary flat expanse —and think the road should certainly go through it, provided they close Magdalen Bridge to most traffic. If they don't, there will soon be just as much going through the city. The Parks are indeed incomparable, though I have a great liking for Worcester county ground, with the river and cathedral alongside.

I fancy Adam may make a fool of himself at Speeches on the Fourth by not knowing the bit of *Don Juan* he has chosen to say. We never saw Duff perform, as he was playing for the XXII and excused. Pray for a warm day. Yes, write here this week—and then! I suppose I shall get everything done somehow. Taking on the whole Oscar job was, as Henry James said in another connection, 'an insensate step.'

P.S. Read this quickly before you lose it!

*31 May 1961*                                                   *Grundisburgh*

Nasty little sarcasm about my losing your letter—like chaffing a man about the loss of a dear friend! I am still full of chagrin whenever I think of it. It shall never happen again.

How on earth you get through your work I can't imagine. The O.W. stuff alone is easily a full-time job for anyone. I expect most of my recent suggestions are baseless: my faint pride about 'far' for 'for' will probably be easily dispersed by you. What a perfectly loathsome man Douglas comes out as—which indeed his father's son could hardly help being. O.W's taking him up again after he left prison even odder than the Murrys' resumption of friendship with D.H.L. after the latter's unspeakable letter to K. Mansfield.

I should like to see *Beyond the Fringe*. It has had very good notices of those spirited young men. You will not, I think, have seen the Crippen trial turned into a musical comedy. There is no limit to what seems to me sheer imbecility, in which class I unhesitatingly put 'The Turn of the Screw' set to music—on the whole the most appalling story I know—making *Dracula* mere commonplace blood and bones.

I don't care much for *Mrs Patrick Campbell*. All higgledy piggledy and surely much too long. At the very start that tale of her petticoat coming down goes on and on up to p. 20. Do we want to know what *every* single critic said about it? And I agree with you about Jock Dent's interpretations. Poor stuff. He would have done better than that when in old Agate's employ, for J.A. was never arch or merely facetious. I expect Mrs P.C. was fairly intolerable. I haven't reached the Shaw part yet.

Interesting about Christ Church Meadow. Did I ever tell you Masterman's reply when I praised the lovely Worcester College cricket-ground or rather the garden in which it is. 'Which garden do you mean? We have five'. The Worcester county ground is good though surely not equal to the Parks. E. Jones the Australian fast bowler once hit a ball into the river and wistfully said to H.K. Foster at the end of the over 'I wish I had got hold of that one', to which H.K. with an unusual flash of wit said 'If you had, you would have smashed the best stained-glass window in the Midlands'. The cathedral is a third of a mile away.

4 *June 1961*                                                    *Bromsden Farm*

Thank goodness we shan't have to attend the Fourth of June for many years to come. We set out yesterday at 9.30 a.m. (taking with us the sixteen-year-old girl of Adam's devotion) and got home, quite exhausted, at 12.30 a.m. It's a little too much for the middle-aged, and the constant bother of parking, deparking and reparking the car is a nightmare. Speeches lasted too long—two and a quarter hours—and varied, as usual. Only two in Greek, one in French and the rest in English. Adam did his bit well, but it wasn't a particularly good bit. The final item was an intolerably tedious chunk of the play Tennyson

64

wrote when he was fourteen, which should have been destroyed by his executors.

Oh yes—I couldn't help thinking how delighted Oscar would be to see a tolerably handsome boy reciting a passage from *The Sphinx* in Upper School in 1961! The best thing about the day was the weather —warm and mostly sunny. Picnic lunch and tea on Agar's, and in between watched some very moderate cricket. If Harrow or Winchester have any batsmen, they should be in clover, judging by the Eton bowling and fielding of yesterday. The Captain (Wigan) re-arranges the field between each ball, and his own bowling did little to improve his average, which the *Chronicle* told me was 1 for 256. I saw almost no friends except Jonah and Vyvyan Holland.

After Adam had attended Absence[1] we took drinks with the Coleridges, and then drove to Monkey Island for a tolerable dinner. Hideous parking problems again, and the poorest fireworks I remember—long intervals between, and too many behind that cypress tree. Posses of police could do little to mitigate the subsequent traffic-jam. What we go through for our children! The whole place was looking its best in the sunshine, but low-flying jets keep on blotting out all other sounds. Adam says it's only the Boeings, but there are lots of them.

Thanks so much for your two last sets of comments—all most pertinent and valuable. I will see whether that 'for' shouldn't be 'far'. I shall hope to send you some more tomorrow, and thereafter my secretary will supply you to the end. Do send them back, with your comments, to Kisdon. By the time you get this we shall be well on our blessed way. Leave Soho Square 4 a.m. Breakfast, Bawtry 8 a.m. Shopping, Bedale 10.30. More shopping, Hawes 12. Lunch on the Buttertubs Pass between Wensleydale and Swaledale about 1. Report to our farmer at 2. In the cottage before 3. I repeat all this, partly for pleasure, partly so that you can follow. Ruth's little Renault has packed up, so she is hiring a new Ford for three weeks, and we may venture onto the earlier reaches of the M.1. You shall hear all.

Last Wednesday Comfort came up for the night and we went to the Mansion House, to the first-ever Midsummer Banquet for the

[1] The Eton name for roll-call.

65

Arts, Sciences and Learning. There must have been four hundred or more guests received in great pomp, between lanes of trumpeters and soldiers in ancient uniforms, by the Lord Mayor, huge, hideous and charming. Fanfares, bands and mace-bearer. Huge banqueting hall with gallery. Husbands and wives all side by side. On my other side I had an agreeable woman, Lady Logan, wife of the Principal of London University. T.S.E. and wife were at the top table—perhaps you saw the list of guests in Thursday's *Times*? Goodish food—and a superb soup: cold turtle soup *en gelée*, with a nest of pink caviare in the middle and cream on top—Russian, I imagine, but certainly delicious. The chief speeches, by Sparrow and Osbert Lancaster, were far too long, and only in part audible, though I'm told heard clearly on the BBC. Eventually we were given a lift home by Hugh Greene, the head of the BBC.

*7 June 1961*                                   *North Foreland Lodge*

I am in the headmistress's study at North Foreland Lodge. We (a small sub-committee) met yesterday to tell the staff they were, in one or two respects, inefficient, and to do so without hurting their feelings —and staff's feelings are very near the surface. Well I, as chairman, poured melted butter over them and all was well—except that I think they dispersed, unanimously convinced that we had come down solely to congratulate them. I used the old trick of describing one or more of their bad practices as what other schools I knew absurdly and lament-ably did. I think I deceived all except the cynical old man who teaches art and fencing who was clearly enjoying hearing his colleagues hinted at and not himself.

Do you know about girls' schools? Virginal starry-eyed, angelic, do you think? Well the headmistress showed me a letter from another school to the girls here, challenging them to a novel contest—how many girls they could get into a bath all at once. The challengers' record was nineteen. And would they kindly send a photograph of the proceedings before, during, and after. The headmistress asked me (non-committally) what I thought, and was delighted when I said what she thought, *viz* that it stank. What do you think? After all *I* am an old Victorian square and stuffy, entirely out of date.

I have long avoided June 4—an intolerable day—and decades ago I swore I never wanted to see another firework. On many ageing parents the day's effect is the same as that which results from attending an old friend's funeral in January, i.e. death. Don't *you* give way.

How lovely the names of your journey are!—Bawtry, Bedale, Hawes, Buttertubs—the diapason closing full in Wensleydale and Swaledale. Ruth and Swaledale—two lovely names and the loveliness doesn't end with the names!

There is literally nothing that I can find in this O.W. instalment, though I am a little distrustful, as I read it against a prattle of childish voices and a backfisch playing the Moonlight Sonata with the forthright vigour that one expects in 'Rule Britannia'.

*11 June 1961*                                            *Kisdon Lodge, Keld*

No need to apologise for the pencil of your excellent letter from North Foreland Lodge: it was noble of you to write at all in such surroundings. Our farmer's son has gone away to work in Kirkby Stephen, and now there is no milking on Kisdon, so we get our post only when we walk down the hill (which isn't every day) or when the farmer comes up on his motor-bike, ostensibly to look at the non-milking cows ('drybags,' he calls them) but in fact to bring us milk from below. So far, ever since we arrived on Tuesday we have been assailed by bitter cold, lashing rain and a whoreson north-west wind. We sleep anything up to twelve hours a night, hug the fire and get ourselves delicious meals. No callers, no telephones, no sound but the wind outside and the tick of the grandfather clock within. Yesterday was Ruth's birthday, for which I usually assemble half a dozen little presents, to be given at intervals through the day. This time, not through any diminution of devotion, but simply because of the crushing weight of things to do in London, I had nothing! She was very good about it, and graciously accepted a tiny fountain pen which we bought on our week-end shopping expedition to Hawes. Our drive up didn't exactly follow my traditional forecast. The hired car—a Ford Anglia—went like the wind, and by making use (for the first time) of the M.I. from its beginning to the Northampton turn we cut *forty minutes* off our total time, without covering any fewer miles! We flashed through Bawtry at 7.40, long before the hotel was open, and eventually breakfasted at Boroughbridge, after whizzing through Doncaster before its interminable traffic had assembled in the bottle-neck. All we now need is a good way of avoiding the loathsome Leicester.

Your Oscar comments and corrections are most valuable. We haven't yet done anything to the index here, for I had to spend the first two days coping with arrears of mess from the office. I have been reading for the first time John Buchan's last (or perhaps penultimate) novel *Sick Heart River*, which I much enjoyed: he is surely under-rated as a story-teller. Now I am ready for Priestley's new novel, and the life of Wilfrid Blunt by his grandson. But in daytime I am mostly occupied with the Oscar proofs. Just finding and filling in those cross-reference page-numbers in the footnotes takes longer than you would think.

As for those schoolgirl pranks, you should have told them that it's most unlucky to have thirteen (or more) in a bath. What next! It sounds to me much like I imagine Rayner Wood's house to have been.

So far you have said nothing of your opinion of Oscar as letter-writer. (I find his letters make most other contemporary ones seem very dull.) Do you find yourself liking and sympathising with him more and more, as I did? Do some of his jokes make you laugh? I am thankful to say that since we found those last three letters in New York no further ones of any importance have turned up, though the book's publication will surely produce another crop.

To our sorrow there seem to be few or no sales in the neighbour-hood during these weeks, but we still have faint hopes. Ruth is waiting to add a little postcript, so goodnight—and love from us both.

---

*P.S. with my adorable new pen*

To you I can confess that I carry a heavy burden locked in my heart for, quite inadvertently, when buying stamps in the post office at Hawes yesterday, I overheard the latest Test Score and may not tell it for fear of spoiling the papers for days ahead (we are always two days behind). I feel dreadfully guilty and may even give it away in my sleep.

You would have laughed to see R. wrapped up to his ears in a rug and crouched over the fire and his O.W. proofs; a tempest without and our last drop of paraffin gone. Why do people like Augustine Courtauld willingly spend a whole winter alone in an igloo? Very odd people are. But we're blissful here in spite of everything. Perhaps that is odd too.

Dear George, forgive these crooked words but I write on my knee which is nearer the fire. And they bring you my love and the nice thought that I shall one day soon again hear the tap tap of your stick on that interminable flight of stairs. My love. Ruth

*14 June 1961*                                                    *Grundisburgh*

How lumpish of me not to have said what I have all the time felt, *viz* that O.W's letters are *fascinating*. But I was, before your letter arrived, intending to tell you how steadily one's liking for him grows. His bed may have been as full of boys as that bath I told you of was of girls, but what is that to me? It didn't prevent him from being far kinder and nicer and wiser and wittier than most of his precious friends. The Victorians really could be unbelievably stupid and grossly unchristian, whatever their lofty professions. His unending poverty in '97 and '98 is a heartrending tale. Why did no man with money and imagination send him £1000. But perhaps the two things never run in harness.

I am vicariously crushed by the amount of work you still have to do on Oscar, and I still remain literally astounded by the amount you have already done. How *did* you find out practically everything? E.g. how did you get on to *Giton* in Petronius's *Satyricon*, or is all literature your province? You never read Petronius up to e.g. Toddy Vaughan. I am very little good to you over the two enclosed lots. One or two tiny printing-errors and one *Bobbie* into Robbie and jolly little else; but the mere reading is sheer enjoyment, though often painful. You praised Constance in one letter, but wasn't she pretty harsh and unforgiving at the end? What *did* they all expect him to live on if his allowance was cut off? Of course she loathed Bosie—and who shall blame her? Except of course D.H. Lawrence, it is hard to think of

69

anyone who could behave more caddishly. And one finds it hard to forgive coarse second-raters like Henley running down the incomparable *Ballad*. General Wavell wrote that it was 'spoilt by insincerity'. I like to remember that when his anthology[1] came out the Lord Cranworth asked 'Is this what we pay our generals for?' Philistine comments are occasionally—even if inadvertently—bull's-eyes.

I agree about John Buchan—a first-rate story-teller—and who is there except V. Woolf and others who profess not to like a story? Did you know him? A very friendly fellow, excellent company. A pretty stout chap too; he paid practically all his Oxford fees by literary work. He died too young. I must get *Sick Heart River*.

I am enjoying Wells and Gissing, especially the former.[2] I think I have read every book he wrote, and enjoyed them all. But how furious he always was when people asked for more *Polly* and less *Clissold*.[3] But he could be unpardonable, e.g. the way he treated old Henry James.

I have lately been re-reading about two great heroes of my youth (and old age) Wellington and Lincoln. Do you realise what a vast volume of opposition, dislike and contempt both were consistently treated with *by their own side*? And neither turned a hair. That picture of Abe—a broken-hearted man—in the last year of his life is one of the most moving things I know. Also the wonderful beauty of the Duke as drawn by d'Orsay. You know it of course. And please look up Carlyle's pen-portrait of him in his journal 25 June 1850. How many biographers etc don't know their business and realise that to find a man unforgettably described you have to look in Carlyle.[4]

---

[1] *Other Men's Flowers* (1944).

[2] *George Gissing and H.G. Wells*, edited by Royal A. Gettmann (1961).

[3] i.e. *The History of Mr Polly* (1910) and *The World of William Clissold* (3 vols, 1926).

[4] 'By far the most interesting figure present was the old Duke of Wellington, who appeared between twelve and one, and slowly glided through the rooms —truly a beautiful old man; I had never seen till now how beautiful, and what an expression of graceful simplicity, veracity, and nobleness there is about the old hero when you see him close at hand. His very size had hitherto deceived me. He is a shortish slightish figure, about five feet eight, of good breadth however, and all muscle or bone. His legs, I think, must be the short part of him, for certainly on horseback I have always taken him to be tall. Eyes beautiful light blue, full of mild valour, with infinitely more faculty and

Wilfrid Blunt I always suspect had a good deal of the four letter man about him—but he was a good friend to some. Why not—after your gargantuan labours on O.W.—produce a biographical sketch of *Skittles*[1] and her sleeping-partners, among whom, did you know it? was the old Duke of Devonshire. I suspect she was pretty good fun.

18 *June 1961*                                                   *Kisdon Lodge*

The weather is turning this holiday into an endurance test, and though we are winning, we do long for a few days of hot sun. So far in twelve days we have sat out for only two hours. A knock-me-down gale has been blowing for days, often accompanied by driving rain, but we managed one lovely long walk, almost all round Kisdon, which took us the best part of four hours. On Thursday we drove sixty miles to a sale at a farm near Thirsk, where we acquired some cups and saucers, two rugs, and a lovely patchwork quilt (this last for one shilling, the only bid). Ruth was delighted at getting a letter all to herself and will add a word to the end of this. Your kind and flattering words about the Oscar editing are most encouraging and come at a welcome moment. The final work (especially the index) cannot possibly be finished here, and God knows how or when it will be done after we get back. Here we do the index together, Ruth controlling the hundreds of cards and fishing them out as I need them. This demands table-space, concentration and no intruders. The final proofs will have reached you by now, and your labours will be done. If mine are ever concluded I shall have to turn to

geniality than I had fancied before; the face wholly gentle, wise, valiant, and venerable. The voice too, as I again heard, is "aquiline" clear, perfectly equable —uncracked, that is—and perhaps almost musical, but essentially tenor or almost treble voice—eighty-two, I understand. He glided slowly along, slightly saluting this and that other, clear, clean, fresh as this June evening itself, till the silver buckle of his stock vanished into the door of the next room, and I saw him no more.'

[1] Nickname of Catherine Walters, a famous courtesan, to whom Wilfrid Scawen Blunt wrote many of his love-poems.

71

SKITTLES
The Story of a *Poule de Luxe*
by R.H-D.
with an introduction on Victorian Prudery,
and special reference to the bathing
accommodation at girls' schools,
by G.W.L.

Am I right in thinking that there is no really adequate biography of the Duke of Wellington? Guedalla is too slick and sly and second-rate. Shouldn't I commission the right chap to do one? Who is he? Gerry W. is very choosy about showing people the documents, having been much harassed by journalists and Yanks, so his approval is essential. I did suggest the idea to James Pope-Hennessy, but he said military history was not his thing, and anyhow he was full up with work.

I am just enjoying Rumer Godden's latest work, *China Court*, in which she has, I think, succeeded in bringing off an almost impossible task—telling the story of a hundred years (1860–1960) of the life of a family country house in Cornwall, with all four generations inter-woven, so that, although they're all quite distinct and separate, they flow into each other and build up a fine continuous unity. Do try it. You may find it too sentimental, but I think you're bound to admire the writer's skill.

I'm sure I've told you before of the tiny shop in Hawes where the eccentric owner of the Wensleydale cheese-factory deposits all the books he doesn't want, on sale for sixpence or a shilling each. In the past the shop has always been shut, and we got the key from the grocer next door, to whom we returned it with our shillings and six-pences. Now the shop is intermittently cared for by an octogenarian retired railway-signalman, who delivers the morning papers in Hawes and then potters about the shop. He knows the Bible by heart, a great deal of Shakespeare, and has a good library at home, he says, including a complete set of the English Men of Letters series. He was much delighted with a life of Beethoven which he recently bought in Kendal. He used to make a day-trip to York, so as to browse through all the secondhand bookshops. There were no books in his home when he was a boy, and none of his family or fellow-railwaymen shared his interest. Isn't it extraordinary? He is a charming old chap.

E. Blunden has arrived at Soho Square, and is to be there, on and off, till August 20, when an old lady from America moves in. What hope for the index? Write here this week: we shall sadly leave on the 27th. Now comes Ruth.

---

I *did* love having a letter from you all to myself and wish I had some fascinating story to fill in my tiny quota of space. One thing I can say. *How G. is my V.* has been taken from its shelf and laid on the window-seat. What this portends I cannot guess, but I will let you know any developments there may be. I read it years ago with enjoyment but shall not press it upon R., as that would be fatal at this stage.

We *long* for sun, just a pale sun would do to begin with, so long as the wind would cease battering us so mercilessly. I dare to hope to-morrow may be better but it is unwise to speak above a whisper about it.

In answer to your question. 'Does R. ever refuse to do something he is asked to do' the answer is, alas, NEVER. And this I cannot seem to change, though, in this one respect, I would dearly love such a change. What *can* we do? Please go on murmuring 'Swaledale'; it may remind someone to send us some sun. I do wish you could see it all—painlessly of course. My love. Ruth.

*23 June 1961*                                    *Lord's Cricket Ground*
                                                  *London NW8*

From the holy of holies—but all the writing-seats are full and this is practically on my knee. And it will only be a wretched scrap. I leave Highgate Village too early for any letter-writing; I wait a long time for a 210 bus to Golder's Green, of all dim spots, then catch No. 13 for Lord's, and the walk from the stop to the nearest entry is curiously long. Then in the evening I wait aeons for a bus home and am expected to talk all the evening between yawns and so to bed, so what would you? You must at last have had good days: surely the last three have been quite perfect. Pamela optimistically opened our garden last Sun-

73

day, in spite of my prophecies of rain and murmurs that no one would pay a shilling, even on behalf of our fourteenth-century wall-paintings, to come and sit and listen to a loud gramophone playing the Water Music, etc. And of course I was quite wrong. Ancient village crones sat about like great loaves of bread (old fashioned shape), and all said how happy they were—*especially*, and surprisingly, *because* there were no lucky dips and guessing-games etc which most people think are what get the crowd to such things.

In twelve minutes Harvey will be batting again—and then O'Neill. All depends upon what sort of a night the wicket had below its covers. Last night I dined with some nice Old Boys at an absurd restaurant in Beauchamp Place, lit—a big word—by glittering candles and cramped, but good food. I drank too many different liquors and slept uneasily. One of the Old Boys' wives whom I had never seen before insisted on kissing me goodnight. A very sinister sign surely, indicating that I am far too old for a kiss to have the smallest meaning. Never mind. The sun is shining, Harvey is in and O'Neill to come. And Gerald Kelly is said to be in Russia.

25 *June 1961*                                                      *Kisdon Lodge*

Goodness knows when this will reach you. They have wantonly moved the village letter-box from outside our dear farmer's house to far down the hill, and now we can't so readily ask him to do our posting for us. Nor shall we leave our hill-top till the sad exodus of Tuesday morning. And if the publication of Oscar is unduly delayed, as seems likely, owing to the editor's failure to compile the index, the blame can be laid fairly and squarely on the shoulders of G. Lyttelton and R. Llewellyn. Almost since I last wrote I have been immersed in that infernal work,[1] enjoying it enormously, and quickly getting used to that lush-Biblical-Welsh idiom. I quite see what you mean about Bronwen. It's beautifully done, and I'm most grateful to you for forcing me to read it. I think I had been put off chiefly by its length and my lack of undisturbed leisure. I finished it yesterday in a dip of

---

[1] *How Green was my Valley.*

74

the hill—the only place where we can escape the gale, which has blown almost incessantly ever since we arrived. *You* may have been sweltering: we are swathed in jerseys. Our farmer cut his hay in the field in front of us, but yesterday when we helped him rake it together, the wind blew it to blazes, and he was thankful to get most of it heaped up under a tarpaulin.

I wish you could see Ruth's bowls of wildflowers: there are three in the sitting-room and three upstairs. The most beautiful is just pink campion, but some of the mixed ones are lovely. This year, for the first time, we have found a new kind of wild orchid which smells delicious—some kinds smell like tom-cats—and there are forget-me-nots, kingcups, wild roses, bluebells, primroses, cowslips, trollius, wild geraniums, cuckoo-pint, and so on. Tonight we are having a fry-up for supper—sausages, bacon, tomatoes and potatoes. The smell is delicious, and I shall stop to enjoy it.

*Later*
It was superb, followed by bread and local butter and raspberry jam. We drink nothing but tea up here—gallons of it—and are all the better.

Your last batch of corrections was most valuable. I have removed the Max appendix altogether: it's out of place there and seemed feeble. We haven't yet got to page 200 in the index: it's an appalling, endless, back-breaking job, and I simply don't know when I shall get it done.

As I write, the sun is setting over Roger and Westmorland, behind a mass of grey clouds, and the hills are shrouded: I fear our last day here will be no warmer than its predecessors. But we shan't mind, for every moment here is incomparable, and the index calls us. I shall be in the office on Wednesday, to face a pile of tiresomeness, and at Bromsden on Friday, so write there. It's nice to think we shall see you before very long. Much love from us both, and now it's Ruth's turn.

---

*Monday.* Now it is our last—but by no means our finest—hour. The sky is grey, the wind blows and I am so thankful, as a brilliantly sunny final day here would have been unendurable. We are packing everything away carefully for next time. I always hate this part and feel as if I was walking out to the tumbril at any moment.

And please understand I am *passionately* interested in cricket and have always been. My father, who captained Herefordshire in its finer days, was a great friend of H.K. Foster—that pippin-faced and delightful man, and played against W.G. himself on a few occasions.

And does this mean that I may never kiss you again without your having idiotic ideas of the kind put forward (fishing a bit I thought) in R's letter? Well—we'll see about that.

My Lyttelton collection grows—two splendid items now in mint condition. But I fear there may be no more for a whole year, which is remarkably sad. And this will be the last notelet too. My love. Ruth.

*June 26 1961*                                          *Lord's Cricket Ground*

The match just over. The last innings was fun and the Australians really had to fight for the runs. The wicket stayed a bit mischievous to the end. *All* the catches at the wicket were off bumpers. O'Neill, whatever they say, cannot be quite in the Bradman–Trumper class, for, as Cardus puts it, a champion is doubly dangerous when frustrated (W.G. first innings b. J.C. Shaw 0; second innings lbw Morley 221). George Hirst, chiselled out by a Lancs premeditated appeal which bluffed the umpire, got *9 for 32* on the next day.

The England side is giving no satisfaction—no guts, no concentration, not playing like a side etc etc, you hear all round. Cowdrey apparently melancholic at the wicket. It is odd but I have never seen him get a run, but apparently on those occasions he is superb. May in both innings looked good, but each time nibbled. Do you realise that if Lawry had let the ball drop from his thigh so as to remove a bail before he had got 10 (as happened to Dexter at 17) it would have been a very even match?

I met the great Ponsford at tea—a charming fellow. I reminded him of how he stayed in with Bradman for two days, and he replied simply 'Those days were fun.'

P.S. It is drenching and I have no hat, coat, or umbrella and there isn't a taxi and all buses are full. The *Daily Mail* man wants Trevor Bailey back and as captain. God in Heaven!

How delightful that at last you have tackled *How Green*. An immense relief to hear you are sound about Bronwen, for there is a great gulf between me and anyone who does not love her. Indeed it *is* lush-Biblical-Welsh as you put it, but also as you say, beautifully handled. It isn't of course the only way to write, but I was sure your catholic taste would not reject it once you were induced to read it. Did the gentle but irresistible hand of Ruth play any part? I make private bets to myself—and always win them.

I had a very good evening with Tim. He tells me old Cuthbert is in a sad way—not *qua* health but finance. Has he been living on capital or what? I remember an old boy in Worcestershire who decided that he could not live past ninety and lived on capital which would last till then. When he passed ninety he quietly shot himself. They brought in the silly verdict that he was insane.

<br>

*1 July 1961*                                   *Bromsden Farm*

The sad week of south-coming was cheered by unexpected letters from you—one sent on from Keld and one waiting for me here. The wind blew to the last, and I daresay all this heat-wave has passed Swaledale by. We got home in record time thanks largely to the M.1. Ruth's daughter was in her house, and E. Blunden in the flat, which, though expected, was tiresomely disconcerting. During my absence the flat had at one time or another housed *six* Blundens, *four* Chinese girls and an old Chinese nurse. To hear my daily talk, you'd think they'd all been there at once, though I think it's scarcely possible. True, the kitchen looked as though a tribe of roughish gypsies had been camping there, but now all is to rights, and only the gentle E.B. in occupation. He's the sweetest man (don't be surprised if he's there when you come) and no trouble, but the fact of his being there means that I chat to him instead of getting on with my work, and since he's on vacation he has very little positive to do. On Wednesday and Thursday evenings I escaped to Ruth's house in Hampstead (her

---

[1] In the Golden Cross Hotel in the Cornmarket.

daughter having left) and did some Oscar index. By means of working most of today in my library, which is blessedly cool, I have dragged the index to page 250—less than a third of the whole.

If I tried to describe our sadness at leaving Kisdon and returning to London, it would sound childish and unbecoming in a middle-aged man, but I think you realise a lot of it, and we try to cheer each other by reflecting that most people don't get even our glimpses of paradise.

I forgot to tell you, by the way, that at one of our sales several lots were knocked down to a lady aptly named Mrs Bosomworth, which delighted us.

Ruth will be overjoyed on Monday when she gets her unexpected notelet. I'm glad to say she has got out of London for the week-end— to a friend in Sussex, but oh! I do miss her. In fact she hadn't anything to do with my eventually reading *How Green*: I just felt the time was ripe, and ripeness is all.

Yesterday, with the temperature at 85, we had our half-yearly sales conference: thirteen people present for two and a half hours, and I talked almost the whole time—I hope with more conviction than I felt. Afterwards, exhausted, I fell asleep in my chair in the flat.

I haven't seen Peter yet, but probably shall tomorrow. Diana Cooper is spending the week-end with Patricia Hambleden at Ewelme, and tomorrow morning I am going to fetch her over for a drink. Bridget is here, Duff and his wife come for the day tomorrow. Adam has sold a competition to *Argosy* magazine for *twenty guineas* and is much elated. Long Leave next Friday, but no Lord's. A good batch of forthcoming books will go off to you next week: I only hope there's something readable among them. I am now reading the little book about Edith Simcox and her passion for George Eliot.[1] You have probably forgotten, but E.S. gets a passing reference in Oscar, as contributing to the *Woman's World*, and I want to improve my footnote on her.

Comfort is despairing because the rabbits have come back and eaten *all* her vegetables and most of her flowers, while squirrels have had all the strawberries, jays and bullfinches every single raspberry. Apart from all that, the garden looks brown and parched, and I dream

---

[1] *Edith Simcox and George Eliot* by K.A. McKenzie (1961).

of the green green fields of Swaledale. Next time you visit Roger you simply *must* engineer a drive to Keld and its waterfalls.

I have had two charming letters from Birley, who seems pleased by the care with which I scrutinised his typescript. The book won't be out till January or so. I found the usual pile on my desk, and I shan't be up-to-date for days. To cap everything, my secretary is leaving some time in July. She has been with me eighteen months and is thoroughly knowledgeable about all the people I write to. Now, if I can find a new girl, I shall have to start all over again—oh dear!

Did you see *The Times* announcement of the death of Dover Wilson's wife? It ran '. . . . bird lover and for fifty years dear wife of John Dover Wilson.' Deliberate, I wonder?

Ruth would send love if only she were here. Please give mine to Pamela.


*5 July 1961*                                              *Grundisburgh*

You are right about me and Keld. I *hate* your not having perfect weather as if it was my own holiday. And for Suffolk to beat Swaledale in the matter of sunshine is absurd. Even so I don't see you spending your next summer holiday at Saxmundham, where incidentally lives the dullest man in Europe, whose sole interest is the Jewish plot against the world, which, with heraldry, is surely the hallmark of the bore.

I still think that E.B. is lacking in perception to take up, however pleasantly, so much of your time and room, but of course you are the last person to snub anybody (I am sure Ruth agrees there). Again and again, when looking through the O.W. proofs, I thought what a hideous mass of work was still before you, dating and identifying and fixing in all sorts of ways. And the reward—unanimous acclaim by reviewers—probably doesn't excite you much, sure though you must be of it. I hope you saw Priestley's little tribute to your *Hugh Walpole* in last Sunday's *Sunday Times*. He condemns Maugham's *Cakes and Ale* but very mildly. I suppose one mayn't use perfectly accurate words like 'caddish' about a still-living writer. What is the new life of M. like?

79

I doubt if I shall read it, having always been rather allergic to him as a man.

I look forward to the batch from you, and hope confidently that they will lift the depression into which the perusal merely of the reviews of Iris Murdoch's new novel has plunged me.[1] I am like Douglas Jerrold after reading 'Sordello'. I haven't a notion what they mean in most of their sentences, or the quoted passages from the book. And I begin to agree with an old friend who maintains that incest and homosexuality are among the most boring of subjects. There is much to be said for being seventy-eight, at which age one *needn't* read modern novels. You will laugh when I tell you that I have been reading of an evening *The Idylls of the King*. The English is largely Wardour Street (a horse is rarely a horse; it is a steed or a charger, or, if a lady's, a palfrey) and the *dramatis personae* are china dolls. But now and then he brings off a charming little picture or a delicious chime of bells, and I don't mind if they do turn the stomach of Leavis or Amis. The latter, they tell me, has been made a Fellow of Peterhouse, where he will meet the shade of Gray who won't think much of him. Oxford is really the place for K.A. I was there on the hottest days of last week—and no place is hotter than Oxford, so I mainly stayed indoors, having found a walk from Merton Street to Carfax equivalent to any Turkish Bath. We had our meeting in 'The Painted Room' (do you know it?) where our choice was between having the windows shut and suffocating, or having them open and being deafened by the passing traffic. We chose the latter and I, for one, got a very sketchy hold of the agenda.


*8 July 1961*                                                    *Bromsden Farm*

With briefest intervals for meals I put in *twelve hours* at my index today—10 a.m. to 10 p.m.—and covered *forty* pages. It's much the most I've ever done in a day, but I've still only got to p. 340, and the end is not yet. I must confess that from 11.30 to 6.30 I also had the radio turned to Headingley, and maybe I should have done more pages if the game had been less exciting. Until recently winning the

---

[1] *A Severed Head* (1961).

toss seemed to be half the battle: now it seems to be fatal. Did you watch or listen?

Our daily (the cowman's wife) reports that a goldfinch, nesting in a lilac bush in her garden, decorates its nest with forget-me-nots and replaces them with fresh ones when they fade. Can it be true? I must investigate.

*Sunday morning, 9 July*

I still haven't quite caught up on my arrears of June correspondence, piles of manuscripts await my scrutiny, and above all the index calls. I must get on with it now, and trust you will on Tuesday express your forgiveness for this half-pint letter. I reckon that with luck my six years' work on Oscar may net me £1200, which is just the minimum we shall need for Adam at Oxford, as well as his £100-a-year Postmastership. You see, I haven't £5 of capital—never have had—a great handicap. I will disconnect all bells on Tuesday.


*13 July 1961*                                       *Grundisburgh*

There is nothing new to say about yet another of those evenings which I enjoy quite extravagantly, particularly that hour before the dinner. E.B. is a charming fellow, yet anyone but you would gently but firmly point out that you haven't really a minute to spare for him. Odd that he doesn't suspect it. As for Ruth—well it would be straining the truth to say that I was aware of her new dress, but it would *not* be to say that she was more attractive than ever to eye and ear. There again I suspect she was every bit as much so in April, but time scatters its poppy, and great charm always contains some surprise. I expect you are conscious of that every time you see her.

I nearly passed out at the end of the evening. I was afraid Tim, who always lifts me home, had gone, but then found he was playing billiards with Peter upstairs. I toiled up and found no one. I came down and asked some genial Garrickians in the lounge where the billiard-room was. They told me it was *two* floors up, and added that they never played the game as they couldn't face the ascent. So once again I climbed (three hours after No. 36!) and not unnaturally found my legs very achy and twitchy in bed that night. Not that I regretted either climb. But what a loathsome place on the whole London is. Misanthropy in the street has all the look of being universal. I hate all I pass or meet in a bus, and they all hate me—and only *black* bus-conductors have good manners.

I am re-reading *A Passage to India* for exam-purposes. Is it as good as some say it is, or is it a bit over-rated? The unpleasantness of Anglo-Indians seems to me rather over-stressed, just as does Jane Austen's irony, but as you can easily see, I am no judge. I was interested to be told by Anthony Powell that he cannot judge any novel, even his own. He has found Iris Murdoch's latest novel more readable than any of the others. I was pleased to find he greatly admires John Bayley. I only had time to tell Harold Nicolson that he had written of John Wesley being at Christ Church *College*, a gaffe for which I—a poor Cantab— had been severely told off by an Oxonian fifty years back. H.N. smiled demurely but made no reply. I hope I did not offend him.

This is rather a poor scrap, but I am just back and the post is not far off. Love to Ruth (with a capital L).

15 *July 1961*                                              *Bromsden Farm*

Yesterday I fell a victim to what I first thought was gastric flu, but now incline to diagnose as a mild recurrence of jaundice. By the time I got down here the internal upset had developed into a fever and I went straight to bed. After two hours I woke in such a heavy sweat that everything had to be changed. Thereafter I slept peacefully till morning, and today am pretty well recovered, though still a trifle wobbly and listless. I shall keep off alcohol and eggs for a bit. What a bore!

So glad you found Tim in the end and got your lift home. Once again I think Siegfried thoroughly enjoyed himself, though his shy-ness still prevents him from talking to anyone but the person next to him. I manoeuvred Harold Nicolson on to his other side, and they got on splendidly. S.S. confirmed his willingness to house E.B.'s books in an empty room in his Wiltshire mansion, so perhaps in September I shall have some room in the flat again. E.B. is an angel, and since he has nowhere else to stay in London I should feel very bad if I didn't take him in. Nevertheless, as you say, his presence does make the index and other work difficult. On Wednesday we lunched with Tommy and Siegfried and they all went together to Lord's, where E.B. reported *no* spectators for MCC v. Cambridge University.

Adam has just learned that he is to spend his year teaching in a college at Raipur in the Central Provinces of India. In the atlas it looks a hellish long way from anywhere, but he is delighted, and at any rate there is no war going on near there yet. I shall give him *A Passage to India* to read on the way, though I agree it's over-rated. *Howards End* seems to me a much better book. Incidentally, E.M.F. wrote last week to say he'd like to give £1000 to the London Library! After all his previous benefactions, this is munificence indeed. He is indeed a good old man.

Nothing you say about London can possibly equal my own increasing distaste for its crowds and ugliness and noise. In the last ten years it has worsened incredibly.

On Tuesday I am to lunch with T.S.E. to talk about the London Library's Annual General Meeting the following week, and on Tuesday afternoon T.S.E. and I are supposed (separately) to record something for a twenty-minute radio programme on the Library *in German* for the Bosches. I said, truthfully, that I couldn't speak a word of the language; T.S.E. said he could read out a sentence or two, and then his pronunciation went haywire and sounded like bad French. So we are both to speak in English and be translated, like U.N.O. Goodness knows what to say!

Do have a look at the Agate anthology[1] and let me know what you think of it. A new batch of books should be coming in soon. My secretary leaves on Friday, and I have agreed to try a girl of nineteen, fresh from the training college. God give me patience.

Did I tell you that Ruth's daughter has taken a seaside house at a place called Forte dei Marmi, between Pisa and Spezia? R. and I are invited for a brief stay at the end of August. It would be heavenly to get some sun, but this infernal index will still be hanging over me, and

---

[1] *James Agate: an Anthology*, edited by Herbert Van Thal (1961).

we still don't know when Adam is leaving for India. Also I have no money, but R. says she will pay my fare.

I suppose I shan't see you till October? It seems a long way off—like Raipur. Are you visiting Roger this year? We long for a few more days of Kisdon, but I don't see how we can manage all that and Italy too. At the moment, my dear George, a private income and no responsibilities are my dream—or mirage. Perhaps it's partly the jaundice.

*20 July 1961*                                            *Grundisburgh*

A million exam-papers infest the house and, as you see, general degradation has set in—no proper paper, biro etc. I don't think I shall go on for many years more, though I admit the pin-money (about £350) is attractive, especially as stocks and shares seem to be in a downhill slither. But no good in worrying.

What *does* worry me is that you should be for any reason under the weather. Because for the life you lead 100% health is absolutely necessary. Jaundice is the devil in person; I once had weeks of it, through taking its onset lightly and *not going to bed at once*. (*Verb sap*) And I remained more or less gamboge for weeks after I had recovered. That pink-and-white complexion which you have noticed took a long time in returning. Some of the candidates clearly have at any rate mental jaundice—notably the one who writes that Macaulay's style is jerky and obscure, conspicuously weak in description and 'on the whole not worth reading.' He is at Winchester.

Adam's appointment sounds exciting. Get him to write full and detailed letters about everything and everybody—thus killing several birds with single stones, for as you know the way to learn to write is to write—there ain't any other. By the way I should have told you, A. Powell was lyrical about the goodness of your *Hugh Walpole* and wasn't old Priestley nice about it too. I enjoyed his articles in the *Sunday Times*, also Waugh on old Wodehouse. Whatever he said or didn't say in Germany in 1939 he has given intense pleasure to hordes of readers for many years. Though there *are* people who don't think him at all funny; you must know some.

I have read the Agate book with huge enjoyment. What an engaging old rascal he was. The extracts are well-chosen, though I am surprised at there being *nothing* from *Brief Chronicles*, which surely contains as good Shakespeare criticisms as there are. I mean of the plays as played. Fancy being able to write six notices of *Macbeth* all as fresh as paint. Different casts of course.

Byron is as inexhaustible as Wilde, both of them mostly second-rate as writers, but not as men. I must have told you that Housman put B. top of all for an evening's company—perhaps because both were what Swinburne in his letters calls Bulgarians. I got Vol. IV from the library—the only one in. I suppose all his 'illness' of 1878 was akin to D.T. Tell me all about this, also about the earlier volumes. He was very verbose and abusive about Zola's *L'Assommoir*. Was he right? Somehow he cuts a queer figure as a champion of propriety. What would he have said to *Lady C*. (our Lady of Pain!)? Tell me how you got on in German. I hope you were finely guttural. It *can* sound a fine sonorous language when spoken by those who manage to avoid the hawking and grunting and a too aggressive 'sch' (though *all* Winston's s's are practically indistinguishable from the German 'sch').

I have had another bout at my papers, and am ready to tell you that my interest in the character of Aumerle (*Richard II*) is every bit as small as Shakespeare's obviously was, and that I am tired of reading for the nth time half-baked dissertations on whether Malvolio was or was not 'notoriously abused'. All the beaks in England dictated what was to be said about Feste, except at Eton, where one candidate had the sense to say that the play could get along very well without him— whereas most of the rest invariably say that without Feste the play would be 'dreadfully boring'.

We shall not be going north this year—I think—though Pamela may well decide otherwise. I suspect I may never see Swaledale. My heart, lungs, liver and kidneys are apparently more or less flawless. None the less I am full of small mysterious aches and seizings-up for which there is nothing at all to be done: 'you must expect such things at seventy-eight.' It bears out old Dizzy whose reply to the young lady who hoped he was quite well. 'No one is ever quite well.'

My life just now is overshadowed by my health—as I imagine
always happens to people who are not often ill. My pain persisted, so
on Thursday I went in London to see a charming elderly doctor, who
seemed to know his stuff. After extended tests and proddings he pronounced the major organs to be in excellent shape, and *no* jaundice
present. The pain, he thought, came from the gall-bladder, and this
mysterious nuisance is to be x-rayed at the Middlesex Hospital on
Monday and Tuesday (two longish visits are apparently necessary).
If they find huge stones in it they will presumably want to operate (I
gather small ones can in some way be dissolved), and I hate opera-
tions for every reason: ordinary cowardice, pressure of work, Oscar's
index etc. Yesterday I felt rotten, with a slight fever in the evening,
and a constant pain, which is still with me: also complete lack of
appetite. This evening, after a quiet day in garden and library, I feel a
little better and more able to cope. Thank goodness dear E.B. is going
to be away all next week. Ruth thinks that I have been suffering from
this complaint, more or less, off and on, ever since my go of jaundice
two years ago, and I daresay she's right. I have certainly felt pretty
listless, depressed and lacking in energy for most of that time, and
who knows but the removal of my gall-bladder might restore some of
my pristine vigour. You shall be kept informed.

Forgive all this tiresomeness. I have dragged the index to p. 416,
quite enjoying it in small doses, interspersed with manuscript-reading
on the lawn. Once again the sunshine has been inadequate and inter-
mittent. Two lovely bullfinches came and drank outside this window,
to my great delight. There are pheasants everywhere, and the hillside
opposite is purple with great expanses of rosebay willowherb. No
children here and all quiet.

I saw none of the University Match, and doubt whether I shall get
to Lord's to see the Australians on Monday or Tuesday—too many
x-rays, and on Tuesday afternoon the AGM of the London Library,
with T.S.E. presiding. I haven't yet tackled the Byron volume—it is
huge and very heavy[1]—and instead am enjoying a gossipy book called

---

[1] *The Late Lord Byron* by Doris Langley Moore (1961).

*The Pilgrim Daughters* by Hesketh Pearson, all about the American heiresses who married English peers: very amusing. The first two volumes of the Swinburne letters are the best so far: the third and fourth seemed to me much duller. Watts may have had a calming effect on the poet: he certainly damped down his natural propensities and flattened his style.

My German broadcast was quite painless: it lasted for two and three-quarter minutes, during which I stopped at the end of each (impromptu) sentence, and a most intelligent German gave a rapid translation. I made him play the tape back to me and it didn't sound too bad. T.S.E. did his bit later in the day.

*Sunday*

I was woken this morning—not too early—by an infant house-martin which flew in my bedroom window and couldn't get out. The sun is more or less shining, and my pain is tolerable. I wish I need never see London or publishing again. But what then would you do for books? Soon the autumn rush will be on us, and I shall have some more to send you.

Adam is in his last week at Eton, much concerned over 'leaving presents'. Next week-end he flies to Norway to camp with the Corps, gets home on August 8, and leaves for India we don't know exactly when. Bridget reports that the weather on the south coast of Spain is mostly cloudy.

Someone is threatening to sue for libel if I publish a novel which is now in proof. I don't think they've got much of a case, but it will mean interviews with lawyers and much fuss. So far I have been very lucky in that respect: it's too expensive to insure against libel, so one simply has to be as careful as possible and trust to luck. My good secretary left on Friday, and the new nineteen-year-old begins to-morrow, God help me.

*25 July 1961*                                                    *Grundisburgh*

This is a brief gap between ten thousand papers on Shakespeare, Macaulay and Scott, and a million on Chaucer. I am gravely disturbed to hear of your continuing malaise—and also much interested. You will be at this moment (Tuesday) full of bismuth and under examination. Well, I should like to tell you that the operation is nothing very terrific and ever since my second I have been, stomachically, as fit as a flea. The gall-bladder is one of those residual organs which we can perfectly well do without. Tell me all about it: all Lytteltons (male) have what others call a morbid interest in medical and surgical details. I used to enjoy a lot of shop with my London surgeon—the great Sir Holburt Waring. When he cut me he was plain Mr and I mischievously told him the provincial (Windsor) surgeon was a knight. When he heard the name Windsor he said coarsely 'Oh yes, those Windsor surgeons; he was probably knighted for cutting King Edward's corns', which, in fact, was not so very far from the truth; he had taken an appendix out of some royal child.

I have got the Swinburne Letters vols I and II. I quite enjoyed the 1880 or thereabouts volume, though it has its dull tracts. And through recent experience I cavil hotly at the editing. To one of *your* 'not identified' this man has ten; many points which you would have roamed half London to ascertain he leaves unexplained, while expressions used by S., such as 'Words, words words' and 'riotous living' are solemnly given their chapter and verse in Shakespeare or Bible. And how comes it that sometimes a figure referring to a note is one already in use on the same page? Old Swinburne's opinions have still a fine adolescent wildness, and I dislike all that reviling of old Carlyle over his reminiscences. He (C.) was distracted with grief and old age, and in any case clearly did not mean the reminiscences to be published. But all lovers of Charles Lamb have never forgiven C's quite accurate notes about the 'insuperable proclivity to *gin* in poor old Lamb,' and sometimes his punning must have been excruciating. And of course he would have deliberately been at his worst with a dour Scot. It is interesting to see that Watts-Dunton really did prolong S's life by about a quarter of a century. Was it you who told me some quite appalling things about W-D.'s sexual habits? Anyway no doubt you know them.

I finished marking *Old Mortality* yesterday. The difference between boys of sixteen and ditto girls is that you have to work hard to give the former 50/100 and equally hard or harder *not* to give the girls 90/100. The sheer *amount* the girls write—often four and a half pages where a good boy writes one and three-quarters. Scott's young ladies are china dolls; I suppose the conventions of his time insisted on that. As a coarse critic put it 'None of them exist below the neck, still less below the waist.' I am enjoying Gissing and Wells of an evening. What a kindly picture H.G.W. makes in his letters. I suppose he knew that *qua* success and reputation G. couldn't hold a candle to him. I imagine he *always* resented Henry James, though below the surface before *Boon*.

Pamela has just returned from a family gathering to the memory of her great-aunts, the one who died youngest being ninety-seven and the largest under five feet. She might say that was exaggerated, but it doesn't exaggerate my impression of them. Aunt Emily's mouth at tea was well below the level of the table, food found its way to it entirely by gravity. But she was a delicious old lady—full of fun.

<br>

*30 July 1961*          *Woolavington Wing, Middlesex*
                        *Hospital, Mortimer Street, W.1.*

Here I am incarcerated, and your letter at Bromsden—Duff will bring it up tonight or tomorrow. The X-rays of Monday and Tuesday (when I reported as an out-patient) showed the gall-bladder blameless, so my doctor suggested further tests in here. 'You probably won't get a bed for some time,' says he, but next morning they telephoned to say I was to report at 5 p.m. that same day. Unable to postpone a dinner with the Master of the Rolls (Evershed) and other Pilgrim Trustees, in a private room at the Travellers Club, I checked in here at 5, went to the dinner, and got back here at 10. On Friday morning I was subjected to tests so exhaustive, humiliating and exhausting that I have only just recovered. The worst of them—a barium enema—consists of their pouring a bucket of whitewash into one while the process is filmed and photographed. The nurses, who are all gay and pretty and twenty or twenty-one, tell me that this is far the worst, so I await tomorrow's tests with comparative equanimity.

I have a little room to myself—at £28. 7. 0 a week, of which I hope BUPA will pay most—quite comfortable but hellish noisy. Yesterday an electric drill outside operated for some six hours. I had the radio switched to the Test Match, but often drowsed off between the two noises. Today being a *non dies* and sunny, they told me I could dress and sit in an enclosed garden in the centre of the hospital block. I read the papers there, and have just come back to my room for roast chicken and a sweet made of bananas. Soho Square is only five minutes' walk, and the Matron (terrifying in dark green) has agreed to my walking gently there and back this afternoon, to change into some old clothes and fetch a few books. Ruth is staying with her sister in Somerset, so I shan't see her till tomorrow, but I have a telephone in my room, on which I have twice spoken to her. I brought Oscar and his index with me, but so far haven't felt up to tackling him. Also the indexing needs a big flat table-top. Goodness knows how long I shall be here, or what (if anything) they will find out. I still have the pain in the region of the liver.

To complete the tale of Friday's woe, I had *another* stye in my eye (I think the *sixth* this year, but have lost count). It has now entirely subsided, but must surely be a symptom of something. (A drunk has just roared down the street, singing lustily. One of the nurses tells me the neighbourhood is full of Greeks, who don't 'respect the hospital'.)

The office will have to look after itself, with Ruth's eye on it. My new nineteen-year-old secretary is a calamity and must go. She is partially deaf and blind and can't spell—oh dear!

I am toying with that new book on Byron, but find it hard to concentrate. Once one becomes a patient one loses all initiative and feels as helpless as a parcel, which may well be sent to the wrong place.

The AGM of the London Library went off well, with T.S.E. in vigorous form. The *Times* report was almost solely concerned with a minor recommendation which the members rejected—rather to my relief. I think all such meetings should be enlivened by some motion on which everyone can speak—and then if possible defeat the executive. On Tuesday all the members went away blissful.

I suppose you'd better write here this week. If I'm happily released sooner than I expect, I'll let you know at once. The whole thing is a great bore, but I suppose necessary. Think of poor Oscar! I wish I was in your summer-house, helping with the exam-papers.

How utterly and entirely damnable! I have been thinking of you all day with a sort of enraged sympathy in your world of bismuth and barium. Please let me hear what they say after all these tests. Pamela says there is a score of causes for pain in the liver. They won't be long surely in finding out what it is. Something to do with the blood causes styes I believe. All things are linked. And of course this would be the moment when you are minus a secretary. Very odd; there are millions. Rose once, among her contemporaries when asked what she was going to be, struck an altogether alien note when she merely said 'Not a secretary'—which *all* of them were about to be. You must have someone with all five senses alert and easy on eye and ear.

This is an interim letter really but I had to write.

What a stuffy little review of old Agate in the *T.L.S.* last week, by a man without bowels. *Per contra* a *first-rate* one in *John O' London* by Moray McLaren. *All* the right pros and cons bonded with exactly the right blend of charity and justice. I shall write and tell him so. Of course you know him. How rare a perfect review is!

My papers are nearly finished and I have no more getting up at 6.15 (which in fact I rather enjoy). The last batch of papers had answers on Bailey's *Shorter Boswell*. One candidate said it was a very dull book, another that Boswell was a very solemn man and very like Johnson; he got few marks. Another of the books was *Ten Modern Poets*—highly praised by most, but from the standpoint that all poetry before 1930 was long-winded, pompous, unintelligible(!) and generally negligible. They know these modern poems very well, but their knowledge is greater than their judgment.

Hurry and get well, my beloved Rupert, I cannot bear your being ill.

I hope you got Ruth's message to say I had been liberated. I got out after exactly a week, to my great relief, although I enjoyed the resting part of it, and the nurses were like gay and pretty butterflies. They (the doctors) have diagnosed my trouble as a diverticulum in the duodenum! There are other diverticula elsewhere, but the one in the duodenum is causing the pain, they say. Apparently it's not an ulcer but a little sac that fulls up with 'roughage', and they believe that medicine and a strict diet will put it right. No raw fruit or salad, bread, pastry etc, nothing fried. I started it only yesterday (the whole week having been devoted to diagnosis), so feel little benefit yet—am, in fact, just as I was a fortnight ago, with a pain in the region of the gall-bladder, and *no* energy at all. Nevertheless I have resumed my labours on the index in a gentle way, but it can't possibly be finished before our trip to Italy on August 21 or so. Will this infernal task ever be accomplished? My love-hate for it is overpowering.

I was delighted to get your letter in hospital (if you wrote twice the second one hasn't reached me yet) and Ruth's daily visits were lovely rays of light. All hospitals, however comfortable and considerate, are rather like prisons, and ordinary outside life seems very remote and desirable. Although I had a pile of books beside me I read little, preferring to drowse or listen to the Test Match. That last day was pretty exciting, wasn't it?

The trouble with the Byron book is that it is so big and heavy— not suitable for reading in bed, needing almost a lectern to support it. I did read a couple of thrillers, corrected the proofs of the new Druon, and toyed with some Oscariana. The good Moray McLaren also reviewed Agate excellently in the *Scotsman*, where he is all agog for Oscar. Other reviews already arranged are Sparrow in *T.L.S.*, Richard Ellmann in *Guardian*, William Plomer in *Listener*, Terence de Vere White in *Irish Times*, probably J.I.M. Stewart (Michael Innes) in *Sunday Telegraph*, and I hope Mortimer and Nicolson in *Sunday Times* and *Observer*.

One good result of all my tests is that heart, lungs, liver, blood, gall-bladder and intestines generally are pronounced A.1. except for these infernal diverticula. All very encouraging.

A postcard from Adam in camp in Norway says he is having fun but the going is hard. He is due back on Tuesday (8th) and sails for Bombay on the 17th. He goes in a cargo-boat with seven other boys bound for various jobs, and I imagine they will stop everywhere, which will be fun for him. From Bombay he is to be flown across the steaming continent to his destination in the Central Provinces.

Peter looked in today, preparing to drive to Scotland for the Twelfth. Duff is playing cricket in Wales, and Bridget is there too, so here all is quiet. If only the sun would shine! I feel completely sun-starved, and sea-starved too. Ruth is spending the week-end with an old friend in Sussex. One benefit of this diet will be that it pretty well prohibits eating out and provides a capital excuse for refusing invitations. I imagine you will soon be submerged under grandchildren, to Pamela's delight.

This afternoon, after lunch, I went right to bed and slept for two solid hours; which will show you how relaxed and listless I have become. The idea of work is disagreeable, and the grasshopper a burden fit for Atlas. No doubt the diet and some Italian sun will re-charge my batteries, but I can't foresee any second Kisdon trip this year, which saddens us both. E.B., charming as ever, is still in the flat, but is to leave on August 20, when my old friend Elizabeth Drew flies in from America. She is almost your age, and a martyr to all sorts of rheumatics. When she leaves (I hope at the end of September) the flat is to be rearranged, so that no sleeping visitor is possible. A night or two one can bear, but weeks and months are quite intolerable. Did I tell you that my Lawrence portrait is to be included in the Lawrence exhibition at Burlington House in the autumn? They tell me it's worth at least £3000, perhaps more! I may have to sell it one day. Now a little more index and then more bed.

9 *August 1961*                                        *Grundisburgh*

I was immensely relieved to hear that all was fundamentally well with the Rupertian interior. And how very kind it was of Ruth to telephone. She got Pamela, and you will be no more surprised than I was to hear that merely to hear her speech over the air put Pamela at once and emphatically among the numerous pro-Ruths. Please thank her most particularly. I know just as little about diverticula as Mr Micawber did about gowns. The diet etc will put you right, but I hope it won't be too severe or prolonged. I don't want to see you at the Lit. Soc. waving crossly away all the offered dishes *à la* Cuthbert. I wonder why the 'roughage' should have behaved like that.

'Sir, you may wonder.' I let you off a second letter last week; not only was the cistern fairly dry, but exam-papers were again silting up. Pleasant little oases were provided by some re-browsing over Wilfrid Blunt's diaries. These are full of good stuff (no doubt you know his admirable page about Wilde's death, as told him by Ross). He was a wilful, and I suspect thoroughly tiresome, old man in many ways. His judgments were always emphatic, sometimes excellent (e.g. on Winston) and sometimes magnificently fatuous. *Your* blood will boil at hearing that he put Yeats *far* below Gilbert Murray as a poet. He also said that it was impossible there should ever have been a worse play than *The Tempest* and that Milton was a 'pompous windbag'.

I must tell you that Pamela a week or two ago stayed at a house where there was a copy of *David* by your uncle. She was greatly attracted, but had no time to finish it. She refused to cadge for a possible copy, but you have deliberately encouraged me countless times to do so. But I expect it is long out of print. I don't remember reading it.

Your groans over O.W. are similar to Carlyle's over Frederick, but you have about another six or seven years to go. I can't think how it didn't kill him (and hasn't yet you!).

I expect the hospital rest did you good, but aren't the days long— partly because of their insanely early start to each one. One thinks it is nearly lunch-time and it is 10.45. How doctors do hate anything *fried*! It is always the first thing they cut off whatever one's complaint. I don't know what is so poisonous about it; why for instance should it raise one's blood-pressure?

There are only half-a-dozen grandchildren here at the moment but more in the offing. P's sister-in-law (a millionairess) has given us a lovely portable hut, or rather two huts, now being erected in the garden (without a permit which they tell me is probably essential, but I am a strong believer in the effect of a *fait accompli*).

*12 August 1961*                                                    *Bromsden Farm*

I'm glad to be able to report that I feel very much better than I did a week ago. For the first time in *many* weeks I begin to feel once again faintly on top of at least a few things, instead of that crushed and hopeless inertia which had for so long oppressed me, and which I now learn is a leading symptom of diverticulitis. The diet is more than tolerable, and my doctor has now agreed to alcohol in moderation—not that at the moment I feel like it, but our trip to Italy is approaching, and the local wines must surely be sampled.

Adam flew safely home from Norway just twenty-four hours before all those children crashed there, and now this infernal organisation that is sending him to India says that the cargo-boat is off (though the shipping line had just assured me to the contrary), and he will probably have to fly. Comfort is putting a good face on it, but there will be a nasty couple of days if he does.

A copy of *David* shall go to Pamela on Monday. You should by now have received Fleming[1], *The Franco–Prussian War*[2], the Whiston book[3] and *Poor Kit Smart*.[4] If any of these has failed to arrive, please send an immediate postcard to Soho Square. My lack of a secretary is an infernal nuisance: that deaf-and-blind girl lasted only a fortnight, and there's no point in trying to get a new one till we're back from Italy.

The Middlesex Hospital didn't wake one till 7.15 a.m.—very civilised. Altogether my week cost £63, part of which I am trying to recover from BUPA. Do you know it.?

I have indeed urged Adam to keep a diary, and he seems to take to the idea. I bought him the three volumes of Somerset Maugham's collected short stories to read on the boat, and *The Legacy of India*, a good Oxford symposium, to teach him something about that humid sub-continent. He is to teach English and elementary Maths and Science up to O. level, or so he gathers. In some ways he is still so childish that I rather quail at the distance etc., but I expect he'll be all right. Now for bed.

---

[1] *Goodbye to the Bombay Bowler* (1961).
[2] By Michael Howard (1961).
[3] *The Whiston Matter* by Ralph Arnold (1961). An account of the running battle between the ʲRev. Robert Whiston, Headmaster of the Rochester Cathedral Grammar School and the Dean and Chapter of the Cathedral (1848–1852), which gave Trollope ideas for *The Warden* (1855).
[4] By Christopher Devlin (1961).

*Sunday morning, 13 August.*

A long but disturbed night, with bad dreams and some pain. My breakfast now is not your manly oatmeal porridge, but a sieved pap of groats designed for babies. As I mumbled this down I re-read Pater's *Renaissance*. Oscar says it influenced his whole life, so I thought I had better have another look at it, in case I had missed some references. So far this is not so, but the gentle tones and modulations of the old aesthete fit well into my frail mood of convalescence.

Soon I shall have to switch over to the proofs of a strident American novel that has been offered to me. The house is swarming: all three children, plus Duff's wife and Comfort's step-mother. Last night they slept all over the place on camp-beds and mattresses, and Comfort cooks and cooks. It is the last reunion before Adam's departure—and perhaps Bridget's too. The sky is a uniform grey and there is a slight drizzle. Owing to a dearth of grass for the cows to eat, Peter's minions have strewn in the adjacent field great swathes of dun-coloured silage, whose sickly stench takes most of the pleasure out of gardening. Adam has a heavy cold and sea-lion's cough—aftermath of eight open-air nights in Norway. I enclose Oliver Van Oss's admirable report on him, which please return. It is very shrewd and perceptive. Has a fold of the mantle of G.W.L. perhaps fallen on O.V.O.?

Write here this week, and next Saturday I will send you our Italian address. I think we set off on Monday, 21st, by boat and train to Pisa, and thence by bus. Neither of us speaks any Italian, but I have a fairly up-to-date phrase-book. Luckily Ruth's daughter knows the language well. I can't wait for the hot sun and the swimming. Much love to Pamela. She and Ruth must meet.


*16 August 1961*                                      *Grundisburgh*

I have pretty well finished my G.C.E. papers now, the last batch being an incredibly feeble lot from a school in Lebanon who regarded Macaulay's English as about on a par with Henry James's last style ('The Old Pretender').[1] Several of them said that Charles II's army

[1] Philip Guedalla (1889–1944) wrote: 'The work of Henry James has always seemed divisible by a simple dynastic arrangement into three reigns: James I, James II, and The Old Pretender'.

was lacking in 'cavalcades'. I wrote a report which will probably result in Lebanon leaving the Commonwealth—which I never knew they were in. Do you ever have a mild black-out, *viz* a spell when the page or manuscript you are looking at conveys no meaning at all? I do after the numbing effect of several hundred scripts. The first one was a little alarming, but I have learnt that the bout goes off in about five minutes and I cease vaguely wondering who on earth Brutus was. I think I shall drop this examining after next year; I dislike it a little more every year of late, though a little pin-money is certainly pleasant.

Thank you for letting me see Oliver Van Oss on Adam, which I return. An *excellent* letter—as such do, throwing much light on both writer and subject. I saw lots of O.V.O. at Eton and (I hope) I to some extent explained Eton to him. Reports are one of Eton's specialities and he may have picked up something in our talks, but I claim no more than that. He is a first-rate teacher and tutor. Is he right about A's humour? I remember no puns at Xmas. Nor somehow can I see his father being very patient with puns.

Pamela is thrilled about *David*, pink with pleasure. I have received all those admirable books you sent except Peter's, which should be good fun. I had great fun all yesterday with the Whiston-Rochester imbroglio. Fascinating. As good in its scale as Bentley and the Trinity Fellows.[1] And I am particularly glad to have *The Franco–Prussian War*, which I have never really read about. I am always fascinated by Bismarck and Moltke (*'der grosse Schweiger'*). I have brought it to Oxford to fill spare hours, and my address this next week-end will be *St Edmund Hall*, where the only defect is the immense distance between one's bedroom and the lavatories. Some younger awarders than I are notably inferior to me in the matter of bladder, though I confess I am not as good as I was (I hope never to descend to the level of dear Harold Nicolson).

I am much interested by your giving Adam old Maugham to read —because I recently recommended him to a parent who was in despair about his son's English writing. For lucidity only old Shaw rivals him.

[1] The great classical scholar Richard Bentley (1662–1742) was from 1700 Master of Trinity College, Cambridge. For thirty-eight years the Fellows of the college vainly attempted to unseat him on the grounds that he had infringed some of the statutes.

If A. is interested in music give him Shaw's Corno di Bassetto volume.[1]
Humphrey battens on it. Please give him my warmest good wishes
(not that he will not feel quite happy without them).

Do you know Pisa? If you don't and the sun is shining you *must* go
to the Campo Santo, mainly ignoring the leaning tower which is a
mere freak, though a lovely tower if *not* leaning. I nearly fell off it in
1902.

<br>

20 *August 1961*                                        *Bromsden Farm*

After an exhausting week, during which my duodenum played up
tiresomely, and I twice retired to bed at 5 p.m., I am now poised for
Italian sun. Tomorrow (Monday) morning Ruth and I leave Victoria
at 11 a.m., lunch heavily (to hell with the diet!) on the Paris train,
chug round to the Gare de Lyon, change into the Rome Express, dine
heavily therein, sleep in our sleepers and alight at Pisa at 11 a.m. on
Tuesday. I fear the only sight-seeing we are likely to do there depends
on what lies between the railway station and the bus-stop, to which
we shall be carrying our luggage. Our address till 5 September will be:
c/o Mrs Goodman, Via Agnelli 16, Forte Dei Marmi, (Lucca), Italy.
They say the posts are terrible, and it is a help to put EXPRESS on
letters, which I suppose means going to a post-office and paying more.
Anyhow I'll send you my regular budget and hope for the best. I am
taking *no* Oscar or other work (I can't remember when this last happened), but simply a few paperback detective stories and the World's
Classics edition of *Middlemarch*. Each day I see in the papers that the
temperature at both Florence and Rome is well into the eighties, so
have high hopes of sun. Ruth is as excited as a schoolgirl, and as she
is paying for *everything*, I tell her that at last I shall experience the full
pleasures of being a 'kept man', which has always seemed to me a
consummation devoutly to be wished.

Meanwhile the index, which is spread around me as I write, has
reached p. 563, with another 300 to go. Darling old Katie Lewis

[1] *London Music in 1888–89 as heard by Corno di Bassetto (later known as Bernard
Shaw)*, 1937.

(daughter of the first Sir George[1]) died last week, aged eighty-three, and left me, bless her, an exquisite drawing of Mrs William Morris by Rossetti—the gem of all her houseful of treasures. It hasn't arrived yet, and must wait for Probate.

E.B. evacuated the flat yesterday, after two and a half months, and apparently his daughter says she will relieve me of his 7000 books (Siegfried first said he would take them, and then thought better of it). My old friend from America, Elizabeth Drew, arrives on Wednesday for the best part of a month, but we shall miss the first fortnight of her. When she has gone I shall *never* have another visitor for more than a night or two: it's too wearing altogether.

Your exam-paper blackouts sound terrifying, and I'm glad to say that not even indexing has yet given me any such.

O.V.O. is not far wrong about Adam's humour, which remains punnish and rather third-form. He is still hanging about, quite happily I think, waiting for his marching orders.

As a bed-book I have been reading Pater's *Imaginary Portraits*, and find them just the thing—exquisitely written sketches of nothing much—four beautiful walls of tapestry with nothing in the middle.


*20 August 1961*                                                *St Edmund Hall*
                                                                     *Oxford*

God knows when this will get to you. You say *your* posts are uncertain, and at this end an Oxford man tells me you may post a letter here for London and it takes a day and a half. Curious how *incompetent* everything is at Oxford. In the exam-room the door sticks, the carpet rucks up, the collapsed bulb took some time to replace because there were no steps long enough to reach it. In this college we are fed like fighting cocks, but there are no bath-mats or corks. I have to be very careful not to slip up on a wet stone floor. The traffic of course is beyond a joke. There are lots of genial men about; several (of course)

---

[1] George Henry Lewis (1833–1911). Leading solicitor. Knighted 1893, created Baronet 1902.

know you, but I gather not well. R.W. David and charming wife, Colin Eccleshare, both of the C.U. Press, and others.

I am annoyed about your duodenum. Oughtn't it to be quieting down? or is more time wanted? You don't seem to be at all fussed about it. You are at this moment browning in the sun while here the cloud persists, though it is (at Oxford) mainly dry.

I shall be surprised and disappointed if you don't like *Middlemarch* with all its (and G.E.'s) defects. V. Woolf rightly described it as one of the few really grown-up English novels. You won't like either Mr Casaubon or Ladislaw, but you will admire the way poor Lydgate's decline is pictured. I am not sure the Garths, if I have got the name right, aren't a bit boring.

Just coming to an end here, the only job remaining being to peruse all the Eng. Lit. examiners' reports and correct their English. It usually takes about two and a half hours. They mostly avoid the split infinitive but are quite prone to the hanging participle and most write 'due to' when they mean 'owing to' or 'because of'. Ignorance to-day is frightening. Hardly any candidates know who the Muses were, their answers ranging from dons, grub street authors, horses, musicians, and 'important people' to (coyly) 'people like Nell Gwyn who lived in the slums'.


*27 August 1961*                                    *Via Agnelli 16*
                                                    *Forte dei Marmi*


Our journey went well, despite a rough Channel, and we ate two stupendous train-meals. In the end we never got to Pisa, since we found that the train stopped at Viareggio only ten miles from here, where we got a taxi.

So far the weather has been superb—a succession of cloudless blazing days in the eighties, with three or four bathes a day, and the rest of the time spent sunning, sleeping (including after-lunch siesta), eating and reading—all done very slowly and with great enjoyment. This is a nice little bungalow with modern plumbing, and I am writing in a garden behind, which is entirely covered by vines and bunches of grapes, rather like Max's 'vining-room' at Rapallo. The sea is an easy ten minutes' walk. There are wide sands, all very clean and well organised. Under pretence of offending the Catholic Church, no one is allowed to undress in public, and this enables countless little bathing-huts to be let for the season, together with deck-chairs and large gay beach-umbrellas. No English, thank God, and the chatter of the numerous Italians is as unintelligible and harmless as birdsong or an opera libretto—'*Ce qui est trop bête pour être joué, on le chante.*'

Close behind the little town, or so it looks when one is swimming, tower the wonderfully dramatic peaks of the Carrara mountains: black and pure white, and the lower slopes pine-tree-green with tiny white villages dotted about. Florence is only an hour away, but I fear we shall stick to the sea. We are both brown and well and, as I say, relaxed to the point of inertia.

So far I have read one thriller, two American novels, and have nearly finished my American friend Francis Steegmuller's splendid book *Flaubert and Madame Bovary*: if you don't know it, do try it from the library. *Middlemarch* comes next.

Occasionally we see threatening headlines about Berlin in Italian papers, and roll over in the sun until it's time for the next swim. The ice-cream is superb, but perhaps this leaves you cold (sorry for the third-form joke)? I don't know whether Adam has yet left for India—in fact all I do know is that I feel wonderfully well—for the first time in ages—and this life suits me fine for a week or two, provided my darling Ruth is with me. Disdaining her normal postscript, she has sent you a p.c. on her own. I'll hope to write more sensibly next week.

Tomorrow is my fifty-fourth birthday, and my duodenum is behaving well.


*31 August 1961*                                              *Grundisburgh*


Your life sounds just right—*four* bathes a day, and huge meals, and seascapes, and a novel or two, and a background of Italian language, and a foreground of Ruth—well if that isn't idyllic!

I have just finished your massive book on the Franco-Prussian war. Very interesting. I admit I skipped airily through some of the battles, of which I can never follow the accounts. Now for your most welcome

P. Fleming, good bedside reading if ever there was. I have to write a tabloid biography of Ben Jonson for Dick Routh. The awful truth is that I have *never* been able to bear B.J., agreeing with Tennyson that reading him is like wading through glue. No doubt I shall find that *Volpone* is your favourite play, as it was A.W. Ward's and Saintsbury's. P. Fleming gets good reviews, which is pleasing. I thought the light 'middle' was out of fashion to-day. Coming back perhaps. Also Bernard Fergusson gets a good press for his sketch of Wavell. But why does his publisher price the book (96 pages) at 12/6? Surely 7/6 would have been right? But what do I know? Old Winston makes a slightly vindictive appearance. And he *ought* to have attended W's funeral— the only general who gave us a sniff of success for two years.

There has been some sad stuff in the recent critiques of war-books. What a pity Paul Johnson, Crossman, Alan Brien, etc were not in command. They clearly know exactly what should have been done.

Is it the Carrara mountains where the marble comes from? Your descriptions are full of sunlight and colour. *Middlemarch* may be a bit Midland English for your surroundings.

*3 September 1961*                                    *Via Agnelli 16*
                                                      *Forte dei Marmi*

Every day here has been lovelier than the last, it seems. Unbroken sunshine, so that instead of dashing out to catch the day's five-minutes-worth, as all this summer at home, here one arranges to avoid the three hottest hours by means of lunch and a siesta. At mid-day the soft sand of the beach is almost too hot to walk on barefoot. We spend some six hours a day on the sand or in the water—this morning I had three long swims of perhaps half an hour each—and except for the area of our bathing-kit we are a most satisfactory brown all over.

I imagine that fifty years ago this was a strip of pine-trees and sand, between the mountains and the sea, with perhaps a little village in it. Now it has been 'developed' as a summer resort, but most attractively —not at all like Peacehaven or Lytham St Anne's. In the centre of the little town—a road's width from the beach—is a large circle of shady pines, under which are a children's railway and numerous carts drawn by donkeys and small ponies. All round the wood there is held every Wednesday a most attractive market, where we have bought this and that. My birthday turns out to be the day of the local saint (St Ermete), in whose honour an extra day-long market was held, followed after dark by superb fireworks on the beach. The Provost and Fellows could get some good ideas for improving the Fourth. The English papers get here at 6 p.m. the same day, so I have kept up with the cricket and drunk to Hampshire's triumph. I am just over half way through the magnificent *Middlemarch* which I am enjoying inordinately. More of this next week, when I shall have finished. Mr Casaubon is certainly a warning ('Oh, he dreams footnotes, and they run away with all his brains'), but a fortnight here has so recharged my batteries that I positively look forward to polishing off Oscar. The book is much *wittier* than I had expected, and within its limits it is masterly—no fumbling or uncertainty in the treatment.

We are due to reach London on Wednesday evening. Write to Bromsden this week. I write in the vine-arbour at 3.45 p.m., but the beach is calling, and I do so enjoy every moment of it. When one swims out a little way the sweep of the mountains is wonderfully beautiful. I haven't left much room for Ruth.

---

There is little more to say in my so small space except to endorse that a 'new man' is emerging, just as good as the old. *Immense* benefit has been had by both and I am convinced it should be an annual affair. The certainty of sunshine is such a delight for a prescribed time. Not for ever.                                                    Ruth.

*10 September 1961*                                          *Grundisburgh*

And now you are facing a mountain of toil and feeling like Sisyphus —*but* feeling in finer fettle than he ever did. Your restored vigour is *very* good to hear of. I was sure you would enjoy *Middlemarch*—to my mind her best, though what that old ass Ruskin called the 'disgusting' *Mill on the Floss* is not far behind. The Rector of Hagley (a particularly good man who hunted twice or thrice a week) wouldn't allow *Adam Bede* in his house. *Tempora mutantur.*

I am setting G.C.E. papers for next year—a curiously sweaty job, especially as one has to provide a crib, and it is hard to find twelve or fourteen consecutive lines of Shakespeare for paraphrase, because there is always a line or phrase in it about the meaning of which I feel quite hazy. I usually put something quite vague which I know Brigadier Thomas R. Henn of Cats will emend, though his version often seems as dubious as mine. Shakespeare is a very difficult author. In the *Macbeth* paper I nearly gave them that magnificent paragraph of Masefield's on how M. should be acted,[1] but Tom Henn would have it out (he is head reviser). If you have in your mind a good question about Conrad's *Nigger* and three other tales, please let me have it. A large general question about the man Josef Korzeniowski.[2] They tell me he is out of fashion now; he would be. But I like the story of a visitor to C. being kept for a bit in the garden, C. still being in the throes; suddenly a window was flung open and a pale, sweating, haggard face looked out and gasped 'I've killed her.' He had just described the death—tremendously moving—of the young woman in *Victory*.

I must go in to tea. The garden reverberates with child-song.

I enclose half-a-sheet for Ruth—very poor measure I know. I am like the saint who had endless things to say to and about the Almighty, but eventually said only 'Lord, Lord!'

*10 September 1961*                                        *Bromsden Farm*

The weather held up wonderfully until the very morning of our departure, when, as though in anger at our going, thunder crashed out over the mountains, and rain fell in torrents. First we took a local train to Pisa, where we spent three hours admiring the Leaning Tower and other antiquities. The Campo Santo was badly bombed, but has been excellently restored. The rain had stopped by this time, but the air was hot and clammy. As we entered the very stuffy Baptistery, Ruth said 'I shall get a migraine if we stay here long,' so we withdrew immediately. I don't suppose the Tower has changed much since you

---

[1] See vol. 4 of these letters, p. 15.
[2] Conrad's real name.

nearly fell off it in 1902—very beautiful and impressive we thought—
but we did not climb up it, for fear of repeating your near-catastrophe.
The bridge over the Arno, also destroyed in 1944, has been very
elegantly rebuilt. We just had time for a drink outside a café before
catching another local train to Florence, and as we crossed the great
Plain of Tuscany, the sun, of which we had seen no glimpse all day,
suddenly appeared in time to set in a blaze over the cypresses and
vineyards and little stunted trees.

We reached Florence in darkness, so saw nothing but the huge,
clean, modern station, where we transhipped to our sleepers in the
express. An excellent dinner, quite a good night, and we reached the
Gare de Lyon at 9.30 a.m. Paris too was sunless but warm. We had
two little walks and some refreshment before boarding the Calais train
at mid-day. A smashing lunch, a roughish crossing, and London on
Wednesday evening. Both of us much sunburned, sad to be separated
from each other and the sunshine. The good lady who is staying in the
flat—Elizabeth Drew—will go back to America before the end of the
month. E.B. is back in Hong Kong, and his married daughter has
nobly said she will take the books, so directly Elizabeth leaves, I shall
at last be liberated from them. All here is well. Adam flew to India
last week, and we have had one good letter from Delhi, where Paul
Gore-Booth (once K.S. and now High Commissioner in India) very
kindly had him looked after. Adam reports the temperature as a
steady 95° and very humid, and I don't envy him the 48-hour train-
journey to his school at Raipur, whence he telegraphed safe arrival.
Comfort misses him a lot, but is bearing up well.

*Middlemarch* was exactly right for that sun-drenched peaceful holiday, with only Italian voices in the offing. I finished it in the train to
Florence, quite sorry to part from some of the characters. For the rest
of the return journey I read *Weir of Hermiston* with sad pleasure: I
think it might well have been R.L.S.'s masterpiece. This passage from
it might be about Kisdon:

All beyond and about is the great field of the hills; the plover, the
curlew, and the lark cry there; the wind blows as it blows in a
ship's rigging, hard and cold and pure; and the hill-tops huddle
one behind another like a herd of cattle into the sunset.

The day after we got back my lovely Rossetti drawing arrived. I'm going to have the mount altered (white instead of gold) and then it will be ready for your admiration some Lit. Soc. evening. It's a massively beautiful head of Mrs William Morris, with whom D.G.R. was clearly much in love, and is to me the quintessence of Pre-Raphaelitism. I don't quite know where to hang it, but it can have pride of place in my office for three months, while my Lawrence is at Burlington House.

Duff has brilliantly contrived to make the *Sunday Telegraph* pay £1500 for the serial rights (one article) of the Oscar letters. Of this £675 will come to me, and not a moment too soon, for I haven't a penny anywhere. Adam's year in India gives me a breathing-space to collect enough for his three years at Oxford. Meanwhile the index has only reached p. 567 and must somehow be finished, though there are mountains of urgent manuscripts awaiting my attention.

Birley, with whom I am now on Christian-name terms, was delighted with *The Whiston Matter* and is giving a copy to the chairman (or whatever) of the Headmasters' Conference. I'll send you some more books next week.


*14 September 1961*                                                 *Grundisburgh*


Your trip really does sound a success. There is something fitting about weeping skies at one's departure from a lovely holiday. But I fear you may not have been long enough in the Pisa Baptistery to hear its really gorgeous echo. The curator sings four or six notes and a celestial chord wanders to and fro about the roof for at least half a minute. The climate of Pisa can be awful but that 'hallowed acre' where the Tower etc are is a blissful memory. A few hours at Florence are not much good; you need a few days, because the views from round about are inimitable, 'at evening, from the top of Fesole'[1] for instance.

Adam sounds well *rangé*; it will surely be a very good experience for him. I am delighted that *Middlemarch* came up to expectation and

---

[1] Milton, *Paradise Lost*, book I, line 289.

hope. There are moments—I say this with bated breath—when *to me* she makes Miss Austen a little thin, but to Roger and all those platoons of women that would sound sheer blasphemy. I horrified a young woman who was here last week by saying that I thought *Mansfield Park* much better than *Emma*. And I am *quite sure* that *Northanger Abbey* is on the whole bad. *Nothing* can surely be said for General Tilney's behaviour—true neither to nature nor art. *Weir of Hermiston* I remember thinking a magnificent start. What an outstanding horror Weir's original, Lord Braxfield, must have been—like a formidable blacksmith in appearance, as Cockburn says. Illiterate, contemptuous, coarse, and often condemning a man to death with a savage joke. Didn't he send to the gallows a man with whom he played chess, with some pleasantry about its being 'mate this time'—the Jeffreys of Scotland? But Scotch judges have always been *sui generis*.

Do you admire that tiresome old ass Bertrand Russell going cheerfully to jail for his principles at eighty-nine? Because I do! And how can anyone be happy about our present bomb-policy?


*16 September 1961*                                          *Bromsden Farm*

With the arrival of two letters from you this week the rhythm is resumed. All week I have been doubled up with lumbago or some kindred complaint, and still am. At least it has served to remove, or sufficiently obscure, all symptoms in the duodenum. If it isn't one thing it's another. My guest in the flat is flying back to America next Thursday, and even the *thought* of having the flat to myself—or rather ourselves—is an immense relief. Someone has been there since the beginning of June! Last week the hot water failed, and the gas people took *four days* to put it right. Also my daily woman is on a week's holiday, so siege conditions have prevailed.

Adam writes happily from India, where he apparently lives on curry and spends every evening playing bridge in Hindi with the beaks. His train-journey from Delhi took three and a half days owing to a landslide, but he failed to describe it in detail, so my letter to him this week is largely composed of searching questions.

I don't spend much time worrying about the Bomb, having plenty of other things to occupy me. As you will long ago have recognised, I have gone stale on the Oscar job, and must somehow regain enough initiative to polish it off. At the same time I feel compelled to strive for perfection. The index is stuck at p. 600, but I have just told the printers that they will have the whole thing back finished by November 30—which should mean publication in May. At bedtime I am slowly reading through Pater's works, finding a few good things buried in layers of pretentious candy-floss, if you can imagine such a thing.

The papers announce parking-meters in Soho by November, and they should greatly lessen the noise and nuisance which now make the whole place hideous. (As I write, the Proms are coming to an end, and Flash Harry is doing his stuff.) I suppose one day I shall feel wholly well and energetic again, and it will be a nice change. One grows weary of all the extra effort caused by feeling perpetually under par. Needless to say, Ruth is forever a light and a blessing: I really don't think I could keep all this up without her. This week-end she has gone to stay with her son in Suffolk, where there is no telephone, so I can't speak to her till Sunday evening when she gets home. We have quite decided to save up for another fortnight of sun next summer, even though it means only one visit to Kisdon the blessed.

Goodnight, dear George, give best love to Pamela, please.

*21 September 1961*                                                    *Grundisburgh*

Lumbago is the devil in person. I used to have a good deal of it, and my sympathy with you is accordingly profound. Old Amsler[1], who was delightfully frank and clearsighted about British medicine, used to say that *all* we know about lumbago is that it comes for no reason and goes for none either, but luckily it always *does* go. Massage they tell me is off nowadays, but heat and electricity are emphatically *on*. I do wish you could have a clear and long run in the matter of health. With health all can be faced, without it, nothing. And your normal programme demands flawless health. Is your leech a good man? Mine

[1] Eton doctor.

is the nicest man imaginable, and knows nothing at all of my recent ailments; his locum cured one on which *he* had thrown no light, a tip from the local policeman another, and Lady Cranworth a third. Anyway your flat to yourself, and not cluttered up with someone else's books, should make a difference—though stairs don't go well with lumbago. I hope for a brighter bulletin next week.

My youngest daughter with family is just off to Kenya—perhaps for three years, maybe for one, or, if Kenyatta has his way, less than that. I of course am obsessed with the morbid notion that I may have passed on before I see her again. I always hate the holidays here coming to an end; I like seeing the place swarming with children. The £50 or £60 extra catering etc is merely equivalent to the trip abroad which e.g. Roger and Sibell take every year.

Old Bertrand Russell of course suffers from that last indignity of the old; worse than bladder, heart, knees, or ears, i.e. his judgment is gone. Fancy not seeing that these sit-downs and marches merely encourage the Russians. But really our governors! The captain of a boys' house in a weak year would have spotted that the way to treat a crowd in Parliament or Trafalgar Square was to do *nothing*. Let 'em sit. If they get in the way of traffic, give abundant warning and then clear a way with a hosepipe. How long would a crowd's spirit last with such treatment? As it is, who minds a one-pound fine? But who would *not* mind looking an ass after a two or three hours' sit, and/or a suit of clothes drenched? But, as I have complained before, they never consult me.

Hammarskjöld[1] surely was murdered, though so far the press has said nothing. That explosion before the crash sounds very fishy. What a hopeless world we live in.

I have been re-reading old H.W. Nevinson's *Changes and Chances* lately—a man I have always greatly admired. I liked 'Most of us deplored and indignantly condemned the atrocious fate of Oscar Wilde, for whom many, like myself, would gladly have offered bail, if, like Stewart Headlam, we could have raised the £1000 demanded.' He became a passionate woman's suffrage supporter later and left the

[1] Dag Hammarskjöld (born 1905), Swedish Secretary-General of the United Nations from 1953, died in a mysterious air-crash in Africa on 17 September 1961.

*Daily News.* He wrote lyrically about Christabel Pankhurst who, I read recently, some genial chap said, was a lesbian. Did you know about this? Untrue, I expect, like most things.

Candy-floss is good for Pater. I never could really do with him 'faint, pale, embarrassing, exquisite Pater' (Henry James) though H.J. did end his paragraph with 'he is not of the little day but of the longer time.' Have you noticed that Pater's favourite adjectives were 'wistful', 'dainty', 'weary', 'strange', 'fantastic', 'exquisite', 'vague'?

Love to Ruth—a routine message and yet always fresh—like the best things in Shakespeare!


*23 September 1961*                                        *Bromsden Farm*


*The Franco-Prussian War* has had a tremendous send-off: leading articles promptly and everywhere, including the centre page of *The Times*, which is seldom given to any book except Winston's. I only hope we sell a few, for it's a three-guinea book.

I hope you got my mid-week note about Jonah.[1] Evy's handwriting is none too clear at best, and her ordeal in Padua had rendered it well nigh inscrutable. I wrote back at once to them both, and encouraged all the friends I could think of to do the same. Tommy responded splendidly. He *is* a good fellow indeed.

All week I have been plagued by my infernal back, seldom able to get into a painless position, except on my side in bed. At last, yesterday, after a fortnight of it I went to a charming osteopath, who said I had a clear displacement between the third and fourth vertebrae, which he was confident he could put right with a few hefty clicks— or 'adjustments,' as he called them. These he duly administered, and by Monday, he says, I should be cured. The pain may be a trifle less today, but it is still very much with me, and much the most painful position is that adopted when writing—or compiling an index—so the temptation to lie down with a good book is immense. I do apologise for harping on my tiresome maladies, but lately they have come to dominate and interfere with everything.

---

[1] He had fallen seriously ill in Italy and been nursed by nuns.

The best news is that my guest flew back to America on Thursday, and for the first time since *May* the flat is my own. Ruth and I had an orgy of tidying, tearing up and throwing away. Now I must get rid of E.B.'s library.

*Sunday morning, 24 September*

There I broke off and slept for nine delicious hours. My back feels much the same as yesterday, and I can only hope.

Now I must attack my index again. My new plan is to limit myself to an hour's work at a time, and see how many pages I can do in it. Thus childishly do I struggle to break through my staleness. As soon as Oscar is dealt with, I must speedily get to work on Max's letters to Reggie Turner, which I promised to do years ago. Everyone concerned has been very patient, but I feel rather bad about it. I had no idea Oscar would take so long. How many things would never get done at all if one knew at the beginning exactly what one was in for! Not long now before we see you. I expect Ruth will get a new dress for the occasion, but you won't know it's new.

27 *September 1961* *Grundisburgh*

That disc I hope by now has yielded to treatment. My son-in-law was treated by the great Syriax, who said he had never seen a worse disc—but perhaps they always say that. Anyway he cured it completely, so we bid you to hope, as Carlyle was always quoting from Goethe, though none the less remaining plunged in melancholy all his life. My back-aches were before the age of discs and happened at just about the time when lumbago was beginning to be called fibrositis. The conclusion of the whole matter is that in England at least nobody knows anything about it.

I wrote to old Jonah on the same day on which I got your letter—airmail, so he should have got it, though I had a feeling he might be moving off to Venice fairly soon. He will not I fear be at the Lit. Soc. (where, by the way, I *shall* be, or rather *chez vous* at 6 p.m. on the 10th).

Cardus's sketch of Beecham was not very well reviewed.[1] Who was

---

[1] *Sir Thomas Beecham: a Memoir* (1961).

it who said it was a brave attempt to pretend that B. was not an intolerable man? We must ask Flash Harry. Did you hear him on the Proms last evening? I wonder how cynical he—and the audience—feels when they all bellow 'Wider still and wider, shall thy bounds be set' etc. Not a convincing picture of the British Empire, or Commonwealth, in 1961 surely. Did you hear or read of the young lady who greeted Flash's quotation from Bach that music should bring honour to man and glorify God, with a shrill cry of 'Alleluia'—which reminds me to tell you Housman's exquisite poem:

> ' "Hallelujah!" was the only observation
> That escaped Lieutenant-Colonel Mary Jane,
> When she tumbled off the platform in the station,
> And was cut in little pieces by the train.
>> Mary Jane, the train is through yer:
>> Hallelujah, Hallelujah!
> We will gather up the fragments that remain.'

I do hope you don't know it, because otherwise I know you will like it. I have a letter from Roger in which he says he was disquieted by a paragraph in the cheap press about you. What would this be? He takes comfort from Macmillan's saying that 'all the graver things of our lives are inventions of the press.' I read hardly anything but headlines nowadays and not many of them.

Old Gow is here—very still-life and practically inaudible. He is annoyed with John Carter's persistence in publishing Housmaniana which for the most part A.E.H. did not wish—in fact forbade—to be published. But what attention do people ever pay to that? I cannot, myself, help being rather pleased at any score off that old curmudgeon, and all his careful defences being gradually flattened. A very ungenial spirit.

At the moment I am re-reading some Gibbon. But I am encouraged to find that Gow found exactly what I do, *viz* that one floats dreamily down the stream of that wonderful style, but remembers very few of the facts recorded. I am just approaching the chapter in which he busies himself in 'sapping a solemn creed with solemn sneer,'[1] but

---

[1] Byron, *Childe Harold*, canto 3, cvii.

expect to be less shocked than e.g. Boswell was. What a good man Diocletian was! He has never been more than a name to me and I was quite prepared to find his record studded with startling notes 'in the decent obscurity of a learned language.'[1] But not one.

Love to R. I look forward to the new dress.

*30 September 1961*                                                     *Bromsden Farm*

Too many of the wrong people are dying. Yesterday I learned of the sudden death of Billy James, Henry James's nephew, an enchanting man with whom I stayed in March at Cambridge, Mass. He was almost eighty, but slim and active and elegant and wholly charming.

Today I drove over to the Devlins', near Marlborough, where Christopher D., who wrote the book on Smart, is fading rapidly from cancer. He looked like a ghost of himself, and one can't wish him any long continuance of this agony of pain and drugs.

To descend to the insignificant, my lumbago is still with me, and I am heartily sick of it. Sitting in the car (fifty miles each way) was a particularly painful position for it. The index is still only at p. 668. I must have a good bash at it tomorrow.

If Gow is still with you, please give him my respectful salutations. I don't suppose he remembers me, but I still cherish the prize (Rupert Brooke's poems) that he gave me in 1923. I don't think he should be too hard on Carter, whose new Housman book is simply, so far as I know, a collection of all the prose pieces that A.E.H. *did* print or publish. And if he didn't want his manuscript poems published he should have burnt them, instead of leaving the decision to his brother whom he despised. Anyhow it doesn't matter a halfpenny. Poets are judged and remembered by their *best* poems, not their worst.

Nancy Cunard once asked George Moore if he could be her father, and he said: 'Alas, my dear, no,' and then added firmly: 'You must never tell your mother you asked me that question!'

Adam writes cheerfully and at length from India. There seem to be a lot of holidays of various sorts, and next week a beak called Mr

[1] Gibbon, *Autobiography*.

113

Purohit is apparently going to take him tiger-shooting! He says the boys love learning English poems by heart and reciting them in class. Also they often ask for more homework! All the teaching is in English except for language-classes in three or four Indian languages. He plays cricket and football with the boys, and bridge with the beaks. He is not allowed to pay for anything, and is apparently given some pocket-money as well.

Now it is Sunday and October, and my back seems worse than ever. My bed here is much softer than the one in London: perhaps I should sleep on the floor.

I was awake for one or two of the small hours and remember saying to myself 'I must tell George that'—but what was it? The sun is shining on my books and cobwebs, and I sit uneasily with a large cushion wedged into the small of my back.

Did you see that Victor Gollancz broke his thigh watching the nonsense in Trafalgar Square? They operated and inserted a pin. I went to see him in hospital on Monday and found him in roaring form. Canon Collins was there—a much nicer man than from his antics one might imagine. Tomorrow I have promised to go back and play bridge round the bed for two hours (6–8) with V.G., his wife and some other lady. As you know, I never play bridge except perhaps twice a year with the Gollanczes, but they refuse to believe this and apparently regard me as a regular player.

Siegfried is coming to the Lit. Soc., but Ivor can't come because he is proposing the toast of Literature at the Guildhall, poor fellow. His word-book, so judiciously dedicated, won't be out till November.[1] Tommy said he had written Jonah a letter so flippant that if Evy came across it she would probably fall into the Po with horror. I've had no further word from her and don't know if they're in Venice yet or where.

---

[1] *Words in Season* (1961). Its dedication runs:

TO
GEORGE LYTTELTON
*whose teaching of English*
*has done so much for*
*others in youth and*
*for me in age*

Yes, I do wish people wouldn't die the way they do. One feels a sort of indignation like James Forsyte: 'What did *he* want to die for? He was no age.' You probably never saw Reggie Spooner[1] bat. You would not have forgotten it—the purest champagne. Even bowlers enjoyed his punishment of them—the lovely grace of the stroke itself and the courtesy, so kindly without anything remotely condescending. It was Colin Blythe who after being despatched through the covers said to him 'Mr Spooner I would give all my bowling to make a shot like that.' Trueman would not have said that. Cardus is sure to have had something good about him in the *Guardian*; he was one of C's great heroes, and got compared with every kind of operatic and musical figure down the years—none of whom dear R.H.S. had ever heard of. He was one of the very *nicest* men I have ever known.

Old Gow alas had left before your letter arrived. He is of course rather proprietary about A.E.H. and it is risky for anyone to encroach on the hallowed ground. I hope John C. will recover all he can. There is something suspicious about leaving a lot of stuff intact and telling others to destroy it. I put *my* poems into the fire myself.

Duff will clearly end up another C.P. Scott[2] or Nevinson. You are silent about the latter, so may have missed his admirable reminiscences. There have been some fine reviews of your *Franco-Prussian War*. I hope *every*body is buying it—also the Agate book, despite one or two criminal reviews. See you on Tuesday if I get upstairs. I have a bad leg which I think is cancer, paralysis, ossification or lupus. P. thinks it is temporary stiffness.

Yesterday I paid a second visit to my osteopath, and I'm delighted to say that his clicks have greatly improved my condition. Ruth says it's almost worth being in pain for the pleasure of coming out of it, but

[1] Lancashire and England cricketer (1880–1961).
[2] 1846–1932. Editor of the *Manchester Guardian* 1872–1929.

I'm not quite sure I agree. Anyhow I'm thankful it was I who had the lumbago, and not she. Lumbago, I find, is not a word used by osteopaths: a compression of discs is my trouble, or was, and he said a fortnight in bed would have put it right after the first treatment, whereas in the rush of office life it may take four to six weeks. Two weeks have now passed, and I only hope he's right.

My dear friend Christopher Devlin died peacefully on Thursday night at his brother's house near Marlborough. I think I told you that when I drove over to see him last Saturday I realised he couldn't last long, but one always hopes against probability. As you know, I rushed out his *Poor Kit Smart* (which he wrote in his convalescence after his fearful operation), so that he should have the pleasure of seeing it out. He was an extremely good, modest and charming man—less like the general conception of a Jesuit than one could imagine, and yet I've no doubt a very able and valuable priest. I shall miss him. He was saying Mass daily up to the last, and in that sense certainly died happy. How difficult it is to imagine oneself similarly comforted!

By the way, the only person I know who has been treated by Syriax was on his back for nine months—I won't say as a result, but afterwards.

I imagine Cardus must have written something about Spooner, but I somehow missed it. No, alas, I never saw R.H.S. at the wicket.

Victor Gollancz's accident reminds me of that verse about a race-meeting in Australia, where: 'a spectator's leg was broken from just merely looking on.' He was 'observing' the sit-downers in Trafalgar Square that night, slipped on the wet pavement, broke his femur, and couldn't be got away for two hours because of the crowds. He has had a pin inserted and was in great form on Monday, smoking a large Henry Clay (he gave me one) and using a pâté-de-foie-gras pot as an ashtray. After three hours of bridge on his bed I was the richer by 6/6, but my lumbago and my index (now at p. 706) were none the better. He is a most amusing and stimulating companion for an evening.

I did read Nevinson's memoirs long ago, and thought them excellent: I must read them again. I have just re-read Percy Lubbock's little memoir of Mary Cholmondeley and think it *first-class*. I expect you've read it. In London, before going to sleep, I'm reading M.C.'s *Red Pottage*, which is rather fun in its way. Were you bowled over by it in 1899? I had a postcard from Evy to say they're coming straight home, but she didn't say exactly when. Flash Harry *is* coming on Tuesday. If your leg won't manage the stairs, telephone and we'll make another plan. If I hear nothing I shall expect you at 6, and so will Ruth. What a pity Pamela can't come too, though perhaps she doesn't agree. My love to her.

*12 October 1961*                                                                                             *Grundisburgh*

Very good Lit. Soc. dinner. Roger and Flash Harry and I had a good crack afterwards, while Tim and Peter F. played slosh. I must tell you that three of the four people to whom I mentioned that I was going to meet old Maugham pursed their lips and/or shook their heads. I suppose he has one way or another trodden on a good many toes. Yesterday when I lunched at White's with my beloved Tim we met Bob Boothby who said that Winston is hardly compos and fills much of the brief periods when he is with angry lamentations at still being alive. When F.E. Smith died who, according to B.B., was W's only great friend, W. said 'Well at least he went out with a bang—one thing I pray is against a protracted old age.' and not long ago he was in a little company which was talking of the Jutland battle and W. sadly said 'Once you know I knew everything about it, but now it is as remote and vague as the Battle of Salamis.' How right the Synge character was in describing old age as 'a poor untidy thing'.

Bernard Fergusson was at White's. He kept murmuring what is actually a fact but also the first line of a music-hall song. 'I'm off tomorrow morn to Singapore.'

Ruth was looking very lovely on Tuesday—what a refreshment for eye and ear—and heart and mind!

Tommy was gloomy about Jonah, and I gathered he thought the poor old thing *might* be a permanent invalid. I do hope not. I shall write to J. to-morrow. I hear he is at home.

We thought you were in excellent form on Tuesday, and at dinner I could see that Flash Harry was eating out of your hand. When you see Willie Maugham ('that old iguana', as Harold Nicolson calls him), it's possible, nay likely, that the subject of his leaving his fortune to the Society of Authors may crop up. If it does, see whether, with the utmost tact, you can suggest that one certain way of helping young authors (his avowed intent) would be to leave some money to the London Library. T.S.E. and his wife, who are sitting for their joint portrait to Gerald Kelly, are going to put this idea up to him, so they should be able to back you up. W.S.M. did give us £1000 at the time of our appeal, but that is chicken-feed to him.

I have had a letter in Jonah's own hand—the first he had written, he said. He is not yet strong enough for visitors, but soon I shall have to fight my way to St John's Wood—'the shady groves of the Evangelist', as a fanciful old baronet of my early acquaintance used to call it.

*Sunday morning, 15 October*
All is obscured by mist, but I can hear the hefty blows of Duff, who is reducing a thirty-foot-high hedge to eight foot or so, and thoroughly enjoying himself. Yesterday week he played for a scratch against the Field and laid himself out cold with concussion. He seems to have recovered completely, but didn't play yesterday for Fred's old Boys v. the Field. He and his wife drove over to watch, and he says the O.B.'s were a trifle lucky to win 3–0: one of those opportunist goals. They saw the Headmaster, who was clearly delighted, and rather touched, to have received a letter from Adam in India. A. himself is being taken by Mr Purohit for twelve days' holiday, which he hopes will include some shooting of all kinds.

My index has reached p. 790, and as I sniff the smell of the stable-door (p. 868), I begin to get the bit between my teeth and bolt for home. When I finish there will be a lot of re-writing, arranging and tidying-up to do, but those are trifles compared to this slogging compilation.

Forgive this half-pay scrap. You shall have more next week.

My lumbago is quite gone. Hurrah!

I shall certainly sow what seed I can about the London Library, though I shrewdly suspect the old iguana's skin is impervious to hints. One discouraging friend tells me there are days when he is impervious to ordinary discourse, neither uttering or attending to, and clearly wishes for nothing but death. I will tell you all about it *quam primum*.

Is Adam really going for a trip with Mr *Purohit*? I suppose he just calls him *Proot*—the only word with which Stevenson could stimulate his donkey.

*Thursday*. Well there is nothing much to report. Old Maugham was friendly, intelligent, forthcoming, unaffected. He might have been a member of the Lit. Soc.! The London Library was mentioned, but he didn't rise much. He knew of your fine work, but censured the 'intelligentsia', whosoever he meant, for the meanness of their contributions. So I fear he may be thinking he has done enough. He looks younger than his years and less corrugated. That Graham Sutherland portrait is mere caricature, but oddly S.M. likes it! Gerald Kelly's portrait of T.S.E. looks to my unsophisticated eye extremely good. He certainly makes him look a very nice man. S.M. was very gloomy about Winston, and it is disheartening to hear that W. welcomes numberless pressmen and is grumpy if they are kept at bay. Also that he resents being asked about his period in the doldrums, before the second war.

Many thanks for your natural history notes on the old iguana. It's amusing that he should have mentioned Winston, since it is generally believed that, apart from diverting his huge fortune from his daughter and her children, his one ambition is to outlive Winston. If they die on the same day their obituaries will take up most of that day's papers!

My best news is that the index is finished—or rather, the first draft of it, for I now have to read it through and re-write some of the messier cards. Also tie up a hundred loose ends, fill gaps etc. The deadline of November 30 is all too near.

On Thursday at 8 a.m. six stalwarts arrived at the flat with an immense van, which they had some difficulty in parking. They unloaded eighty tea-chests and set to work. Their foreman was a stocky little ex-pugilist with a broken nose, a face the colour of raw meat, and scarcely any hearing, but he worked without stopping, and after four and a half hours every E.B. book and bookcase was loaded and off. When they arrived, more than five years ago, it took three men *eight* hours to carry them up and unpack them.

Now I am trying to find a 'little man' to paint the spare room, and when that's done I shall be able to use all those shelves for my own books. On Monday I'm going round to help Diana unpack some of Duff's, so that looks like fitting in very well.

My Duff has been down to-day, shooting with Peter. They got some partridges, pheasants and hares, and one fox (shot by Duff). They saw *five* wild deer, but did not bombard them.

I was sorry to read of Bernard Darwin's death. He was in College with my father and was always very nice to me. His death makes no difference to the Lit. Soc. election, since he had become an Honorary Member.

Siegfried has been asked to unveil the tablet to Walter de la Mare in the crypt of St Paul's at the end of November. Tommy has promised to chaperone him, but already S.S. is saying he is sure to be having bronchitis just then. I lunched with Jonah and Evy on Tuesday, and found him wonderfully better than I had expected. He has lost a good deal of weight but otherwise looks fine. He gets up and dresses for meals, and goes back to bed in between. He says he has written enough stories for a second volume and is soon to present them. He is wildly enthusiastic about the Linklater novel, *Roll of Honour*, which I had sent him, and roundly proclaims it a masterpiece. I think he's right and shall eagerly await your judgment.

T.S.E. is much delighted with the French translation of *The Owl and the Pussycat*.[1] Have you looked at it, or hasn't it reached you? I

---

[1] *Le Hibou et la Poussiquette*, freely translated into French from the English of Edward Lear by Francis Steegmuller (London, 1961).

think we ought to sell quite a lot of it. But everything depends on the Durrell book, which appears on Monday week.[1] I have printed 50,000 copies, and have already orders for more than 23,000. If only I had a few more authors of that selling-capacity!

Heinemann, and their big-business owners, are getting increasingly restive at the unprofitability of my business, and I foresee a fairly early crisis. If they would let me go I think I could find someone else to buy the business and leave me to run it, but Heinemann seem to think my leaving would in some way damage their prestige. Nonsense, I say, but if you really think that, you must be prepared to pay for the privilege of keeping me. What I can't tell any of them is that in general I've had quite enough of publishing and would welcome retirement—but what should I use for money? It simply isn't on.

There I went to bed, and it is now a weeping Sunday morning. The empty pond completely filled up during the night and all is drip and squelch. Comfort is making Christmas puddings, with Bridget's assistance. Yesterday I read *The Worm of Death* by Nicholas Blake (C. Day Lewis) with enjoyment. (Now comes a crisis. They have peeled almonds and made breadcrumbs and mixed a great bowl of flour—and there is no candied peel! Comfort has driven to Henley to try and knock up a friendly grocer.) When I was in New York in March I paid £50 for an option to have first look at a full-length biography of Sherlock Holmes, which one of those crazy enthusiasts has compiled from the stories, and now the typescript has arrived—more than 400 pages of it, and my spirit quails a little at the prospect.[2] I have never had much sympathy with the Baker Street Irregulars, though I love the stories. How many people would read or buy this book? What do you think? Assuming that it's decently done. I may consult S.C. Roberts.

Comfort has returned in triumph with peel and the Sunday papers.

[1] *The Drunken Forest* by Gerald Durrell (1961).
[2] *Sherlock Holmes, a Biography of the World's first Consulting Detective* by William S. Baring-Gould (1962).

I say Duff's *fox*! What will the huntin' neighbourhood say when they hear of it? Shooting a fox was the only crime the Murgatroyds in *Ruddigore* accepted as a pukka crime without cavil. Do you know the opera? We go to see and hear it this evening. I have never seen it before, and though both G. and S. respectively thought they had never done anything so good, the public has never much taken to it, and on such matters the public is usually right. Gilbert's humour seems to me to last less well than e.g. P.G. Wodehouse's, though some cannot bear *his* brand. I like to think I am in the company of Asquith, Balfour, M.R. James, Ronnie Knox etc, who at least were not trivial and foolish people. The simple truth is that we share an intense delight in seeing language *perfectly* handled, no matter what the subject. But I was amused by a recent review of him in which there was a complaint that his young men and women who fall in love are altogether *too* virginal—that the only idea the sight of a double bed puts into their minds is 'What a grand apple-pie could be made of it!' And that is true. I don't want any *Chatterley* muck, but shall we say a little more red blood in his love-affairs. I hope the new Penguin P.G.W.s will revive a few which for some reason have been out of print for years, though every bit as good as the rest. Did any popular author ever remain more constantly at his best?

I too have deeply enjoyed Eric Linklater's *Roll of Honour*. The unusual setting is entirely successful—not wholly unlike Masters's *Spoon River Anthology* but much less bitter. Hardly a week goes by without some contribution to Letters from Lit. Soc. members, and there is your O.W. just round the corner. The Linklater book is always giving one what Mark Twain called 'a spell of the dry grins.' And *The Owl and the Pussy Cat* is delicious—illustrations and all. I imagine the French to be the last word in neatness.

S.C. Roberts would be a good man to ask about that Holmes book. I am no judge, but my impression is that all that clever investigation —which as you say, was rather overdone—has had its day. 400 pages is staggering. I may be quite wrong in thinking the fashion is past; I generally am. I too am a fan of the stories (especially *Adventures* and *Memoirs*, in which I once could have passed any exam) and S.H. still cuts a brave figure. (But if there is a poorer tale than 'The Noble Bachelor' I should like to see it.)

And *The Christening Party*[1] too is extremely pleasant reading. What immense pleasure your generous gifts fill my days with. I have not yet embarked on the Walpole,[2] but I have been dipping again into *your Hugh Walpole*. These people who airily fling words like 'fake' and 'bogus' about are stuffy little folk. They forget that in the Almighty's eyes we are all to a large extent fake and bogus. (Not you or dear Ruth, to whom my love.)

*28 October 1961*                                                    *Bromsden Farm*

Last week was much occupied with publishing discussions. Just when my relations with Heinemann had reached breaking-point and there seemed to be no possible satisfactory solution except the closing down of my business, or my resigning and starving, a splendid *Deus* stepped *ex machina*, or rather out of a jet air-liner, and all may now be well. My saviour is a chap called Bill Jovanovich. His father was a peasant in Montenegro (as you may know, the Montenegrins are proud mountainy men who rightly consider themselves superior to all the other Jugoslavs), who managed somehow to emigrate to the U.S.A. and worked in the Pittsburg steelworks. He married a Polish girl and produced Bill, who won every conceivable scholarship, ending with a Ph.D. in Eng. Lit. To cut a long story short, by the time he was thirty-four he was President of Harcourt Brace, one of the leading U.S. publishers for quality, though not then for size. He had worked his way up through the textbook department, and in the last six years he has turned H.B. into the second or third biggest publishing house in the world, with an annual turnover of $33,000,000.

Nine-tenths of this comes from textbooks, but the general list is still good, and Bill is the most extraordinary mixture of literary man and tycoon. He is still only forty. For some reason he seems to think

[1] By Francis Steegmuller.
[2] *Horace Walpole* by Wilmarth Sheldon Lewis (1961).

a lot of me and is prepared to buy my business from the loathly Heinemann. He would leave me to run it, as now, helped by books from his list, and would bolster it with a textbook business, which today is the only hope of survival. It's all too good to be true, and the chief hurdle is to get Tilling's (who own Heinemann) to agree. On the face of it, they would be crazy not to get rid of a losing subsidiary for cash, but they have an idiotic idea that to sell to an American buyer is in some way to sell the pass, and I am busily engaged in trying to persuade them this is not so. Their meeting is on November 10, so keep your fingers crossed. I shall never get used to the speed of modern communications. Yesterday morning I spoke to Bill on the telephone at Claridge's before he left for home, and at 9 p.m. I called him at his home in Upper State New York to report progress. Directly Tilling's agree in principle he is prepared to fly back to discuss terms.

All this makes ordinary life very difficult, and as you can imagine, everything is piling up round me. But I feel wonderfully well, with a new and very welcome upsurge of hope. The awful thing is that *everything* belongs more or less to Heinemann—my flat, my car, my office and so on.

*By the way*—all this is hideously secret, for obvious reasons, so mum's the word.

Despite all those preoccupations last week I managed to spend two afternoons unpacking Uncle Duff's books, dined my poetess from Lancashire, spent a long evening playing bridge with Victor Gollancz (I lost one and sixpence), visited my aged father, lunched a beautiful authoress one day, an ugly literary agent another, and had tea with a delightful octogenarian at the Goring Hotel. The combination of the Motor Show, the Dairy Show and almost incessant rain didn't help the traffic at all.

I have said I will publish the Sherlock Holmes book, if all questions of copyright can be cleared up, and in due course you may be called on to read its proofs as an expert.

Adam has got a ticket for the Calcutta Test on New Year's Eve or thereabouts. He reports a total absence of liquor in the Central Provinces, and a great shortage of razor-blades.

And now yesterday's Johnson Club dinner. Your absence was regretted but the Secretary was very nice about it and put it down to an even busier and fuller life than you actually have—and that takes some doing. There sat with us a lively and pleasant doctor called Hubble, who has apparently been a member for twenty years. We dined reasonably well at The Cock (but regrettably there was no plump head-waiter[1]), but let me tell you the dinner was (1) less good and (2) more costly than those *you* provide at the Garrick. Old Powell[2] made a speech about his birthday. He looks far younger than he did when I first became a member. Probably the presence of old R.W. Chapman kept everybody old.

I will certainly and with pleasure help in any way I can with the Holmes book though I claim to be no expert with the stories after his return. There is a pleasant vignette of old Doyle in P.G. Wodehouse's *Performing Flea*, which I bought yesterday. But the Penguins haven't really got down to publishing five out-of-print ones. Only one of these have I not got, *viz Full Moon* of which I had never even heard.

Today Comfort and I drove to the Cotswolds and took C's aged stepmother to lunch at the Lygon Arms at Broadway. It was a day of miraculous autumn beauty—cold, but with clear blue sky and hot sun. The trees every colour imaginable, and comparatively few cars on the road—very enjoyable. On the way I snatched three-quarters of an hour in Blackwell's, which I always enjoy, but the crush in the Oxford streets made it a struggle just to walk along.

You will remember my mentioning my dear old friend Katie Lewis, who died this year and left me that lovely Rossetti drawing. Forty years ago she bought for £200 a derelict farmhouse and six acres at the end of the main road through Broadway. She converted it into a

---

[1] 'O plump head-waiter at the Cock' (Tennyson, 'Will Waterproof's Lyrical Monologue').
[2] L. F. Powell, Johnsonian scholar and editor (1881–1975).

thoroughly comfortable house with a lovely garden, lived there for the rest of her life, and the other day it fetched £17,000! The purchaser is reported to be an American who wanted 'a place in England'.

No more news of my *Deus ex machina*, but the vital Tilling meeting is next Wednesday. I have a strong and increasing belief that they will agree, and then there will only be the price to be settled. Another few weeks should prove decisive.

The Sherlock Holmes book is temporarily held up while I attempt to get a clearance from the Estate through John Murray. I gather that Conan Doyle's son Adrian is both dotty and litigious. He recently tried to sue someone for saying that *Holmes* was Semitic! Also he lives in Geneva, which doesn't quicken things up. I'll let you know if any light breaks.

On Thursday Jonah and Evy turned up at Soho Square in a hired car, Jonah looking astonishingly better in his overcoat and bowler hat. He even talks of coming to next week's Lit. Soc. We thought the stairs, even to my office, would be too much for him, so I got into the car and we drove round and round the square till Evy got giddy. Jonah gave me the typescript of his new collection of stories (all written before his illness). I haven't yet had time to read any of them, but I like the book's title, *Trepidation in Downing Street*.

Here is the joke I promised you. A couple, twenty years married, had a fearful row. The wife told the husband exactly what she thought of him, ending: 'And on top of all that, we've had your mother living with us for ten years.'

HUSBAND '*My* mother? I always thought she was *your* mother!' End of story.

Can you get old novels (1946 or so) from your library? If so, and you haven't read it, ask immediately for *States of Grace* by Francis Steegmuller. He gave me a copy, which I have just finished with chuckling delight. It's light and witty and altogether a joy. Now I am reading Evelyn Waugh's latest[1], which as usual is compulsively readable, I find. Only twenty-six more proofing days before I part with Oscar.

Ivor came in and signed some copies of his book, including one for

---

[1] *Unconditional Surrender* (1961).

you, but you won't get it for another week or so, since he said he thought it best to keep them till just before publication day.

I simply hadn't time to read his proofs, and fear there are a lot of misprints and errors in the book. You might be an angel and let me have a list of any you notice. Ivor seems delighted with the book's appearance (and indeed it is quite elegant), so if he's satisfied, all is well. I have printed only 2500 and look like selling half of them before publication, which is rather good. He says he hopes to come to the Lit. Soc.

Try and go to the Lawrence exhibition at Burlington House when you're in London. I haven't been yet, but hear that my picture is well hung—sounds like game!

*9 November 1961*                                                          *Grundisburgh*

I was fascinated by *Horace Walpole*, and I am glad to see that many of the reviews praise its sumptuous get-up. One actually said that the firm of Hart-Davis were outstanding for the appearance of their books! Meanwhile we pray for the soul of Tilling; all must have been decided yesterday. I am excited about it. How splendid it will be if the situation is established when you have nothing to think of but the quality of your books.

I came across a fine 'gaffe' recently when a reviewer complacently referred to the hero of 'Mr Anstey's famous book'[1] as Mr Bulstrode. Surely every reader of the book in existence has *Bultitude* in his mind for ever. I met Anstey once, bicycling in France with Monty James— a very absurd little man. He told us that he saw 'Bultitude' over a shop-window from the top of a bus but couldn't remember where. If I weren't too lazy I would write to the paper in which Bulstrode appeared and point out that the error is in the same crime-catalogue as, say, *Foster* for Falstaff. Anstey was childishly pleased when we quoted *Vice Versa* to him. M.R.J. knew it by heart, and I wasn't too bad at one time. I suppose it is dead now.

I have just got from the library Mrs Langley Moore's immense

[1] *Vice Versa* (1882), which has now been continuously in print for a hundred years.

book on Byron. It looks good browsing, but how can one remember all the ramifications? Luckily she tells us many things more than once. I suppose B. shares with O.W. that extraordinary posthumous vitality. We simply cannot let them rest in peace.

I look forward to further information about Holmes—and the imbecile Conan Doyle. But I agree with him in rejecting the theory that Sherlock was a Jew. I cannot think what evidence supports it. He was a misogynist—except for Irene Adler—and I am surprised no one has yet suggested that he was a homo. What about that gang of Baker Street Irregulars? Highly suggestive surely to anyone but Watson ('You see it, Watson, you see it?' 'But I saw nothing.' Might be the motto of the whole chronicle).

That is good news about Jonah. I am drifting through his *Victorian Boyhood* at odd moments, e.g. at meals when P. is out. Excellent reading, though full of inaccuracies, most of them small. His character-sketches of beaks are good. I wish, after his two years at Lowry's he had come to Arthur Benson's. I cannot quite say of A.C.B.'s 'Sir, we were a nest of singing-birds',[1] but with people in it like Percy Lubbock, Edward Cadogan, L.H. Myers, we were, I am sure, the least Philistine house at Eton. Kindersley was a fine man and hopeless beak.

<br>

11 November 1961                                          *Bromsden Farm*

On Wednesday the Tilling board agreed 'very reluctantly' to sell R.H-D. Ltd, 'provided they get their price.' John McCallum, vice-president of Harcourt Brace, flies over tomorrow to negotiate, and the great Jovanovich himself follows on Thursday. So keep your fingers permanently crossed. All should be settled this coming week, but not by the time I see you on Wednesday. If and when (not a phrase I like) they come to terms, there will still be a hundred details to be settled and a great deal of work to be done. Somehow in the midst of it all Oscar must be despatched by the end of the month. Reading, correcting and rewriting the index has got as far as DOUGLAS, LORD ALFRED, who has sixteen closely written cards to himself. I am

<br>

[1] Doctor Johnson on Pembroke College, Oxford.

heartily sick of it all, but still in an awful way fascinated—and the quest for perfection in editing dies hard.

Doris Langley Moore's book on Byron is on the short list for this year's Duff Cooper Prize. I think Duff would have found it fascinating. And surely the last thing either Byron or Oscar would have asked was to be allowed to rest in peace. By the way, the German and the French translation rights of Oscar have been sold—each for £400 advance, of which I get half. I am now sure that this book will pay for the whole of Adam's Oxford career. Perhaps one day I'll produce a book whose royalties I can spend on myself?

Adam reports the sudden death of the energetic and popular Vice-Principal of his Indian college. He writes: 'I attended the funeral procession and cremation on Monday. This lasted from 9.15 a.m. until noon. The temperature was 90 in the shade, and there was no shade. The procession involved a rapid walk of about three and a half miles in fifty minutes, and by the time we returned I was dished.' Not surprisingly he went down that afternoon with some kind of dysentery, but seems to have made a rapid recovery. There is a hospital (and post-office) in the college, and they seem to be looking after him well. Comfort (who has a heavy cold) has taken it all very philosophically.

Jonah's new collection of stories seems to me much inferior to its predecessor, but I shan't tell him that, so mum's the word. They seem to me, the stories, to be getting steadily more juvenile, and somehow I must try and prevent his hoping for a third volume. The trouble is that he has nothing else to do, and loves writing them. Short stories are notorious non-sellers at best, and I have half-a-dozen books of them in my next list: not purposely: things have just worked out that way.

Last week I dined out twice, and on the second occasion at the Droghedas' in Lord North Street, I met Hugh Gaitskell for the first time, and to my surprise found him most charming, intelligent, amusing, and easy to get on with. An admirable Lit. Soc. member, I should say. I wonder if you know him. My chief impression was astonishment that anyone so seemingly sensible should want to spend his life in the filthy power-grabbing welter of politics. If I ever see him again I must ask him why.

Diana Cooper, who was also of the party, lent me her Mini (Morris) for the evening. 'It's like driving a swallow,' she said, and indeed it was: an ideal car for traffic. When I fetched the car I found stuck under the windscreen-wiper a piece of paper on which Diana had written 'HAVE MERCY. AM TAKING SAD CHILD TO CINEMA.' Apparently it had effectively prevented her being charged for parking in the wrong place.

Last night, as soon as I got here, I drove to Oxford and dined with Laurence Stone, a very nice historian, at the high table at Wadham. They still do themselves pretty well—soup, grilled sole, good veal and veg, apple tart, and some admirable little confections which can only have been 'cheese remmykins'. Plenty of sherry, claret and port, nuts, fruit etc. I drove home stupefied and fell asleep without reading a word—a rare occurrence.


*17 November 1961*                                          *Grundisburgh*

This is miserable work. Not for donkey's years have I delayed writing till Friday. I should really have written *before* the dinner. This has been a full week—a meeting—only one of pleasure—on every day of the week plus next Monday. All G.B.'s except to-morrow, when again I come to London to face the Revisers of the G.C.E. papers who usually tear over half my questions, their main reasons being apparently that a Reviser's job is to revise. It was amusing to find Harold Nicolson *cagey* about the real cause of Byron's separation from Lady B, as if it was too bad to reveal a century afterwards. (Do you, by the way, approve of the Oxford protest at a young student of St Hilda's being sent down after being found in bed with her boy-friend? It is all very strange to an old Victorian like myself.) I was in luck on Wednesday as while Tim was playing slosh with Peter I found Clive Burt in the lounge and had a good crack. I know quite a number of Garrick members.

Ivor's book is splendid. I have read only forty-five pages so far and discovered *one* misprint—'ra*nucu*lus' on p. 45. But I will look more carefully. It is first-rate reading. Now, my dear R., let yourself off writing this week. This scrap deserves no recognition.

It was splendid of you to write at all, in such a busy week, and so soon after our meeting, and I must certainly respond, if only with a half-charge.

You will be pleased to hear that the great deal is safely through. There was a nasty period—about three quarters of an hour—on Thursday morning, when the negotiations broke down altogether, and I had lost the business and everything. I think that perhaps the opposition had a faint hope that I might cave in, but luckily I didn't, so they capitulated instead. Now the lawyers and accountants are drawing up the documents, and an announcement will probably be made about Tuesday. I can't tell you what a relief it is to have escaped from the Heinemann Group, which I'm sure was the cause of all my recent illnesses. Incidentally I shall also be earning a bigger salary, which will be a great help. I feel a great resurgence of hope.

Meanwhile, since most of last week was taken up with all this, I am more than ever behind with my ordinary work. Only twelve more days of Oscar, and much still to be done, though the index, thank God, is checked and ready.

One day Ruth and I sneaked out to the Lawrence exhibition at Burlington House. My ancestor stood up very well, we thought, in distinguished company; there are half a dozen smashing portraits there.

Adam has recovered from his dysentery and is preparing for a tiger-shoot at Christmas.

So glad you're enjoying Ivor's book: it comes out on Monday. I'm delighted to say *Le Hibou et la Poussiquette* is selling like hot cakes: the 10,000 copies I printed won't last till Christmas, and I'm desperately trying to get some more printed in time. That's the worst of publishing—either one has far too many copies, or far too few, usually the former. Durrell too is going splendidly.

I really am delighted about the great deal which you must have transacted in the most masterly fashion. It must be a vast relief to you to be free of Heinemann. What you say of your illnesses is interesting, because old Mat Hill[1], who was well ahead of his time, always maintained that the connection between body and mind was much closer than the faculty realised. Once when I had lumbago he asked me if I was worried about anything.

Fancy your being descended from old Lawrence. Very distinguished. He is, as they say, coming back, isn't he? These up and down fashions are very ridiculous, as I am going to tell the girls of North Foreland Lodge on Monday. The gist of my address is what a lot they can do to educate themselves by merely reading what they like—*and ruminating* about it. My line will be largely anti-G.C.E. Eng. Lit. (in which I examine them) and anti-Leavis, of whom they have probably never heard. I expect they will be quite a good audience, but one can never be entirely sure. And one of them, no doubt, will be the English mistress who will not like it when I tell them that at their age it is quite right that they should enjoy flamboyant verbiage and urge them to indulge in it sometimes in an essay. 'Probably your teacher will be sick, but that is one of the things she is there for.'

I had a glorious flop not long ago with a speech to the Old Boys of Ipswich—an entirely carnal and philistine crowd who had no interest at all in the history and traditions of the school but were wholly satisfied by such tales as what Smith mi said to the matron about the lavatory in 1944. A depressing evening, as I said to the Archdeacon of Suffolk who was also there. 'But you must remember,' he said, 'that they are all shop-keepers and sanitary inspectors, who have never heard of Cardinal Wolsey' (who is supposed to have founded the school—erroneously).

Did I tell you I had been reading about the intolerable *Prof*?[2] I cannot remember so strongly disliking anyone whom I had met only in a book. He seems to have had all the faults commonly charged against scientists, *viz* arrogance and narrowness and Philistinism. He had some very odd habits, e.g. his refusal ever to wipe his brow in public,

[1] Former Eton master.
[2] Frederick Alexander Lindemann (1886–1957). Professor of Experimental Philosophy at Oxford. Personal assistant to Winston Churchill from 1940. Created Viscount Cherwell 1956. Known as The Prof. His biography, *The Prof in Two Worlds* by the second Earl of Birkenhead was published in 1961.

however hot the day: and his diet seems to have been largely confined to olive oil and the white of egg. He would have been no good at a Lit. Soc. dinner.

Also Hankey's vast book all about the running of the 1914–18 war —one of the very few men who was really indispensable.[1] And how on earth we survived the incessant disasters of three and a half years is ungraspable. I suppose the solution is that, though we did not realise it, the Germans were really more incompetent than we were— and their top men more quarrelsome among themselves even than ours with the French—a very huffy and pigheaded lot these, conspicuously and persistently devoid of anything remotely resembling gratitude to any of their allies—and in fact I read not long ago that gratitude has never been one of the French virtues—coupled closely with conceit, for what else are you to call the settled conviction that only the French are and always have been truly civilised?

The news about my publishing plans broke in Tuesday's *Evening Standard*, with a piece on the front page headed by a blown-up reproduction of my fox.[2] Thereafter I had long telephone conversations with chaps from *seven* daily papers, all of which printed the news, more or less accurately, next morning. I was particularly anxious not to cast any aspersions on the efficiency of Heinemann, and mercifully all was well: no feelings hurt or umbrage taken. Now we are hard at work planning to resume power in January—the first *hopeful* planning that has been possible for years!

Did you see the leader about Henry James in this morning's *Times*? It was written by the Editor[3], as a result of my lunching with him at

---

[1] Maurice Pascal Alers Hankey (1877–1963). Secretary to the Cabinet and the Committee of Imperial Defence 1916–1938. Knighted 1916. Created Baron 1939. His book *The Supreme Command 1914–1918*, after being banned by three successive Prime Ministers, was published in two volumes in 1961.

[2] The emblem of my publishing firm, engraved by Reynolds Stone.

[3] Sir William Haley.

the Athenaeum on Monday, and is a splendid Puff Preliminary.[1]

On Wednesday I took most of the day off and travelled to Oxford with Raymond Mortimer, Peter Quennell and my cousin John Julius Norwich, for the choosing of this year's Duff Cooper Prize. At Oxford we were joined by Tony Powell and his wife, and given an excellent lunch in the Warden's Lodging at New College by the Warden (William Hayter, lately Ambassador in Moscow) and his lady. After some discussion the Prize was awarded to Jocelyn Baines's Life of Conrad (mum's the word till the Presentation next month), and then we were shown some of the College treasures, including the superb El Greco which Major Alnatt presented to the Chapel. He suddenly wrote out of the blue to say that he had been looking round the Colleges and thought the El Greco would look best in New College Chapel! I imagine he did just the same with the Rubens and King's.

That evening I dined with Wyndham Ketton-Cremer (whom I first met at my prep-school in 1917)—again at the Athenaeum: twice in one week puts a strain on the toughest constitution. Next day I lunched with Diana Cooper and talked some more about Duff's books. In fact, one way and another, I was out to every meal last week.

*Sunday morning.* I slept for the best part of ten hours, and still feel cosily drowsy. I've just finished Leonard Woolf's second volume of autobiography, *Growing*, which I found extremely interesting, and now I am reading Priestley's new Pictorial Life of Dickens, which is an excellent job with first-class pictures.

I fear my last letter misled you: I am not descended from Lawrence, but from one of his sitters. You ought to visit that exhibition on your next visit to London.

The 'Prof' I met only once, when Roy Harrod took me to lunch or dine in the Common Room at the House, and I took an immediate dislike to him, on exactly the grounds you describe.

---

[1] For the first two (1961) of the twelve volumes of *The Complete Tales of Henry James.*

I saw more than one respectful reference in the press to your Heinemann transaction. It is all very interesting to hear about. I like to think that you are at last really having the only thing really essential to life, *viz* peace of mind. Though of course the fates are pretty niggardly with it. *Il-y-a toujours de quoi*, as my doctor, had he known any French, would have said recently when I complained of small aches and pains which I suggested he should deal with.

I saw and liked that Henry James article with the impressive announcement that exactly the publisher one would have expected is undertaking the short stories. And I was glad to read that you will be mainly ignoring H.J.'s own corrections in later editions—almost all of which, I remember thinking, were for the worse. Did you read Connolly on *A Christmas Garland*[1] in the *Sunday Times*, in which he said that of the authors parodied only five were really familiar to-day (Conrad, Hardy, Kipling, James, Shaw) 'not because the parodies killed Baring, Benson and Co but . . . because their eclipse forms part of the *general subsidence into oblivion of the whole of English Literature*.' Is this really the truth—outside the schools who are still set books by Galsworthy and Wells and Bennett (who C says are 'under eclipse')? And if so, cannot one say that it always was true? C. implies that 'the leisured reader' is vanishing.

And I was talking about reading to the girls of North Foreland Lodge last Monday and telling them how pleasantly and profitably they could teach themselves. I read them Conrad's account of the return of the *Narcissus* 'Under white wings she skimmed low over the blue sea like a great tired bird speeding to its nest', and they were wonderful listeners. Do you think I was fantastic to tell them that that sentence alone contained the ideas of speed, sunshine, loneliness, spaciousness, welcome, happiness, earth's solidity v. sea and sky's opposite, and to sum up drew a lovely picture? Well anyway I did and they seemed to swallow it. With equal avidity they delighted in Ivor's officialese reproduction of the Lord's Prayer, though I didn't dare to quote more than 'We should be obliged for your attention in provid-

[1] By Max Beerbohm (1912).

ing for our own nutritional needs, and for so organising distribution that our daily intake of cereal filler be not in short supply.'

Pamela has ordered several copies of his new book for Christmas presents, and is still immersed in it, so that I still have not read any more. She is no etymologist but delights in Ivor's miniature essays. They *are* very well done.

Another book I have just read—with increasing dismay—is the Pelican *Modern Age* in their Guides to Eng. Lit. The language of modern criticism is to me so fearfully pretentious that again and again I cannot grasp the meaning, and am constantly merely guessing at it. Such a sentence as 'The final death of Gerald in the snow is only the symbolic expression of the inexorable consequence of his life-defeating idealism' means so little to me that I have decided to avoid modern criticism in future. There are some pretty grim sentences about dear T.S. Eliot too. I wonder what he thinks of them. One Bantock insists that my old Evelyns, Eton, and Cambridge contemporary, L.H. Myers, is really a most important figure. I knew him up to about his twenty-fourth year, and I think this judgment puts him rather high. He committed suicide in 1944 for the simple reason that he 'despaired of humanity.'

*3 December 1961*                                               *Bromsden Farm*

This may be the last of my interminable letters, for at eleven o'clock on Wednesday morning I am to take wing for New York, returning on Saturday. Were it not for my morbid fear of flying, it would be something of a spree, but as it is you can imagine me boarding the bus at the Air Terminal as though it were a tumbril taking me to the guillotine. The knowledge that hundreds of people fly safely each way every day is no comfort to me, and I doubt whether the tranquillising pills I have been given will have much effect either.

Last time I flew the Atlantic (in 1952) there were no jets, and the flight took the best part of twenty-four hours, with unscheduled landings in Iceland and Newfoundland. Now, if all goes well, we leave at 11 a.m. and arrive at 2 p.m. (U.S. time) the same day. I am to stay with the Gleaveses, as in March, and to spend almost all my time in conference with Harcourt Brace. If only Ruth could come with me! She doesn't mind flying at all—women are much braver than men—and would thoroughly enjoy it, but it costs £321, and one fare is enough for H.B. Anyhow, if I survive, I shall have something to tell you next Sunday.

Meanwhile Oscar is done! The proofs go back to the printer to-morrow, and thereafter only proofs of the index will remain to be done, and I shall probably spend a day at the printers' at Frome in Somerset, looking over all their corrections before the machining begins. Luckily Tony Powell lives at Frome, and has offered to put me up for the occasion. You can imagine what a relief it is to be shot of the whole caboodle, and if only I were travelling to New York by boat, the trip would be one long celebration.

That's a magnificent sentence about the *Narcissus*: no wonder the girls were good listeners. You simply *must* stop worrying yourself by reading rubbish like that Pelican book about modern literature. L.H. Myers is a deadly writer, and Mr Bantock should be condemned to read nothing else for a year.

Meanwhile the advent of parking-meters in the Square has proved an immense blessing. One can now drive right up to the door of the house, and the vans can load and unload in peace. No one is allowed to park for more than two hours, and that only in fixed areas on payment. This knocks out all the monsters who used to leave cars there every day for eight hours. The meters stop working at 6.30 p.m., so it fills up again for the evening as of old, but no cars are left there all night, and the tireless Jamaicans have a chance of sweeping the roadway before the office-workers start to arrive.

Last Wednesday Ruth and I took her guests to the dramatisation of C.P. Snow's novel *The Affair*, which proved an excellent evening's entertainment, somewhat in the Galsworthy manner. If all Snow's works could be served up in this painless way I might find them less rebarbative.

I also lunched one day with Diana Cooper, another with Eric Linklater and generally rattled about, with final attacks on the Oscar proofs up to midnight each night. One evening I dined agreeably at the Beefsteak, and as I hadn't been there for a couple of years my

dinner must have cost me the best part of £40. Harold N. was there—
it is his main eating-place—very sweet and woolly.

Yesterday morning I attended a requiem mass for Christopher
Devlin at Farm Street, the Jesuit church. For non-believers who didn't
know the service by heart no word could be recognised except twice
*Dominus vobiscum.* I tried to think nice thoughts and take it all seriously.

*6 December 1961*                                        *Over New Brunswick*

I think your best chance of getting a letter this week is to endure
a serial one, part written today and part during my return journey on
Saturday. I only hope this Biro (the best I have found) is legible.

I daresay, with perhaps pardonable pride, that this is the first letter
you have ever received which was written at 35,000 feet above the
earth. So far on this trip I have found the preliminary dread greater
than the fear in the air, though that is ever with me. Perhaps the two
tranquillising pills I took have helped. When I arrived at the Victoria
Air Terminal at 9.30 this morning I found that the absence of my
vaccination-certificate, which I had mislaid since my American trip in
March, might land me in for fourteen days' quarantine in the U.S., so,
at the Terminal, for a fee of ten shillings and sixpence, in five and a
half minutes, I was re-vaccinated and given the necessary certificate.
All along it has been a day of clear blue sky, and though we are said to
have a 50 m.p.h. wind against us, this is apparent only in occasional
bumps. This plane (a Boeing 707) is so much bigger than any I have
ever been in before that it's more like a train, and therefore a little reassuring. I am sitting next to the President of the Shell Oil Company
of America, who might well be most useful to Adam after he gets his
degree—a most charming and civilised man. For lunch I consumed
two large Bourbon whiskies as an aperitif, then caviare, lamb chops and
beans, fruit tart, Stilton, *three* glasses of claret, coffee and brandy—all
very good and boosting to the morale. I have also been able to smoke
my pipe with impunity. When we passed over Iceland, *seven miles up,*
the island looked like a mud-flat intersected by trickles of water.
Since then we have had a carpet of white cloud below, clear blue sky
and sun above. We are due to arrive in another hour, and the terrors

of landing still lie ahead. The trouble is that I shall by then have endured a full day's trials, but it will only be mid-afternoon in New York, and many more hours of bright activity may well be expected of me. I *hate* leaving Ruth, even for a moment, let alone on so long and hazardous a journey. Never again I swear. Goodbye for now. More on Saturday at latest.

*8 December 1961*                                      *Grundisburgh*

I hope Jonah is not missing the Lit. Soc. for health reasons, though I expect Tommy L. is not fit enough yet. My exam-papers start coming in on Saturday, and, as always, there are a good many more than I bargained for. One lot I shall have to mark on a book whose contents I have almost completely forgotten. My cynical colleagues assure me that it is quite easy. I think, as Swift would have put it, that they are saying the thing that is not.

Your condemnation of that Pelican *Modern Age* pleases me; a great deal of it seems to me awfully bad. I appreciate too your derision of my pathetic attempts to keep abreast of the moderns. But habits are not easily uprooted. I must tell you that, having so repeatedly read that *Women in Love* is one of the greatest of novels, I have again started re-reading it, after about twenty years, and am about halfway through. There are fine things in it, but I remain convinced that when the D.H.L. *Schwärmerei* has died down the general opinion will be a lot of it is pretentious and unconvincing. So many of his subtle probings into man-woman relations are far outside any of *my* experience or the furthest range of my imagination that they strike literally no chord in my mind. If your answer is that this merely shows I am too stupid or at least too old-fashioned, I shall be quite ready to agree. But do have a look at the chapter headed 'Rabbit' and tell me how and why it isn't pointless not to say silly.

*10 December*                                      *Bromsden Farm*

My plan to write some more yesterday was thwarted by my charmingly talkative neighbour—an attorney from Ohio with the reassuring name of Weller. The return trip (though equally well victualled and liquored) was less attractive than the outward one. A strong tail-wind caused such bumps, even at 30,000 feet, that we were several times ordered to fasten our safety-belts. Eventually (having taken off from New York at 10 a.m. their time (3 p.m. ours) we reached London airport at 10.15 p.m. (our time), three quarters of an hour late. When the sickening, deaf-making descent was almost completed (down to a few hundred feet), the pilot decided there was too much fog, went into a steep climb, and announced our departure for *Ireland*! An hour later we landed in *pouring* rain at Shannon Airport. When I was last there (also unwillingly—I wonder if anyone ever goes there on purpose?) the building was a sort of converted shack. Now it is a huge emporium like the ground floor of Selfridge's, with dozens of counters at which one can buy *anything*, an efficient telephone service and a twenty-four-hour bar, at which all drinks were free (i.e. paid for by Pan-American Airways). I rang up Ruth in London, and Duff here, to find that Comfort was waiting with the car at London Airport.

Then followed an exceedingly tedious wait of two and a half hours. When I could take no more whisky I turned to coffee and ham sandwiches. Eventually we took off again in the still heavy rain, and after another hour's flight came down safely at London A. It was then almost 3 a.m. and poor Comfort had been there for five hours. We got home and to bed by 4 a.m. I slept heavily, but all this morning could feel the aircraft throbbing under me.

My trip was, I think, a great success. All three days were cold, crisp, sunlit and blue-skied. I ate and drank and talked prodigiously, and drove almost three hundred miles to and from a seaside village in North Connecticut, where a novelist lives. Lunches and dinners were given for me, and I was presented with the magnificent Parker pen with which I am writing this. To fill it you simply hold the other end in a bottle of ink for a moment, without pressing any levers, and the ink flows in by capillary attraction! In a modest way I think my publishing fortune is made, and the whole thing is most exciting. *And* Oscar is finished. *Laus Deo!*

Next week you shall be brought up to date with home affairs, and your excellent letters shall be answered. Oh yes—Harcourt Brace are going to reissue my *Hugh Walpole* in a paperback edition in the U.S.A.

Very good budget of interesting news from you, and now you are safe home in port. Those air-pockets must be supremely beastly and then the fog which sent you on to Ireland. Whenever one hears from anyone about a flight in winter one has the impression that the margin of safety was nothing to boast about. Humphrey was once ordered—with the other passengers—to throw all his luggage out, and the plane, after avoiding one foggy place after another, eventually landed with fifteen minutes' worth of petrol left. Diana in one plane accompanied two others to Yalta or somewhere—one of the other two planes crashed.

I am nearing the end of *Russia and the West* by George Kennan; it seems to me wonderfully good, though not making one exactly cheerful—except in comparison with Bertrand Russell's last book of essays, which literally hold out no hope.[1] In Boots I bought secondhand a book of L.P. Hartley's called *Facial Justice*. A failure, *qua* me. A sort of blend of Orwell and Aldous Huxley all about life after the third world war, when all life will be compulsorily underground. All very jolly and boring, as George Mathew said of some Wagner opera. My exam-papers pretty well fill my day.

What a grand writer for the young Macaulay is—so lucid and emphatic. They have been tackling his great Chapter III and I am stifled with exhaustive information about the Navy in Stuart times, the country gentleman, the new advances in science etc etc. They love such climaxes as 'In Charles II's navy there were both sailors and gentlemen, but the sailors were not gentlemen, nor the gentlemen sailors.' Simple and obvious no doubt, but a good true point.

Fog and Christmas between them must have prevented your letter from arriving this week. I was lucky getting down yesterday, for the fog was dense, and if I hadn't walked into the 4.18 to Reading at 4.55 (it left at 5.5) I might have had a long cold wait at Paddington.

[1] *Has Man a Future?* (1961).

Let me have your address at Eton: which day do you go there? Special preparations are being made for your luncheon on Boxing Day. Bridget will be here, and perhaps Duff and wife, though they may be out shooting.

The Lit. Soc. was shadowy without you. Only nine stalwarts turned up. We ate scampi with rice, roast duck and a pear dish or soft roes. Ivor was particularly sad at missing you again. It was just as well you hadn't got to negotiate the stairs at Soho Square last week, since the decorators are in charge, with scaffolding, planks and splashing paint. They are also in the flat, where confusion reigns, but all should be ship-shape and glistening by January. So far I have bought *no* Christmas presents, and the days are running out. I had hoped to find some little thing for Ruth in New York, but I simply hadn't a moment, and in any case the furious steam-heating of the shops there exhausts one in a few minutes. I can see that next week is going to be a busy one.

*Sunday morning*

Clear and frosty and sunny. We are just going to drive down to Henley to inspect a new Standard Vanguard, which the garage-proprietor is trying to persuade us to have instead of a new Morris Traveller (our present car is an M.T.).

It seems funny, after all these years, having no Oscar to do, and in a perverse way I slightly miss it, though for the most part I rejoice—and there is plenty of other work. This afternoon I must start reading the typescript of the second volume of Leon Edel's life of Henry James, which is immensely long and detailed. The new publishing arrangement is so exciting and many-sided that my office-time looks like being pretty full. I already have more work than one secretary can cope with, and may get a second one, or perhaps a dictaphone. Forgive this scrappy half-pay letter. Next week there should be two letters from you to answer, and I'll probably send a line to Eton before your visit.

*Boxing Day 1961*                                                    *Bromsden Farm*

This is a poor substitute for several hours of your company, and we are all most disappointed—not least Comfort, who had prepared specially succulent dishes to tempt you. I do hope poor Pamela will soon be better—though I daresay bed's the best place in this icy weather. The little gifts you should have had at luncheon will be posted to Eton tomorrow, and I shall hope to see you at the January Lit. Soc.

On the Christmas tree I was given a magnificent new bird-table, specially made by Peter's estate-carpenter, but I shan't be able to instal it until the ground is a bit softer. Meanwhile the old one is increasingly popular and gives me much pleasure. Since I arrived on Friday evening I have scarcely set foot outside the house—it's quite cold enough inside.

Did I tell you that, in small print and double column, my Oscar index will occupy *eighty* of those large pages? No wonder it took me so long! I have now arranged to scrutinise each sheet of the book, after the final corrections have been made and before it is machined. They hope to send me one or two sheets (each of sixty-four pages) each week, so that will take several months. Also, when the first sheet is ready for press I shall go down to the printers at Frome and encourage them with well-deserved praise—a jay has just come on the bird-table, the first I've ever seen there. It dwarfed the other birds, but stayed only a moment.

Your description of the Grundisburgh Parish Council is most depressing. We are in the parish of Bix, but of its churchgoing or council I am woefully ignorant. I'm sure you're right, however, in thinking that nowadays everything depends on the personality and popularity of the incumbent. (The jay has returned—and departed.) Last time I took up Macaulay's Chapter III, I simply couldn't stop reading it. Soon I must try it again.

I'm sure you would be well-advised to put in oil-fired central heating. It requires *no* attention, except the occasional checking or alteration of a thermostat. If I ever amass enough money, I'll put it in here, and so greatly improve the value of Peter's property. Duff has gone shooting with P. this morning.

*Evening*

Duff shot two woodcock and two pigeons, walked *miles* in freezing cold, and seems to have enjoyed himself. During the holiday I have read the manuscript of the second volume of Leon Edel's biography of Henry James, which I greatly enjoyed, and also the second autobiographical venture of Vyvyan Holland, Oscar's son, which alas is very thin and banal. I don't know how on earth to tell him without hurting his feelings. Also I have done some work on Birley's proofs, and in bed have read or re-read *Kipps*, which on the whole stands up very well. The whole of Wells's first draft of the book, much longer than the published version, has turned up, and I felt I couldn't judge it without refreshing my memory. I'll report more of this next week.

A friend and contemporary of Adam's at Eton, James Loudon, went abroad at the same time as A., under the same scheme, but was sent to teach in a school in British Honduras. He had hardly got there when the whole school, and most of the town of Belize, was reduced to rubble by a hurricane, followed by a tidal wave. The boy wrote to ask if I could do anything about books, of which no single one survived. I sent him a parcel, and persuaded our trade paper, the *Bookseller*, to print a letter in which I appealed to all publishers and booksellers to send what they could: I've no idea whether they will respond. Birley, whom I met at a bibliographical dinner in London last week, told me the boy had written to him too, and he asked the school to help. This produced more than £500. Isn't that splendid!

Last Thursday the Duff Cooper Prize was presented most effectively by Mountbatten, who spoke easily, without notes and much to the point. He gave just the impression of unflappable *sang-froid* one would expect from the Navy. Champagne flowed and Diana was much pleased.

One evening Ruth and I went to Covent Garden to hear Tchaikovsky's opera *The Queen of Spades*, which we quite enjoyed. On the whole, opera is beyond my musical comprehension, but I want to see all the best ones at least once each, to make sure, and to see what they're about. Ruth has been spending Christmas with her son and his family in Essex. No telephone there, so we have been sadly separated, and I have been worrying about her ability to keep warm there. Tomorrow we shall be happily reunited. The stairs at Soho Square are now clean and bright, and the workmen start tomorrow on the bedrooms in the flat. Mine is to be painted dark red!

Pamela is still pretty feeble, though thanks be, it is not a severe attack. This house is fairly warm. Finndale, I expect, is frozen solid, but we haven't heard. The good plumber may have turned all the water off by now. I hope to come to the Lit. Soc. but I have been having bouts of 'aural vertigo' which make me *pro tem* entirely incapable of walking unsupported or even of standing up. So I may not be able to go to Cambridge on Tuesday. I will let you know. If it comes on in the underground I shall have to go round the whole circle before getting out. It is apparently connected with some kinds of deafness. Something happens in the inner ear which upsets the balance. Damnable!

I do practically nothing here except read. Neither my daughter nor her husband ever reads, but luckily my grandson has quite a readable library, though most of his books are at Oxford. He works every day at haberdasher Caley's in Windsor and is amassing quite a nice little pin-money. I have just re-read D.H. Lawrence's letters. There are far too many of them (880 pages). Many are very dull and not worth printing. What is the point of printing 'Frieda has just got herself a big coat because it is so cold'? What a bad critic he was—all prejudice and exaggeration. But I grant you there is something refreshing about his describing Joyce's *Ulysses* as 'a clumsy ollapodrida'. I don't like him; his way of biting most of the hands that fed him is not an amiable trait.

Do you know Ivor's *Master Sanguine*? Some fine satire in it about educational theories, party government, militarism, in fact most things; very good bedside reading—till one's hands become too cold.

What you say of Macaulay Chapter III applies to all of him. Fatal to look something up; you just go on reading. But I suppose to admire him is wholly out of date now. What bilge literary fashions are.

That is a heartening tale about the Belize hurricane and that school library. Eton did well and so will the booksellers and publishers of whom, you remember, Johnson always spoke warmly. Those hurricanes are a great strain on anyone's faith—as in fact a good many things are. I hope Adam won't come across one. Is he enjoying the work he is doing? Almost the only thing that matters.

Tell me all about the *Kipps* affair. I have not read it for many years, but remember liking it, although less than *Mr Polly*. To admire either is always said to have infuriated H.G.W., but I don't suppose it did really. Who said he sold his birthright for a pot of message?

You omitted to mention the insertion of a *lift* at No. 36, no doubt inadvertently. Not that my vertigo minds stairs; no one knows what it does or does not mind. Its usual moment for coming on is when I am sitting in a chair. The leech says it sometimes comes on in bed.

*30 December 1961*                                                    *Bromsden Farm*

I hope you're pleased about Bernard's taking over from your nephew.[1] I don't see why your grip on that great Dominion should be in the slightest relaxed by the change, and I imagine it's an excellent appointment, though I'm doubtful as to B's soundness on the subject of cricket. We must educate him in that all-important branch of sovereignty.

Yesterday Birley came to the office, hot from addressing the School Librarians, and we went through his proofs. He is not a good proof-corrector, but lightning-quick in the uptake, and apparently grateful for my attempts to polish up his prose. I wonder what he'll do when he leaves Eton: write books, I hope. He tells me he has plenty of ideas for such.

Adam writes enthusiastically from his camp in South India. He has shot a spotted deer and explored the antiquities of Mysore and other neighbouring cities.

Today Duff and some farmer-friends of his shot 109 hares in a blizzard. The older I get the less do I sympathise with the systematic slaughter of birds and beasts—not that I was ever very keen on it.

The point about *Kipps* is that it was originally planned as a much longer, almost Dickens-sized, novel, and then reshaped in its known form. Wells believed that all the discarded chapters had been lost, but they have now come to light in the H.G.W. archive in the University of Illinois, and have been offered to me as a literary curiosity. I read

---

[1] As Governor-General of New Zealand.

almost half the new stuff this evening, and it's vintage Wells all right. The trouble is that I doubt whether, just now, many people are interested in *Kipps*—or Wells, for that matter. One day they will be again. Anyhow, if Illinois will take 1500 or so copies for America, I think I could sell a like number over here, and lose no money thereby.

One of my American colleagues (Jovanovich's No. 2) is over to conclude arrangements with Heinemann, and with any luck all should be tidied up sometime next week. Meanwhile there is plenty to be done—hiring new staff, buying machines, taking extra offices etc. All in the right direction and therefore stimulating. Now I shall go to bed. More in the morning.

*Sunday morning*

After more than *ten hours* of deep sleep I woke to find this new soft-fallen mask of snow over everything. Duff says it is eight inches deep on the front lawn, and I fear it may drift on the exposed part of the road between here and the main road. How and when we shall all get to London is a matter of conjecture.

Bridget has just announced that in ten minutes she is going to battle her way to the post-office, so I think I'd better send this, even if it's not full measure. Somehow I must be in London tomorrow morning, and maybe it would be wise to go up in daylight this afternoon.

Have I sent you a forthcoming book called *The Fleet that Jack Built*? I meant to send it, but probably forgot. I think it might amuse you. Jack is Jackie Fisher, and it's about the Navy and its admirals between 1868 and 1918—written by an admiral too.[1]

I am thinking of putting the price of Oscar up from three to four guineas, which I think it will stand.

Now Bridget is off—so I must stop.

*3 January 1962*                                                    *Cambridge*

A good letter which caught me up at the University Arms Hotel Cambridge, where, judging by the forecasts, I may easily be marooned for many days, though my purpose is to leave on Saturday for 67

[1] Rear-Admiral Sir William Jameson.

Chelsea Square (Diana's). The prospect, climate, and general feeling here is Siberian, and how they delight in telling us that there is no sign of a change.

My vertigo *may* be improving, but I don't trust it yet. A friend here knows all about it as his brother-in-law has it. It *can* end in an operation which makes one ear stone-deaf but cures the vertigo. But somehow I don't think it will with me. I shall come to the Lit. Soc. if possible and will telephone to Soho Square on Monday if impossible. (And I never thought I should ever fill a page on my own health! How right Johnson was in regarding an ill man as a scoundrel.)

Yes, I was pleased to see Bernard's appointment—a very good one I thought it, though he won't hit any sixes against a visiting team. I wonder how handy he is with speechifying. To my nephew that is the real burden, as he always spends a lot of time in preparation, as all good men do except the born speakers like old Quickswood. Odd that he so bungled his speech in the prayer-book debate when a crowded house expected him to make the speech of his life. Somehow his heart was not in it. Birley is tremendously long-winded they say, Alington was as good as any, and my old uncle Edward too was very good. I have a strong suspicion that R.H-D. is too.

I agree with you about shooting. I was no great shakes at the art, but I gave it up deliberately after a few years because, simply, I did not enjoy killing things, though more than ready to devour the results of others' efforts. A roast pheasant in perfect maturity I always regard as a dish for the gods. Do you agree?

*Kipps*? H.G.W. is of course dead as a prophet and priest, but as a storyteller, I simply don't know. *K.* was a fine tale. *I* should like to see it at Dickens length. I rather hope you will have a stab at it.

Colin Eccleshare is here. He has somehow heard of your recent Heinemann transaction and wishes you luck. How right you are about Kitchener. My old uncle, the general, always disliked him intensely on much the same grounds as you do—an unscrupulous and heartless careerist. He also maintained that he was a very moderate general. He said nothing about his being a homosexual, repressed or open, you will be surprised to hear.

Your letter has been lying on the table while I write this and two of my colleagues have both commented on the elegance of your handwriting. How right they were. I am always writing on my knee and my writing has gone to pot. I hope only temporarily but it may be due to latent vertigo. Who shall say?

I don't know *The Fleet that Jack Built*, though I have a feeling I have seen it reviewed. My old friend Admiral William Fisher always had a great admiration for Jackie F., who surely was a great man, and no doubt at the end quite impossible.

*6 January 1962*                                                     *Bromsden Farm*

I was afraid you might have been snowbound at Eton, and was relieved to know you had got safely to Cambridge. The snow was so deep here last Sunday morning and the roads so tricky that I went back to London that afternoon. Duff managed to get me to Henley station in his little car, but we couldn't even reach the main road until we had persuaded one of the farm-workers to go before in a tractor to flatten out a track for us. Altogether it took me *four hours* to reach the flat from here, but I was warm all the time, and able to read. Next morning, I learned later, the roads were worse still, and to cap it all my usual Monday morning train crashed into the buffers at Paddington and twenty people were taken to hospital. It's an ill wind . . . Most of my office staff failed to arrive till after lunch, and then we sent them straight home again. My American colleague John McCallum was in London all week, and we spent long hours, day after day, with lawyers and suchlike, before all was brought to a happy conclusion on Thursday evening. On Tuesday I never left my own office from 9 till 6.30, sending out for sandwiches for lunch, and on Wednesday I left the house at 9 a.m. and got back at 10.30 p.m.

My darling Ruth tactfully chose the week to get some sort of bronchial flu—tactfully because (a) I couldn't have spent any time with her if she had been well and (b) she had staying with her a devoted old retired lady-doctor, who nursed her delightedly. I'm hoping R. will be back by Tuesday, but she still sounds pretty feeble. If you can't face the rush-hour journey and the stairs, ring me up and we'll meet at the Garrick or elsewhere. If R. is well enough she will be longing to see you.

The painters finally evacuated the flat on Thursday, and I am now happily installed in my new scarlet-walled bedroom. Also a huge re-arrangement of books is in progress, since now for the first time I can use the shelves which so long harboured E.B.'s library.

Yes, I must confess that I thoroughly enjoy roast pheasant, so long as someone else has shot it, out of my sight, but I shouldn't really *mind* being a vegetarian if need be, though I daresay one would soon get heartily sick of nut cutlets and all such.

I finished the Kitchener book simply *loathing* K, and almost pleased at his hopeless bungling of the War Office and the War. The knowledge that a massive attack at Gallipoli when it was first mooted would prob-ably have taken Constantinople and perhaps ended the war is almost unbearable. Winston was right all along in that matter.

The Fisher book shall go to you on Monday. I stupidly thought I'd sent it already. It doesn't appear till the 22nd. Now I shall go to bed and finish in the morning. I am happily re-reading *The Diary of a Nobody* (rationed to one chapter a night, to spin it out) and *Edwin Drood*, which I had never read before and am much enjoying. Have you any strongly held theories as to what was going to happen? There's a vast literature on the subject, and most of the contestants are as cracked as Baconians.

*Sunday morning*

The snow has almost vanished, and everything is suddenly very green and soft. I expect you are safely in Chelsea Square. Bridget and Duff are making plans for a fortnight's winter sports in the Italian Alps at the beginning of February. Twelve of them are planning to take a chalet. I can't think of anything I should hate more—nonsense, I can think of plenty—but all the same—

Last Monday night, before Ruth took to her bed, she and I took the McCallums to a remarkable entertainment called *Stop the World, I Want to Get Off.* It was all written, words and music, by a chap called Anthony Newley, who is never off the stage all evening. Besides him there is one woman and perhaps a dozen pretty girls. Only one set, with very little in it. Newley is dressed as a clown, and the whole thing is a sort of satire on modern life. I thought it brilliant and en-

joyed every minute. Goodness knows what the McCallums made of
it, for a lot of the jokes are very English, if not Cockney.


*13 January 1962*                                          *Bromsden Farm*

Despite your prohibition, I think you must have at least a half-
length letter to cheer you in your giddiness. You looked exceptionally
well on Thursday, though I'm sure it only irritates you to be told so.
   Yesterday morning I took my sister to the Augustus John memorial service at St Martin in the Fields. Apart from an abnormally high
ratio of beards to pews, it was all immensely decorous and tasteful,
and might have been in honour of any ambassador or social dignitary.
A crowd of gipsies on a mountain-top, with plenty of wine and girls,
would have been nearer the mark. I'm sure A.J. never set foot in a
church after his childhood. David Cecil gave a well-written address,
but his super-U accent, his tail-coat, and his position in the pulpit,
made it all grotesquely unsuitable. Many of A.J.'s children and grandchildren were there, and I wondered how many illegitimate ones. He
knew he was a genius and came to think it his duty to people the
world with others. Did you know that Peter F's mother had a child of
his? A pretty girl called Amaryllis, with his red hair and Mrs F's
features. I remember the appearance of this baby when P. and I were
at Eton, and even then in my innocence I thought Mrs F's account of
how she had adopted this child, through Lord Dawson of Penn etc.,
rather unnecessarily protracted. Now she is a cellist of, I suppose
thirty-seven, very good-looking and withdrawn. The most moving—
the *only* moving—part of yesterday's service was when she suddenly
appeared in the choir, looking very young and slim in black, with
flaming red hair, carrying her cello, on which she played some unaccompanied Bach—rather too much I thought.
   The first index-proofs of Oscar have arrived, and I am ashamed to
see how often the compositors have misread my handwriting. Illiterate boors, I cry, wondering at the same time whether perhaps you and
everyone else have the same difficulty.

My vertigo (I am pleased to find, in the teeth of all my Cambridge colleagues, that the i is long and not short as they said) is being held at bay *pro tem*, though I don't feel it to be very far away. It is, as you say, mildly vexatious to be told one is looking well and, *a fortiori*, when a leech, never yet suspected of being a humbug, says he has never seen a fitter man of seventy-nine.

Talking of pronunciation, several G.C.E. examiners maintained that ambiválent was the right pronunciation (some, it is true, were scientists) so after a bit I demurely asked for a word with an equiválent meaning, and also brought in preválent. Sheepish, my dear R, is the only word that sums up their demeanour.

The John funeral sounds very incongruous. How immensely absurd the English can be in such things. Victorianism has not really lost much of its grip. That is very interesting about Peter F's mother. But 'such a mistake' as old Sir G. Sitwell would have said, to play *un*-accompanied cello music, where very little goes a long way. The cello is (to me) the most splendid of all instruments, but not unaccompanied. A few bars emerging from the orchestra (as in the Mendelssohn violin concerto) always get me in the wind, as horns so often do in Beethoven.

Fancy the compositors boggling over your writing. I have never had a second's hesitation anywhere. They must be like those children who complain that they can't read the Italic hand (i.e. perfect legibility) because they are used to bad writing. Give these men the rough side of your tongue; they deserve it.

Rather a setback over *Edwin Drood*. My set of Dickens is by way of being complete, but *E.D.* is not there. Nor is it at the Ipswich Library. Is there a reasonably cheap edition of it? I have read *The Fleet that Jack Built* with great pleasure. What fine chaps good sailors always are. I particularly liked Tyrwhitt, who got into the navy at his third attempt thirtieth out of thirty-one! He has a splendid face—in fact they all have. Odd that old Fisher should have ignored the defensive equipment of the big ships. Anyone who knew the Germans must have known they would hit hard and accurately. The fact must be faced that Jutland really was a defeat. That the Germans never came out again merely shows that they never really acquired the naval spirit.

(Hitler didn't either.) But we had a lot of bad luck over those raids, when fog kept on saving them.

I am writing a day later than usual, since I only got back from Scotland yesterday, and it took twelve hours of solid sleep to get me back to normal. I travelled to Edinburgh on the Thursday morning train, eating a huge breakfast and lunch (neither first-rate. Oh for the food on French trains!), and jotting down a few headings for my speech. After Darlington I had the carriage to myself, so could try out a few sallies *à vive voix*. Robin Walpole (Hugh's brother) met me at 3 p.m., and we just had time for a cosy tea of scones etc at his house before catching the train for Glasgow. There was a good deal of preliminary talk and drink in a stifling bar, and then the annual dinner of the Scottish Bookmen, which was attended by seventy-four stalwarts, mostly booksellers or publishers' travellers. My speech went down tolerably well, and we just caught the last train back to Edinburgh. There was a bar on board, whisky flowed, and I was ready for bed when we got home soon after midnight.

Friday I spent peacefully in Edinburgh, visiting booksellers and looking at secondhand books, which I always adore. Robin Walpole lives in great comfort with *two* maids! and it was rather fun to find one's pyjamas cherishingly wrapped round a hot-water-bottle, etc. The city was looking very black and wintry, but as always beautiful, and the Castle dramatic. I enjoyed my day. I caught the 11 p.m. train, slept fairly well in a first-class sleeper, reached the flat at 7 a.m., had a bath and breakfast, and got down here in time for lunch. The new car has arrived and looks very smart, but I seldom enjoy change, and each new model seems less roomy and comfortable than its predecessor.

Steady rain has fallen ever since I arrived, and everything is awash. Tomorrow I am going down to Frome to see the ritual machining of the first sheet of Oscar. I have now passed 256 pages for press. The proofs of the index, which are still coming in, look as long as an ordinary book!

I am to stay tomorrow night with Tony Powell and his charming wife Violet (née Pakenham), and get back to London on Tuesday afternoon. Ruth came back to work last week, but is still a little feeble after her flu.

In his new book of memoirs, the actor Cedric Hardwicke is asked by an interviewer whether today he would recommend a young man to go on the stage, and answers: 'Certainly not: there's far too much competition. He'd do better to go into Parliament, where there's none.'

If you look at the current (February) number of a paper called *Encounter* you will find an article by Sparrow which seeks to prove that *Lady Chatterley's Lover* is in fact a handbook to buggery. What next? Some old Wardens of All Souls must be rotating in their coffins. I much prefer *The Diary of a Nobody*, which I am enjoying more than ever. When did you last read it? Have you got a copy?

Adam writes regularly and cheerfully from India. His coloured parrot has escaped: otherwise he seems to have no complaints, and is planning to visit Kashmir and the Taj Mahal in the next holidays, whenever they are.

So glad you enjoyed the Jackie Fisher book: it appears tomorrow, with three other books—my first publications of the year. We have managed to take eight more office-rooms, not in Soho Square but in Dean Street, immediately across the well outside my office-windows. Here we are assembling the accounts and invoicing departments which were disbanded when we entered the Heinemann group. We shall need all the new rooms—and more I daresay—when our educational books start to appear. Harcourt Brace's head textbook man has just arrived for a three-months stay, in which he is to investigate and report on the whole question. He is said to work sixteen hours a day and exhaust three secretaries: I haven't yet found him one. Perhaps the more sedative air of London will slow him down a little.

The Max B. plaque is now ready, and as soon as it is in place in the crypt of St Paul's I shall have to arrange a consecration and unveiling ceremony. If it isn't one thing, it's another. Now I must go to bed.

Your Scotch trip sounds good (except that surely breakfasts *used* to be good on English railways?). Pamela grinned complacently when I read out how at R. Walpole's your pyjamas had been wrapped round your hot-water-bottle because she always does that with mine. She has recovered from a nasty bout of flu at Christmas, when she did not avoid pneumonia by a large margin, but still rests for two hours in the afternoon. Tell dear Ruth she must do the same. Our good doctor says the main thing about this onset of flu is not to *hurry*. What a damnable complaint it is! My vertigo has not attacked lately, but I long to get rid of the feeling that it isn't far round the corner. P. robustly maintains that is nerves, and she may be half right—but not more.

Is Hardwicke's book good? I always liked his acting. Yes, it must be a dreadful, fluky, up-and-down life. 'Overpaid casual labour' was what Gerald du Maurier called it, and he was a star—and apparently always plunged in depression. Old Arthur Benson once told me the most dreadful thing about melancholia was, as Shakespeare put it in one line 'With what I most enjoy contented least', for of course some quack told him to carry on with all his favourite ploys—and they all turned to dust in his mouth. Is it not odd that if A.C.B. came into the room, I should respectfully get up and generally kowtow—and he died when fifteen years younger than I am now? Once your tutor always your tutor is no doubt true.

I am re-reading *Pickwick*. Do you realise what an old tippler Mr P. was? I suppose they all were in the 1830's—just as a reader in 2050 will see our age as one of fornication, not of drink. But the end is not yet; something much more portentous than 1914 or 1939 is on the way. Some demonstration by the Almighty that he is not mocked, or what?

I am also reading (don't laugh) Leavis's *D.H. Lawrence, Novelist*. I must try and find out what the man's greatness is supposed to be— particularly in that sticky *Rainbow* and *Women in Love*. So far F.R.L. is disappointingly peevish and sneery with those who don't agree with him, and anyway I know *that* is wrong. You seem to be wavering in your support of *Lady Chatterley*. I shall certainly get the February

*Encounter*. John Sparrow may be much lazier than he should be, but he has never written anything that was not abundantly worth reading.

I haven't read *The Diary of a Nobody* for a long time, but I remember enjoying it, though my favourite in that genre was always Burnand's *Happy Thoughts*, which I shall quote from to you when we next meet (February 13 unless I am still vertiginous). I am full of hope. I look forward to seeing your renovated flat, and speeding aloft in the lift. It is clear the R.H-D. publishing business is on the crest. Fine. Love to Ruth. Mind you *insist* on her resting daily.

27 *January 1962*                                                   *Bromsden Farm*

Aren't you glad you're not dressed in a space-suit and waiting to be rocketed to blazes? That man must have nerves of steel, and I shall be in a much worse dither next Tuesday, when I am to have a decayed wisdom-tooth removed. I am insisting on a general anaesthetic, since I hate the suffocating feeling of the gas-mask, and a local anaesthetic leaves the horrors all too visible and audible. Ruth has promised to hold my hand and take me home afterwards.

Warmed pyjamas are heavenly: I might have known that Pamela would so cherish you. Ruth told me yesterday that she was *just* beginning to feel human again after her flu. I keep trying to persuade her to rest after lunch, but it is seldom easy to arrange.

Thank goodness you're reading *Pickwick* to counteract that frightful Leavis. One day you must just forget all about D.H.L. Life without him is fine, I promise you.

Last Monday I travelled down to Somerset and spent a delightful evening and extremely comfortable night with the Powells in their charming house near Frome. Next morning I drove over to the printer's to see the ritual printing of the first sixty-four pages of Oscar. Needless to say, after a few minutes the machine broke down, and to allay my disappointment they took me on a ruthlessly conducted tour of the works. Seeing round any factory soon produces a state of acquiescent coma, as the exact performance of each monstrous engine is bellowed out at one above the din. After a couple of hours I was mercifully driven to Bath, where I caught a train to London and had quite a good lunch on it.

That night Ruth and I went to a private showing of an excellent movie that has been made from a first novel we published called *The Custard Boys*: do you remember it?[1] On Thursday we dined with the Reichmanns (Mrs R. is Elisabeth Beerbohm's sister) and were given a dinner so deliciously rich and enormous that we felt peculiar for the next twenty-four hours. First a soufflé filled with salmon and asparagus, then a haunch of miraculously tender venison, with cranberry sauce and sauerkraut; then a pudding of the shape and consistency of a cake, which was in fact a rum-laced trifle, then some cheese. All washed down by quantities of Rhine wine that tasted of grapes. They had clearly laid it all on specially for us, and my word we did full justice to it! Talking of venison, I saw six or seven deer in the next field as I drove home from the station last night.

*Sunday morning, 28 January*

I am reading, with great enjoyment, that first volume of the life of J.A. Froude that appeared some months ago. I ordered it immediately, but the O.U.P. has only just vouchsafed a copy. The great merit of the book is that most of it is in Froude's own words (hitherto unpublished) and he wrote beautifully. His prose is a joy to read. Do get the book from the library. The author's name is Waldo Hilary Dunn, and he hails, believe it or not, from Wooster, Ohio. Here is Froude on his first school:

> The master, Mr Lowndes, was rector and patron of the living. He was assisted in the teaching department by his brother and by three ushers, as they were then universally called, though converted now into masters by the ambitious vulgarity of the age.

That was written in the 1890's. What would the old fellow think of *our* age, I wonder?

The devoted old lady who sends out all the Lit. Soc. cards absent-mindedly addressed Sparrow's to All Souls College, Cambridge. Some wag in the Cambridge P.O. wrote 'Try Oxford' on it, and

[1] By John Rae (1960).

it eventually arrived safely. The post seems to have speeded up a little this past week, but the only way to make certain of quick delivery is to express a letter or parcel. Stuff from abroad seems to arrive quicker than anything else. I think I can dodge tomorrow's chaos by getting a lift in someone's car from Paddington—if my train ever gets there. Quite a lot of my staff come from south of London and probably won't arrive at all. That happened in the freeze-up at the New Year, and we had nobody in the building who knew how to work the switchboard, so the telephone was happily silent. You are well out of London these days, but I do hope your vertigo and the traffic will let you come to the February Lit. Soc.

*1 February 1962*                                                    *Grundisburgh*

Let me know about that tooth. I had one of my two surviving wisdom teeth out a fortnight ago—local anaesthetic, never felt a thing. I wonder what *visible* horrors you refer to; there is nothing to see but the determined face of the ivory-snatcher. I face now a lower plate, which all say is much more uncomfortable for some reason than the top one. At present I bite only on one side.

*Pickwick* of course was very refreshing. I skip a good deal—all about the boring fat boy, Mr Winkle, Mr Snodgrass, Solomon Pell, but there is plenty of compensating richness. I am now re-reading all the U.S.A. part of *Martin Chuzzlewit*. The Yanks' chief claim to greatness is that they forgave Dickens his really blistering picture of them. Jefferson Brick, Hannibal Chollop, Mrs Hominy, Elijah Pogram—they all scintillate with gems of absurd speech whose appeal never dims. But what an ass Dickens could be. Pecksniff should have been left a figure of fun, not become a plotter and a villain. Similarly Squeers in *Nicholas Nickleby* should have been left a grisly comic instead of developing into a serious swindler. And all the Gride etc part of *N.N.* I find unreadable, in fact I finish more or less when N. has met the Cheerybles. Sir Mulberry Hawk won't really do. (By the way, have you ever heard any explanation of the *twenty-five*-mile walk which Dickens sent old Wardle, Pickwick etc on on December 24? They would hardly have got home before breakfast on December 25. I believe Bernard

Darwin maintained that D. meant it as a joke—surely a very inferior one?)

I have every intention of coming to the dinner, but cannot yet be certain. Almost all the time I feel slightly sick, which takes all the *joie de vivre* out of one—which at seventy-nine is in any case rather a fragile plant. Many risks can be taken—heart, asthmatic onset, lumbago etc., but not actual sickness. But no one surely has *always* felt sick; there must be an end, though it may still be some weeks distant.

That was fine feeding you had with the Reichmanns. Venison needs very careful timing if tastelessness is to be avoided on the one hand and a dreadfully pungent over-ripeness on the other, though no doubt dear Dr Johnson would have relished the latter. I have a grim memory of a parent's gift of venison for my boys. I don't think it was really very long past its prime, but of course it smelt far worse than it tasted and very few boys faced it. No domestics of course will ever touch game of any kind however perfect. The only reason I have ever heard is the slightly mean one that they aren't going to eat anything that has not been paid for.

Froude has been on my list for weeks. He has always seemed to me a good man, but how they did pitch into him. His English is lovely—without, oddly, the smallest tinge in it of Carlyle whom he so greatly admired.

I am very glad the Prince is not going to Eton. The snob tourists would have made the place quite intolerable. From one or two parents who have had experience of it, Gordonstoun sounds an excellent school—with *apparently* less dead wood than many schools. Education is in just as much of a mess as anything else, in fact what isn't? Starting from my stomach.

*4 February 1962*                                   *36 Soho Square*

The decorators are at work on the hall, stairs, landing and bathroom at Bromsden Farm, so the house is pretty well uninhabitable and Comfort has gone to stay with a neighbour for a few days.

Yesterday Ruth and I went down to Brighton for the day, which we much enjoyed. It was a soft grey misty day, the sea calm and benign, as we walked the length of the front, breathing in the lovely seaweedy air. I was distressed to find that the secondhand bookshop in Hove that I had patronised since my earliest bookbuying boyhood had gone out of business. I can remember my mother urging me along the promenade with promises of this shop at the end of the walk, and I grieved at this snapping of another link with what Henry James called 'the visitable past'. However, we picked up a few trifles at other Brighton bookshops, ate an excellent lunch of fish-and-chips followed by treacle roll, breathed in a little more ozone and came peacefully back to Soho Square, to await the End of the World. I haven't yet had Adam's account of Indian reactions, but according to the press they are in a fine stew. When nothing happens they will doubtless attribute the miracle to the efficacy of their own prayers.

As a foretaste of judgment last Monday's traffic-chaos in London was quite enough to be going on with. I was lucky enough to get a lift from Paddington in a friend's car, and thereafter managed on foot. For miles round here the streets were solid with stationary vehicles for most of the day, and my poor Bridget, who had owned her first precious car for only a week, was run into broadside by a motor-bicycle in Eaton Square. No one was hurt, but it was clearly a beastly shock, and the car got a nasty bash.

The worst thing about the extraction of my wisdom-tooth was the apprehension beforehand. At the time I felt nothing—Pentothal works at once and leaves no aftermath beyond a slightly tipsy feeling for an hour or two. The chap who skilfully administered it turned out to be the man I sold our Highgate house to in 1946. Ruth came with me to hold my hand and waited next door. That evening I graciously (but with a trace of guilt and dishonesty) consented to be treated as an invalid and given my dinner in bed, but the whole thing was very little trouble. My objection to a local anaesthetic is first of all *hearing* it all happening, and then I imagine gouts of blood. Anyhow I much prefer Pentothal.

I must soon read *Martin Chuzzlewit* again: it used to be one of my favourites. I'm sure that the changes in so many of Dickens's characters (Pecksniff, Squeers etc) were due to the difficult and unnatural way he had to write his novels, for the monthly part-issues. He was seldom an issue ahead, and I imagine had only a rough plan of what was to happen, and how the characters were to develop. Also, he several times wrote two novels at once. In fact it's a wonder the plots hold together as well as they do.

*8 February 1962*                                              *Grundisburgh*
                                                              *(Summer-house)*

First of all *I am* coming on Tuesday, unless there is a railway strike. I am not *quite* well yet, but at seventy-nine who is? And I was encouraged recently by a friend who said he once had six months, during which he felt sick every day, but after finding he never *was* sick, he got used to and ignored it. If I turn out to be too optimistic next Tuesday evening, well that will be jolly bad luck on the Lit. Soc. The vertigo has been in abeyance now for a month and more.

I am sending this to Soho Square as you may be still unhoused. For all I know you are also unaneled,[1] but I am not precisely seized of its meaning.

To-morrow I start a lower-jaw plate, which everybody (except my dentist) says is always uncomfortable for weeks. My only originals left are the eight front ones in the lower jaw, which apparently are always the last to go. I may possibly be writing next week to the dentist, as the old woman pensioner did 'My top ones are all right but those in my bottom are very painful.' The worst thing about the local anaesthetic, to my mind, is the piercing of the gum. The actual extraction is completely painless. Of course for some seven or eight hours afterwards that half of one's face seems to belong to someone else.

My memory is awful. I read in some recent book that R.H-D's biography of Hugh Walpole was one of the really outstanding books of the last twenty years, and, ass that I am, cannot remember the author. Clearly a man who knew what was what. I was pleased to read a strong complaint by Connolly in the *Sunday Times* about modern criticism, which never says that a book is good reading, but talks aridly about technique. Apropos of Leavis's remark recently about Max Beerbohm in the *Spectator*, I nearly wrote a letter quoting Lamb's

[1] *Hamlet*, act I, scene 5.

very sharp-pointed question to Coleridge, 'whether the higher order of Seraphim *illuminati* ever sneer', because a great deal of Leavis's line about poets or novelists that he doesn't like and their admirers is not that they are mistaken but that they are contemptible. I do wish someone like H. Nicolson would blow him sky-high.

All here is still confusion and smell of paint; moreover the library stove has given out, and the experts are slow in coming. Instead I have got an oil-stove in temporary use: it gives out lots of heat, but occasionally emits a disconcerting gurgle. Snowdrops and crocuses (yellow) are out, but winter seems otherwise very much with us. No news from our winter-sporting children beyond a postcard to say their aeroplane had reached Geneva safely. The headmaster of Adam's school (a Sikh) is clearly a most enlightened and imaginative man. He recently told A. that he (A) was doing just as much work as any of the other masters, and it was ridiculous that he should only be paid £1 a week. He proposed therefore, not to pay him a larger salary, but to pay for his first-class fares and expenses in any travel he wanted to do, since he had come to India to see the country as well as to teach. Isn't that splendid! Adam took immediate advantage of this generous offer and travelled in state to Delhi, where he witnessed a gigantic Republic Day parade. He is now back at the school, but has designs on Kashmir and the Taj Mahal. I must write and thank the excellent Sikh.

In the middle of my last bout of correcting this afternoon, I took half an hour off, to clear my head, and read the opening chapters, one after the other, of *Oliver Twist*, *Nicholas Nickleby* and *Great Expectations*. All are good and made me want to re-read all three books immediately, but *G.E.* is infinitely the best—much the most sharp and assured. I wish I had time to read *all* Dickens in the right order, so as to observe his growing mastery of technique (the overflowing genius of creation was always there).

Last week Ruth and I went to *The Cherry Orchard*, which we enjoyed enormously. It is superbly acted, very funny and continuously moving. Also I had a final session with my Uncle Duff's books. Many they are keeping, some are to be sold, some given to the London Library, some given to me.

Bernard F. rang up yesterday to say he can't after all come to the Lit. Soc. because he and Laura have received a royal invitation for that evening. He is tremendously pleased and excited about his appointment, but has been overwhelmed by *seven hundred* letters of congratulation. After living in Scotland with two daily women, it will be fun for them having A.D.C.'s, ladies in waiting, butlers, chauffeurs and goodness knows what.

*Sunday morning, February 11*

The sun is shining, and Comfort is putting me to shame by digging outside the window. If I had one of those jobs that finish when one leaves the office I should probably be a busy (if fine-weather) gardener. As it is, each week-end I hopefully bring home more work than I can possibly do, and the garden suffers. Don't misunderstand me: all I do anyhow is the rough work—weeding and repairing the brick paths, tidying, clipping and so on. All the real gardening is done by Comfort, and she is very good at it. Duff loves really hard work, like cutting down trees, and the other children are prepared to work the motor-mower in moderation. I wish to goodness we could get a man to do it, but we are too far from everywhere, though nowadays even the cowmen seem to have their own cars.

My increase of salary since the H.B. take-over means that in a month or two I shall have no overdraft, and I simply can't remember when that was last the case. I have grown so used to hand-to-mouth economy, and never knowing where next half's school-fees are coming from, that this new situation is quite disconcerting.

*12 February 1962*                                                                 *Grundisburgh*

*De profundis*—not quite in the O.W. sense but from a welter of humiliation, rage, disappointment, and malaise. The fact simply is that with this beastly feeling, I know that at no gathering, however alluring, could I either get or give pleasure, and there you are. One can only back out. Please give my special regrets to Ivor and Jonah *qua* the dinner and, *a fortiori*, much stronger ones for missing you and Ruth beforehand.

I am now starting on *Dombey and Son*. I believe it is Jock Dent's favourite.

I still remain the leech's headache. A liver-complaint hitherto confined to the entourage of the Akond of Swat is *my* diagnosis. The faculty's only suggestion is that in about a week, if no better, I should go and be investigated and x-rayed etc at the Ipswich hospital, so no doubt some day all will be as serene as it ever can be at seventy-nine.

You will of course be letting me know all about the Lit. Soc. (and the fare thereat). I don't often quote T.E. Brown—except of course 'God wot' etc in mockery, but I have recalled another poem of his in which I seem to recall the refrain 'And I not there!' And on Tuesday evening I felt every bit as sentimental as he did.

I like the idea of your taking a spell of *Dickens* to *clear* your head; but I suppose he is rather like a plunge into the sea. I have left off *Dombey*—found I must have read it too recently and remembered it too well. Also I found Miss Tox and Captain Cuttle a bit wearisome —as also is the incredible Dombey himself. Carker's teeth are mentioned *every* time he appears; so are Captain Cuttle's signature remarks. But I am embarking on *The Moonstone*, which I last read when a boy at Eton and have forgotten every word of. Tell me what you think of it—it may I suppose be called the first detective story. Shall I be disappointed? The Clough book is on my list.[1] The young reviewers have been, *me judice*, all wrong about him. He was much better than they say. Of course there is something faintly absurd about a man who loses his faith and then bemoans the fact, but I am blowed if there isn't a lot of good stuff in 'Dipsychus'. Easy enough of course to be superior and sniffy about hexameters and varsity reading-parties of a hundred years ago, but I enjoyed 'The Bothie' at Cambridge.

A joke I wanted to mention to Ivor (and you) is that the Prince o

---

[1] *Arthur Hugh Clough: the Uncommitted Mind* by Katherine Chorley (1962).

Wales's headmaster at Gordonstoun was once H.M. of Salem wherever that may be, and Mr Creakle (*David Copperfield*) was Headmaster of Salem House. But I have a frightful misgiving I may have told you that already. Don't tell me if I have. Only forgive.

Your picture of Bernard F. cosseted by a battalion of servants is too rosy. *All* domestics leave in troops directly they find that at any other job they get higher wages. Their whole wage-scale is even more monstrous than ours; it has been a constant worry to Charles's wife.

Well, that is all I am strong enough to write, and far more than you are strong enough to read, and that is that.

P.S. Clough. I should of course have mentioned 'Amours de Voyage'.


*17 February 1962*                                              *Bromsden Farm*

Your last week's letter was waiting for me in the office on Monday morning, and on Tuesday I got your pathetic signing-out note. Too bad: we were all, including Ruth, most disappointed at not seeing you. It was a week of ceaseless activity. On Monday Ruth and I attended a cocktail (or rather, thank heaven, a champagne) party on Campden Hill in pouring rain, then went on to dine at the Café Royal with Allen Lane, the originator and head of Penguin Books. It was the night of the National Sporting Club's annual do, and the whole place was swarming with outsize bruisers in dinner-jackets. Tuesday was the Lit. Soc., of which more anon. On Wednesday I went to the theatre with Flash Harry, Princess Marina and her sister Princess Olga. The play was *Becket*,[1] which I saw in New York last year but enjoyed again. After it we were conveyed in a huge Rolls to the Savoy Grill, where we had an excellent dinner. Flash H. told a number of near-dirty stories, which the royal ladies clearly knew they couldn't avoid, and then Princess Olga told a charming one: 'Once upon a time there was a king who had two daughters, one blonde and beautiful, the other dark and exceedingly plain. The son of a neighbouring monarch came in search of a wife, and the two girls were paraded for

---

[1] By Jean Anouilh.

165

him, the dark one in superb clothes and the blonde one clad only in her flowing hair. Which one do you think he chose? The answer is that he chose their father, for this is a fairy story.'

I like both the princesses very much, and was much flattered to think that they must have suggested my making a fourth, as I'm sure Flash Harry didn't, though he couldn't have been nicer. On Thursday Ruth and I went to *Don Giovanni* at Covent Garden: a superb production of a superb opera, but it went on for three and a half hours with only one interval, and the seats weren't made for anyone my size.

When I tell you that I was also out to lunch every day, and dictated more letters than my secretary had time to type, you will realise why I arrived home exhausted last night. And what did I find? The two painters, who had already reduced the house to piles of paint-pots, dustsheets and heaped furniture, both collapsed with bronchitis on Tuesday and haven't been seen since! Chaos reigns, but thank God the library stove has at last been mended, so all's well in here, and I have a mass of overdue manuscripts to occupy my week-end.

If you had to miss a Lit. Soc. this was quite a good one to choose—for two reasons: (1) the dinner wasn't as good as usual (and, as I have long feared they would, the club is putting up the charge from 21/- to 25/-) and (2) Lockhart was all too present. I had prudently insulated myself by asking Sparrow and Tony Powell to sit on either side of me, but Lockhart was on Tony's other side, with poor Ivor beyond him. I thought Lockhart (whom mercifully we hadn't seen for a year) was looking very old and ill, but it soon became apparent that his wits have gone. *Four* times in as many minutes he asked Ivor who was sitting on Tommy's right, four times Ivor said 'Alan Moorehead', and four times Lockhart countered 'He wrote a very bad book', meaning, I suppose, the one on the Russian Revolution, in which L. thinks he has a prescriptive right. At the coffee-stage Ivor asked if he could come and sit next to me, leaving Harold Caccia to cope as best he could. There is unfortunately nothing in the rules to remove members when they become gaga, so we must just hope he doesn't come often. Tommy has promised to take him on next time, but I don't think he fully appreciates what he's in for. Afterwards Roger walked back with me to Soho Square and stayed a little while, gossiping agreeably.

How is your lower-jaw plate? I feel most sympathetic about it, since I dread false teeth, and so far rely on my own, which are mostly metal.

Adam has visited the Taj Mahal, but ran out of money there and had to get through the day on a bag of peanuts. No doubt this fasting sharpened his aesthetic propensities. The other two are due back from the Alps tomorrow. When we last heard, only one member of the party had broken a leg.

21 February 1962Grundisburgh

I was rather disappointed when your last letter came to find no reference at all to anything in *my* last letter, but then I realised I had been rather late in posting it and it might well not have arrived till Monday. I was wrong. It was posted all right but *was* carefully addressed to the secretary of a girls' school who returned it yesterday. She is a puffick lady and I am pretty sure did not read it, but I rather apprehensively re-read it, and was reassured to find it was not 'scored with startling blasphemies' as Dr Jekyll's holy book was by Mr Hyde, or even with the mildest Rabelaisianism. But it annoys me much that you must have thought that sour little grouch about my shirking the Lit. Soc. was regarded by me as my weekly letter. And in the end it is you who suffer, because you get two letters by one post, which is what the evangelist meant by full measure pressed down and *running over.* And you made no complaint about my apparent lapse!

Roger told me that Lockhart's mind seemed to be giving way— like my old uncle, who was however eighty-six; he used to be reminded, when he got to the end of a story, of the beginning, so it went like chain-smoking—very hard for the audience to keep its face. Otherwise it sounds a good party. *The Moonstone* is fine—no sign of it coming to an end for several more days. I feel there may be some tragedy to come, either via the Indians or the Quicksand which has already had one victim.

I have paid another visit to the leech and am now to go and be examined by the hospital consultant. There is something vaguely wrong round about the liver. You can't surely have gall-bladder adhesions thirty-seven years after the operation. Nature is a good deal of an ass but surely not such an ass as that.

Flash Harry of course *does* bound for all his amiability—the kind of man who, I am sure, is at his most bounding with women. Does Ruth know him? I trust her judgment. Sorry about your constricted seat at the most delicious of all operas. It always takes the edge off one's enjoyment. As Winston once said of oratory 'The head cannot take in more than the seat can endure.'

How right you are about regrets for books one has discarded. I am always wanting the books I got rid of when leaving Eton for here. I wonder what Adam's reactions to the Taj Mahal were. To my eye the mere pictures of it show it as of overwhelming beauty. Does it ever disappoint?

I must stop—slightly short measure, but I feel compunctious about inflicting a sort of *Mabinogion*[1] in one post. Love to Ruth. I bet she revelled in *Don Giovanni*.

P.S. My plate, thank you, is perfectly comfortable, and I can now eat anything—except caramels for obvious reasons.


*24 February 1962*                                          *Bromsden Farm*


Two excellent letters in one envelope were waiting for me here last night. My only fear last week was lest you might be feeling too groggy to write, and I am much relieved, even though your doctor's diagnosis doesn't sound very certain. Let me know what they say at the hospital. Perhaps you are suffering from that diverticulitis which I seem to have made so popular of late?

I didn't mention the fare at the last Lit. Soc. because it wasn't good. Harold N. (just back from his cruise) admits that Lockhart's wits are going and says we must just hope they go quickly. Harold was responsible for Lockhart's membership in the first place. I thoroughly enjoyed *The Moonstone* when I last read it (ages ago) and am sure I should again. Did not T.S.E. write an introduction to the World's

[1] A series of Welsh tales, mostly about Arthur and the Round Table. An edition in three volumes was published by Lady Charlotte Guest in 1838–1849.

Classics edition? I should also try *The Woman in White*, which I also thought great fun.

Adam was bowled over by the beauty of the Taj Mahal and used a whole roll of coloured film trying to capture some of his pleasure.

Last week was mercifully a little less strenuous than its predecessor, but on Tuesday I took part in a lunchtime *divertissement* in the Holborn Central Library. There were three performers, allotted fifteen minutes each. First I read some poems from books I publish; then Pamela Frankau spoke very charmingly about her books and others; then my dear friend William Plomer read some of his own poems. 150 stalwarts attended (free of charge) and seemed to enjoy it all. Afterwards we were regaled with sandwiches and whisky by the Mayor and Librarian.

I still have the final proofs of some 150 pages of Oscar to correct (or rather check) when they come in, but already I have begun, in a desultory, shuffling sort of way, to assemble the materials for two minor projects which have been held off for ages by Oscar's continuance. They are (1) the editing of Max's letters to Reggie Turner[1] and (2) the compiling of the definitive bibliography of the works of E. Blunden. This last is a labour of love and requires only time and a clear head, for in my office I have the most complete collection of his writings that exists. I am so accustomed to having some editing or kindred work on hand that I feel rather empty without any, and neither of these jobs will tax me unduly.[2]

I have at last managed to get Max's plaque erected in the crypt of St Paul's, and the Dean has promised to dedicate it in April, when S.C. Roberts will make a speech. In August Max's ninetieth birthday is to be celebrated by the publication of a large anthology of his work.[3]

*28 February 1962*                                                                 *Grundisburgh*

I am writing before the hospital visit, so there is nothing new for the moment. I don't know that I expect much, and I suspect I may be

[1] Published in 1964.

[2] The Blunden bibliography eventually passed from my nerveless grasp into the capable hands of Miss Brownlee Kirkpatrick, who published it triumphantly in 1979.

[3] *The Incomparable Max* (1962).

involved in a long series of 'trial and error' transactions. *Nous verrons.* I should like to feel perfectly well again. How impressive it would be if one day you announced to the Lit. Soc. that one of its members was suffering from diverticulitis.

I note your recommendation of *The Woman in White.* Is it still in print I wonder? How refreshing it is to make one's way through a long story full of human beings who behave as such, and when one really wants to know what is going to happen. I have finally decided (quite impenitently) that I am a square, a fuddy-duddy, an incurable middle-brow, the sort of reader he who shall be nameless sneers at, as one who thinks Housman a good poet.

I have now read *A Question of Upbringing*[1] and much enjoyed it though I am mystified about its exact significance. I like his neat and pertinent English. Le Bas has a good deal of Goodhart, not much of McNeile I think, who was a frightful ass. He succeeded to my beloved Arthur Benson and had every boy agin him in three weeks with his persistent fussiness and suspicion, and all the staff too. How good Tony P's picture of that French *pension* is and its inmates, and I feel I know Widmerpool nauseatingly well. What is Tony P's next one?

Shall we Maximilians be notified of the Max B. ceremony? Not if it depends in any way on Jock Dent who must be the least efficient secretary that ever was.

(Later) I have just had an immense interview with the leading Ipswich doctor and am in for a spell of x-rays and blood-tests etc with God knows what results. All that is so far certain is that I have a slightly enlarged liver, but he added reassuringly that very many people have. I shall report to you what they say—obstinately ignoring the truth that you do not in the least want to hear it. But even Dr Johnson did sometimes report, e.g. 'Dropsy threatened, but seasonable physic averted the inundation.' I hope to feel less of a worm in a week or two. I couldn't feel more.

Love to dear Ruth. The idea of her being a grandmother is ridiculous.

---

[1] The first volume (1951) of Anthony Powell's *A Dance to the Music of Time.*

[*My letter of 31 February has vanished, amazingly the only one of the whole correspondence to do so.*]

7 *March 1962*                                        *Grundisburgh*

I become daily more like a Russian diplomatist capable of no answer to any proposal but 'No, no.' They keep postponing their exploration of my interior, and till that has happened, I am still too dicky to face a Lit. Soc. What particularly dishes me is the walking and stair-climbing etc, all the things one has to do in going from place to place in London. It is all thoroughly damnable, and at times I think it is going on for ever. But Pamela does not allow me to express that view.

You are determined that I shall remain a square, and I expect you are right. I shall never make the other grade. I await with hope C.P. Snow's riposte to all those mannerless dogmatisms of the Downing seer, but he perhaps prefers silent contempt. I shall go on with Tony Powell, but he is pretty popular and the library is usually short of his books. I look forward to reading the Irish tales you have just kindly sent. I see you are publishing two Ibsen plays. I hope they are better translated than the Archer ones. A. seemed, from what I can remember, to think that 'Hem' was a common English ejaculation. It always pulled one up.

I have had rather a failure with *The Return of the Native*. Not much interested. My fault probably. Among the countless questions the consultant asked me were several which seemed clearly to be investigating my sanity, so it may be that I am in the position of the sieve which complained of the pump for not filling it. You will be reminded of me in Jocelyn Brooke's literary article in today's *Times*. He admits to doing what you always urge me to do, i.e. abandon the struggle to keep up. J.B. finds D.H.L. unreadable. A man after my own heart.

I have just heard that the x-ray cannot be done for at least a fortnight. Depressing. I may score off them by passing out with an un-diagnosed gastric ulcer. Unlikely, but these delays do one's nerves no good.

My outlook at the moment on practically everything is pessimistic. I am only cheerful when reading a letter from you or writing one to you. A worm and no man. Love to Ruth.

I am outraged at the way these doctors keep you waiting for their idiotic opinions. No wonder you're depressed, but you must try not to be. The spring is coming, and you will soon be holding the Lit. Soc. table in thrall once again. In fact I couldn't recommend the youngest and healthiest person to come to London as it has been just lately, with that cutting east wind and an insufficiency of taxis. Today has been warmer, but at the cost of incessant rain. Compton Mackenzie has got things properly organised: all the winter he hibernates in his warm Edinburgh flat, emerging only with the daffodils, or even later. I suppose that, if it wasn't for our hellish winter, we shouldn't appreciate the spring so much, and that to live in Southern California where the sun shines *every* day might grow wearisome—but there are days when I have my doubts.

I think you will enjoy the book on the Marconi Scandal.[1] The author started out without any *parti-pris*, and wrote the book for the best possible reason—that she wanted to read a book on the subject, and there wasn't one. Gradually she came to realise, as any unprejudiced reader must, that Isaacs and Lloyd George were saved by Asquith and the Liberals, who covered them up with whitewash. It's a disgraceful story, and I think Isaacs was one of the nastiest bits of work that ever schemed his way to the top in everything. Kipling's daughter, who is a friend of Reading's widow, has refused permission for the reprinting of 'Gehazi', though it has already been printed in countless other books. G.K. Chesterton's executor was similarly churlish about a relevant and amusing poem of his.

Have you read your friend Leavis's swingeing attack on C.P. Snow in the current *Spectator*? It's high time someone took this line, and I only wish it had been a less woolly and repetitive writer than Leavis. He says everything several times, wanders about, and, as always, writes without any style or distinction. I wonder whether Snow will answer. I fancy he must. Would you like to have the new Ibsen translations? So far I have published eight of the sixteen I agreed to bring out. Such reviews as there have been have been favourable, but the

---

[1] *The Marconi Case* by Frances Donaldson (1962).

public is not exactly stampeding for the precious volumes.

Don't be put off T.H. by *The Return of the Native*. Have another go at *Far from the Madding Crowd* and *Tess*. I wish I had time to try them all again.

Last Monday Ivor and Mrs B. gave a dinner-party for ten in the Lit. Soc. room at the Garrick—excellent food and agreeable company, including Edith Evans and Ralph Richardson. Another day I had a good gossipy lunch with Frank Swinnerton. He is seventy-eight and full of beans. He is an excellent mimic and gives lifelike reproductions of dialogues between his old friends H.G. Wells and Arnold Bennett. I introduced him to a visiting U.S. professor, who is writing on Wells and was thrilled to hear something from so near the horse's mouth.


*17 March 1962*
*(St Patrick's Day)*                                    *Bromsden Farm*


All this and the flu as well! It really is too bad, and I am all sympathy. Please thank Pamela for her letter: it was most kind of her to write. I was planning to ring her up this evening to ask after you, but this morning some woodmen of Peter's who are felling trees in the valley-bottom with a circular saw neatly brought one down across our telephone-line, so we are cut off till goodness knows when. Ruth is expecting me to ring her up tonight—hell!

The Lit. Soc. on Tuesday was as good as could be without you. We ate scampi with rice, *escalope viennoise*, and angels on horseback. I had Ivor on one side, Sparrow on the other. Sparrow and I have put up Patrick Devlin the judge (now Lord D) as the first candidate for next November. As you may have seen, Balliol has just sent out an appeal for the best part of a million pounds, and as we discussed it, we gradually realised that of our eleven diners, no fewer than seven were Balliol men! There are 4000 old Balliol men living, so they'll have to give £250 apiece if the target is to be hit. Not very likely, I should say.

Earlier in the day I had been through Jonah's proofs with him, and the book should be out in June. I told Tony Powell you had enjoyed his book, and he was much pleased. He said the only characteristic of Goodhart's that he had deliberately given to his housemaster was G's

173

habit of standing with both his feet pointing sideways in the same direction.

I have enormously enjoyed, and strongly recommend, Osbert Sitwell's *Tales My Father Taught Me*. They are most entertaining, and short enough to prevent O's getting involved in those endless sentences that made some of his autobiography such heavy going. Sir George is a superb character—and this whole book is about him.

*Sunday morning, 18 March*

I was happy to see your Diana had been safely delivered. Does that make twenty-one grandchildren? I wonder whether they were hoping for a girl this time. Diana is so lovely that she ought to have a beautiful daughter.

Apart from the Lit. Soc., last week was a great rush, since on Wednesday morning Bill Jovanovich, the dynamic head of Harcourt Brace, turned up for a week's stay. There are hundreds of business details to be settled, and we shall be at it non-stop till he leaves next Thursday.

I expect you noticed Dr Attlee's death. If his advice had been taken in 1921, and my mother had not intervened by taking me to London for an immediate operation, I should probably have died in a matter of weeks. I remember her saying to Jelly: 'I can't help it if the boy has to leave Eton. I'm not satisfied with the diagnosis and I'm taking him to London.' Jelly agreed meekly, but in later years chose to forget the incident, and always maintained that Attlee had been right.

You are not to dream of writing until you are really strong enough. I shall ring Pamela up from London tomorrow for the latest news. Now I must read a manuscript about Nepal, and some proofs about the Channel Tunnel, neither of which at the moment interests me enormously.

*22 March 1962*                                   *Grundisburgh*

Grand man you are! I have sent you practically nothing for a fortnight and here you are with four excellent sides. What can I do in reply? I tell the doctors I am very ill and they deny it, pointing to thoroughly well-behaved heart, lungs, and kidneys etc. I say 'What do they matter in view of the fact that I am tired all the time, sunk in apathy and lassitude, and faintly sick-feeling much of the time. The x-ray process yesterday (two and a half hours) was acutely uncomfortable. You lie face downwards for about seven minutes eight times with ten minutes' interval during which you relax (ha!) by lying on your *back*. You lie on a practically bare board.

I suspect that part of the treatment will be drastic dieting. And what sort of a guest shall I be then? Is there any precedent at the Lit. Soc. for a member dining off bread and milk and saying no to all the scampi and angels on horseback? Would it be in the records?

Your kind heart prompted you to ask about me and Ibsen. Well the truth is I *loved* Ibsen when I read him years ago, but I have been too tired to read much lately. I tried Crabbe whom I hadn't read for fifty years, but it didn't do. That thudding relentlessness got me down with which he grimly shows up every friendship and love-affair ending in disaster. His pictures of Suffolk do nothing to enamour one of the county.

I didn't know that habit of Goodhart's, but please ask T.P. if he knew that G. had in a drawer numberless advertisements of women's shoes. Mat Hill of course recognised at once one of the commonest signs of suppressed or sublimated sex. Human beings get odder and odder. Do you ever dream about snakes or keys? Because if so you must look out.

The Hoods are pleased about their third son. Diana always said— and I think truly—that she would not be good at dealing with a daughter, and Alexander for some reason passionately wanted another son. It is to be called James. Number 21 grandchild.

Leavis does reduce poor old Snow to monkey-dust, but one doesn't like or admire L. any the more. As you say, his style is what I call rebarbative, though never quite sure what it means. You will know. He writes as if his opinion was clearly the truth, and anyone who disagreed with it must be fool or knave. Surely Snow *must* reply: in old days he would have with sword or pistol. But I doubt if he carries the guns.

Attlee wasn't my doctor, who was old Amsler who suited us very well. How impressive lay interferences with medical ukases are. My father-in-law forbade them to do a mastoid operation on my delicate mother-in-law. He said quite simply that he knew nothing of medicine but was quite certain it would kill her. She got quite well, and lived for another fifteen years.

In latter days many of Jelly's memories were very unreliable, and of course he would *always* back Eton doctors (and others) against swells from London.

This letter is a striking example of the victory of mind over matter. I got up feeling like death and very nearly fell asleep in the bath. But I formed *one* resolve—to ignore all else but to write four sides to you, and though I must now go and lie down for a bit, I feel all the better for having done so.

I told the North Foreland Lodge governors last week that I was going to retire from the chairmanship this year. I was amused to find that their reaction was not one of horrified protest, but of quiet congratulation on having gone on so long (eleven years). In other words what they *really* meant was 'And high time too'. Such is life. I get deafer (certainly) and I suspect stupider as the weeks pass.

Bless you Rupert and give my best love to Ruth. Pamela is a wonderful nurse—and wife generally, but I have plenty left over for R.

*24 March 1962*                                                      *Bromsden Farm*

It was heroic of you to write those four fine pages last week, but also very wrong. I told you particularly not to write till you were strong enough, and you *must* be sensible. I only hope the effort didn't bring on a relapse. But I must admit that the sight of your writing on Friday evening was most encouraging.

If you do in fact have to diet, I will guarantee to produce whatever you're allowed at the Lit. Soc. dinners. For some time Ivor was allowed only certain things, and we coped with that safely.

I'm glad to say I never, to my knowledge, dream of snakes or keys, but I'm sure Rayner-Wood dreamt of little else. You were clearly right to resign from North Foreland Lodge, and I think you ought also to give up all that correcting: you have done more than your whack, and earned a rest, surely. I can hear you answering: 'How the world is managed, and why it was created, I cannot tell; but it is no feather-bed for the repose of sluggards,' and I can only say that I often wish it was. From that quotation you will know what I have been reading, and here's some more of it, just for the fun of copying it out, and despite my fear that you may earlier have copied it out for me:

> If a man will comprehend the richness and variety of the universe, and inspire his mind with a due measure of wonder and of awe, he must contemplate the human intellect not only on its heights of genius but in its abysses of ineptitude; and it might be fruitlessly debated to the end of time whether Richard Bentley or Elias Stoeber was the more marvellous work of the Creator: Elias Stoeber, whose reprint of Bentley's text, with a commentary intended to confute it, saw the light in 1767 at Strasburg, a city still famous for its geese .... Stoeber's mind, though that is no name to call it by, was one which turned as unswervingly to the false, the meaningless, the unmetrical, and the ungrammatical, as the needle to the pole.[1]

If only Leavis could write like that! But he has no ear, no taste, no judgment. How *can* a man who writes as he does teach anyone *English*?

*Sunday morning, March 25*

Comfort always refuses to recognise the beginning or end of Summer Time, and this makes for some confusion to begin with. Bridget has just arrived from London, blithely unaware that she was an hour wrong. The wind has changed and they tell me it is slightly warmer.

Bill Jovanovich's week in London consisted largely of conferences lasting several hours each—stimulating but at the same time exhausting. He stayed at Claridge's, where I ate several meals with him. In my youth it was a resort of riches and distinction: now most of the *clientèle* look as though they had been swept up in a third-class international air terminal. Ichabod! The gradual but complete social revolution which we have lived through has undoubtedly improved the

[1] A.E. Housman, preface to his edition of Manilius, Book I (1903), reprinted in *A.E. Housman, Selected Prose*, edited by John Carter (1961).

lot of millions, but it has largely destroyed elegance and *la douceur de vivre*. What would Old Jolyon say to the bearded youths in jeans and open-necked shirts that one sees in stalls at the theatre and Covent Garden?

I am now reading *A Pride of Terrys*[1] with much enjoyment. Despite the author's lapses of taste she does know and love the theatre, and the early chapters, *circa* 1850, are fascinating. At the same time, in bed, I am reading Compton Mackenzie on *Moral Courage*. It is the book of a tired old man, just rambling memory, gossip and ideas, without any appreciable design, but he is a full man, and I much prefer the weary old to the angry young. I think you might well get it from the library.

Tomorrow I am promised the final pages of Oscar for approval— the index and the first thirty-two pages of the book (which they always print last). I shall return them to the printer on Tuesday, and all will be over—very nearly seven years since I took over the job in July 1955. I hope to have complete copies by Easter. So far we have orders for just over 1000 copies, but that is without the London shops, which should take as many again. They won't order at all until they see the complete article, whereas the wretched booksellers in the provinces and abroad see only a 'blurb' and sometimes a dust-jacket.

Months ago *The Times* sent me Edmund Blunden's obituary to revise and tidy up, but I find it almost impossible to do. If, which Heaven forbid, the dear fellow died tomorrow, I could do all that is needed in an hour or two, under pressure of emotion, but in cold blood it's another matter. And yet I'm always nagging them to have proper obituaries ready. I promised to write them one on Diana Cooper, but can't bring myself to do it. Have you ever written any?


*28 March 1962*                                           *19 Burton Ward*
[*Dictated to Pamela*]            *East Suffolk & Ipswich Hospital*
                                                                    *Ipswich*


I write *de profundis*—which is the right address of the Ipswich Hospital, as I think you will admit, when you hear my life is one of

[1] By Marguerite Steen (1962).

crushing boredom, often variegated by discomfort and sometimes by pain. What more need of words? There shall be none. Pamela supports your contention that I should give up examining, but on the other side is what Stevenson called 'the still small, unanswerable voice of coins.' However I promise not to let it be a burden. That is a lovely bit of Housman you quote, all I remembered of it was the famous 'a city still famous for its geese'.

I say, Leavis! Have you ever known opinion so unanimous about a man's spite, bad manners, injustice, bad English and conceit? It will surely do him a great deal of harm. I don't know why you have your knife into old Snow, though I admit I don't know much about him. He is perhaps a bit too omniscient. I agree with you about *la douceur de vivre* and what old Jolyon would have said about many modern things and men. With a few prejudices his values were surely mainly right.

Did you ever see Irving act? And if so did you see the genius of him through all the faults? It must have been a great handicap to a young actor to be apparently unable either to walk or to enunciate like Edmund Kean too. Marie Tempest told a young actress that if she worked hard for a year, she might be able to walk across the stage properly.

Obituaries. I was for some time in charge of them for Eton Masters, and did several. I had a certain amount of grisly fun, e.g. in getting Eggar to do Mat Hill's, and Mat Hill to do Eggar's.

Well I mustn't fag poor Pamela any longer. I had an enchanting letter from Ruth which I will answer with my own hand as soon as I can. Give her my love.


*31 March 1962*                                              *Bromsden Farm*

All that and hospital too! It's really too bad, and I am delighted to learn from Pamela that you're probably going home tomorrow. My week in the Middlesex last summer is still vividly in memory and I can truly sympathise. Pamela is a splendid amanuensis, and her hand is beautifully clear. I haven't in fact got my knife into Snow, but I do dislike his literary scheming, superiority and self-election as pundit.

I find his novels third-rate, dull and humourless, and the sight of his fat face reproduced life-size in newspaper advertisements for the *Daily Herald* is enough to put anyone off their breakfast.

I never, alas, saw Irving act, being only two when he died, but his was clearly a triumph of personal magnetism over natural handicaps. The most magnetic performance I ever saw was Chaliapin's in *Boris*, which I thought terrific. It was in 1930 or 1931.

On Wednesday Ruth and I had drinks with the Eliots in their Kensington flat. They are just back from six weeks in Barbados, and T.S.E. was looking better than he has for years. Gerald Kelly is painting his portrait for this year's Academy, and regaling him during sittings with ripe anecdotes of the last fifty years. In many of them Willie Maugham figures more or less discreditably.

On Thursday I lunched with Tommy and Joan in their royal stables. Clemmie Churchill, Veronica Wedgwood and Peter Lubbock were the other guests, and we ate a delicious steak-and-kidney pudding. One simply can't believe that C.C. is seventy-seven, so young and alert and active and pretty is she, and so charming. Tommy was at his gayest and most mellow. He said that the only stinker of a letter he ever knew George VI to write was to Ambassador Kennedy, about his defeatist pronouncements. Winston and others persuaded him to water it down to the version that is printed in Jack Wheeler-Bennett's biography.[1] Later Tommy referred to Jack's Appendix B as the best, indeed the only accurate, account of the duties and difficulties of the sovereign's Private Secretary. Last night I read it with interest and pleasure, suspecting that Tommy inspired all of it that he didn't actually write. Then I realised that I hadn't time to read the book properly when it appeared, so I am at it now. It's pretty good, I should say, but Jack hasn't got Harold Nicolson's magisterial sureness of touch in English prose, and occasionally slips into careless cliché. I can't remember whether you read the book. (If our correspondence goes on long enough, we shall *both* have forgotten what we wrote ten years ago, and shall then be able happily to start the record all over again.)

On Thursday I passed the utterly last pages of Oscar for press, only

---

[1] *King George VI: His Life and Reign* by John W. Wheeler-Bennett (1958).

to be told next day that the printers will need a month more than they originally said! So now publication-day is shifted to June 25, and I shall hope to have finished copies by the third week of May. It's infuriating, but after seven years' work I suppose one month is neither here nor there.

Just to show you that I'm not idling, I should say that last week I also visited old Lady Lovat to discuss a possible volume of Maurice Baring's letters, attended a cocktail party at Veronica Wedgwood's where I got trapped by a stalwart hunting lady, gave lunch to an American publisher, presided at a two-and-a-half-hour meeting of the Phoenix Trust, interviewed an estate agent about the London Library freehold, sat through a long meeting to give relief to starving book-sellers and their relicts, went through my firm's accounts for 1961 with *three* chartered accountants—but that's enough.

Ruth is very pleased because last week she sold at Sotheby's a dreary Henry Moore drawing which she had had for years and didn't care for. They told her it might fetch £300. She went to the sale, and it was knocked down for £550! If you saw it you'd realise how ridiculously out of proportion such a sum is, but how right she was to cash in on the prevailing fashion. In imagination she has already spent the money two or three times over.

*5 April 1962*                                                                 *Grundisburgh*

George has asked me to write and say that he feels too ill to write any letters, but is most grateful to you for yours. At the moment he says he feels he can't cope with either receiving them or writing them. I am afraid he does feel horribly ill and I have an awful feeling that there is nothing they can do. We have not yet had the hospital report. Your friendship and letters have meant so much to George, I really can't tell you *how* much, and by the same token I do thank you so much for your sympathy and understanding. Love from Pamela.

*6 April 1962*                                                        *Grundisburgh*
[*Dictated to Pamela*]

I send a postcript to Pamela's of yesterday to tell you that they have at last found a name for the damned thing. It is Hepatitis. It is rarer but apparently much the same in foulness and duration of time as Jaundice, and you know all about that. So evidently I am out of circulation for some time. The odd thing is that when I had jaundice ten or twelve years ago, though it was unpleasant, I was nothing like so miserably depressed as I am now. But in some queer way it is a relief to know that the beastly thing has a name.

---

P.S. The doctor told me that the tests were inconclusive. A clear negative would have been better. The above, i.e. Hepatitis, *is* true and a good answer to kind enquirers, and one which I am adopting. He is a bit happier having a name and some treatment.[1] Love Pamela.


*7 April 1962*                                                      *Bromsden Farm*

I was so glad to get your dictated letter, and dear Pamela's, but I absolutely forbid either of you to spend any more time writing to me until you once again feel up to writing yourself. Pamela assures me she doesn't mind being telephoned to, so I shall ring her up once or twice a week, to hear how you are, and I shall go on writing regularly, as long as you promise not to feel obliged to read my letters until you're better.

Hepatitis, rather than jaundice, is what I had in 1959, and I remember your once or twice commenting on the depth and extent of my inertia and depression, so I can utterly sympathise with all you are going through, and to cheer you can only say that though I was heavily under the weather for several months, I thereafter got quite all right, as you assuredly will. I can't help thinking too that if the spring ever comes, some hot sunshine may work wonders for you.

[1] He was in fact suffering from cancer of the liver, but he wasn't told so and apparently never suspected it.

I am reading a forthcoming book called *Great Cricket Matches*,[1] which I am enjoying. I have ordered a copy to be sent to you, ready for you to read lazily in your summer-house a little later on.

This week I met for the first time, and greatly liked, Dennis Silk, a master at Marlborough, who plays cricket for Somerset and captained the last MCC side in New Zealand. He is a great friend of Siegfried S. and knows Edmund B.

I can't tell you how *delighted* Ruth was with your letter. It was angelic of you to write it when you were feeling so low.

15 *April 1962*                                                    *Bromsden Farm*

I am most relieved to learn from Pamela that you have got a nurse to look after you, for I was beginning to worry that Pamela would have too much to do. I wonder if you have felt well enough to look at *Great Cricket Matches*. I am about half-way through, enjoying it all, remembered matches and forgotten ones. I find it best to read one match each evening, so as to keep them separate in one's mind.

All the members of the Lit. Soc. asked most solicitously after you on Tuesday. Tommy couldn't come, so old Cuthbert presided, very thin and shrunken, with one foot in a carpet slipper. Peter sat on one side of him, and Gerry Wellington on the other. Gerry was full of his journey to Australia and New Zealand, which he adored. He said the popularity of your nephew Charles in N.Z. is unbelievable, and all declare he is *far* the best Governor General they've ever had. Bernard (who was also there) realises that to follow Charles will be hellish difficult.

Max's plaque in the crypt of St Paul's was duly dedicated by the aged Dean on Thursday, and S.C. Roberts gave a charming and extremely apt address. Jonah and Evy were there, and other friends of Max's. Afterwards we were all given a good lunch at Kettner's by the Reichmanns.

[1] Edited by Handasyde Buchanan (1962).

183

[*Dictated to Pamela*]

We both love your notes and enquiries. That cricket book is full of interest and also strange omissions. Fancy leaving out Jessop's great match at the Oval in 1902, and the famous, though possibly apocryphal, 'Come on Wilfred, we'll get 'em in singles.' Uncle Edward on Fowler's Match I find a little prolix in places and I think there are better accounts, but it is all right. It calls up numberless memories, and as you may imagine I live during the day largely on reminiscence. One of the most persistent is those hours before the Lit. Soc. Bless you. I do wish I didn't feel so awfully ill, but *tout passe* no doubt.

-------

P.S. The poor darling is very low today and I'm afraid feels very ill, but no pain and no nausea which is something to be thankful for. He doesn't feel able to do anything but he has enjoyed the cricket book.
Much love Pamela.


*25 April 1962*                                               *Grundisburgh*
[*Dictated to Pamela*]

There is nothing in anything except my gratitude and the wonderfulness of Pamela (she mustn't cross that out). So what then? I am not even a chaos—I am a vast infinity. She will write you any more, if there is anything. Love to Ruth and bless you both. Oh the boredom!

# EPILOGUE

George Lyttelton died on 1 May 1962. His sister-in-law Sibell Fulford said that in his last days he looked like a splendid effigy, with a face which bore the marks of the dignity and strength of his mind.

Ruth and I travelled to Grundisburgh for his funeral. *The Letters of Oscar Wilde* appeared on June 25. Adam crowned his academic triumphs with a First in Chemistry at Oxford and a Ph.D. at the University of York.

In 1964 my dreams came true. After eighteen years of waiting Ruth and I were able to marry. I thankfully retired from publishing, we found a lovely old house in our beloved Swaledale and lived there blissfully, until on 31 January 1967 Ruth died suddenly of a heart-attack.

Sixteen years later, on 6 January 1983, forty Old Boys of George's Eton house dined together in London to celebrate his hundredth birthday. They generously invited me to be their guest, but I was unable to accept. Instead I wrote this letter, which was read out after dinner by Sir Geoffrey Agnew:

*6 January 1983*                              *The Old Rectory*
                                       *Marske-in-Swaledale*

My dear George

Now that you have reached your century (*how* you would dislike hearing it called a 'ton') I feel I must add one last letter to the six hundred or so that we exchanged over those six crowded years long ago. For years after you died, whenever I saw, heard or read anything amusing or interesting, I found myself thinking 'I must remember to tell George that'.

Our published correspondence has been accused of 'elitism', snobbery, name-dropping and old fashioned 'squareness', but happily the praise has far outweighed the denigration. I have had many hundreds of appreciative letters from all over the world, many love-letters from delightful old ladies, countless references to reading-lists compiled from our letters, and two separate strangers have written to say that our correspondence had changed their life. The first two volumes have already been reprinted, and all six are soon to appear in America. So we can't complain.

When Jock Murray quixotically undertook to publish the first volume, neither he nor I had any idea of what was going to happen. My only sorrow is that you and dear Pamela weren't here to enjoy the fun, but I take comfort in the knowledge that your rich personality, which might otherwise have largely died with the last of those who knew you, is now safe in six volumes, hardbound for posterity.

As we often agreed, letters are almost always nuanced—or, as they now say, slanted—to suit the recipient, and I couldn't have written my letters to anyone but you. Raymond Mortimer, who loved the first volumes, thought it extraordinary that two people with a difference of twenty-four years in their ages could share so very many tastes. Extraordinary perhaps, but so it was. Your depth and breadth of reading, your excellent memory, your willingness to accept new ideas and suggestions, your splendid sense of humour, made you an ideal correspondent.

As I have pointed out to many of our fans, my share in the correspondence was comparatively easy, since I was leading such an active life that all I had to do was to recount my week's doings, using you as the diary I never kept. But your task was far harder. Sitting whenever possible in your beloved summer-house (the only time I tried it I *just* escaped *rigor mortis*) you had little straw for your magnificent bricks, since (except for reading) correcting exam-papers and attending examiners' conferences were almost your only occupations, until the Literary Society drew you to London once a month.

I am now several years older than you were when we made our compact at the dear Nugents' dinner-table, and though I am still busy with literary work, I couldn't now react as you did to a younger man's suggestion of a regular correspondence. You, dear George, were a wholly exceptional and remarkable man, and a born letter-writer. I wish I had been in your house at Eton.

You always dreaded your Old Boy Dinners, and always enjoyed

them enormously when the day came. I hope perhaps you are enjoying this one in the Elysian Fields, alongside Max Beerbohm, Thomas Carlyle and Doctor Johnson. Let us hope that Leavis is in another place! Wherever you are, I send you, as always, my unending admiration, gratitude and love.

Yours ever

Rupert

# INDEX

Gibbon, Edward, 112, 113
Gilbert, W.S., 5, 10, 13, 15, 16, 122
Gilligan, A.E.R., 37
Gissing, George, 70, 89
Gladstone, W.E., 26
Gleaves, Charlie & Suzie, 12, 24, 30, 32, 39, 137
Godden, Rumer, 72
Goethe, 111
Gollancz, Victor, 114, 116, 124
Goodhart, A.L., 173, 175
Gore-Booth, Paul, 105
Gow, A.S.F., 33, 112, 115
Grace, W.G., 76
Gray, Thomas, 80
*Great Cricket Matches*, 183, 184
Greene, Graham, 3, 8
Greene, Hugh, 66
Gregory, Lady, 38
Guedalla, Philip, 72, 96

Haley, Sir William, 133
Hambleden, Patricia, 78
Hamilton, Jamie & Yvonne, 18
Hammarskjöld, Dag, 109
Hankey, Maurice, 133
Hardwicke, Cedric, 154, 155
Hardy, Thomas, 135
Harrap, Walter, 54
Harrod, Roy, 134
Hart-Davis, Adam, 1, 2, 12, 14, 15, 16, 18, 19, 22, 26, 40, 42, 53, 63, 64, 65, 81, 83, 84, 87, 92, 95, 96, 97, 99, 101, 105, 106, 107, 113, 124, 129, 131, 144, 145, 146, 154, 160, 162, 167, 168, 169, 185
Hart-Davis, Bridget, 78, 87, 93, 96, 121, 125, 142, 147, 150, 159, 160, 177
Hart-Davis, Comfort, 12, 42, 45, 65, 78, 95, 96, 105, 121, 129, 140, 142, 163, 177
Hart-Davis, Duff, 1, 11, 12, 14, 15, 17, 18, 19, 22, 25, 26, 40, 42, 44, 45, 60, 63, 78, 89, 93, 96, 106, 115, 118, 120, 122, 140, 142, 143, 146, 147, 149, 150, 163
Hart-Davis, Richard, 49, 57–58, 120
Hartley, L.P., 53, 141
Harvey, Neil, 74
Hayter, Sir William, 46, 134
Headlam, Cuthbert, 7, 22, 41, 42, 77, 93, 183
Headlam, G.W. (Tuppy), 55
Headlam, Stewart, 109
Henn, T.R., 104

Hill, M.D., 132, 175, 179
Hills, John, 21
Hirst, George, 76
Holford, William, 60
Holland, Vyvyan, 65, 144
Holmes, Mr Justice, 8, 17, 33
Hood, Alexander, 4, 175
Hood, Diana, 6, 141, 148, 174, 175
Hornby, J.J., 14, 29
Housman, A.E., 9, 41, 45, 112, 113, 115, 177, 179
*How Green was my Valley*, 23, 49, 51, 52, 54, 73, 74, 77, 78
Howard, Michael, 95
Howells, W.D., 33
Hubble, Dr, 125
*Hugh Walpole*, 12, 79, 84, 123, 140, 161
Hutton, Len, 33

Irving, Henry, 179, 180
Irving, Laurence, 5, 7
Isaacs, Rufus, 172
Ivor, *see* Brown

James, Billy, 25, 60, 113
James, Henry, 58, 60, 70, 89, 96, 110, 133, 134, 135, 142, 144, 160
James, M.R., 122, 127
Jelly, *see* Churchill
Jerrold, Douglas, 80
John, Augustus, 151, 152
Johnson, Dr, 128, 145, 148, 159, 187
Johnson, Paul, 102
Jonah, *see* Jones, L.E.
Jones, E., 64
Jones, Evy, 110, 114, 117, 120, 126, 183
Jones, L.E. (Jonah), 5, 13, 20, 23, 24, 30, 65, 110, 111, 114, 117, 118, 120, 126, 128, 129, 164, 173, 183
Jonson, Ben, 102
Jovanovich, Bill, 123, 128, 174, 177
Joyce, James, 145

Kelly, Gerald, 47, 74, 118, 119, 180
Kennan, George, 141
Kennedy, Joseph, 180
Kennedy, President, 27
Kent, Marina Duchess of, 18, 165, 166
Ketton-Cremer, Wyndham, 134
Kipling, Rudyard, 135, 172
*Kipps*, 144, 146, 147, 148
Kiss in the Car Case, 20

Nugent, Tim, 5, 12, 56, 60, 77, 81, 82, 117, 130, 186

Olga, Princess, 18, 165, 166
O'Neill, Norman, 74, 76
*Owl and the Pussy Cat, The*, 122, 131
*Oxford Apostles*, 3

Pankhurst, Christabel, 110
*Passage to India, A*, 82, 83
Pater, Walter, 96, 99, 108, 110
Pearson, Hesketh, 87
Penn, Eric, 56
Peter, *see* Fleming
*Pickwick Papers*, 155, 156, 158–159
Pinero, A.W., 16
Plomer, William, 92
Ponsford, W.H., 76
*Poor Kit Smart*, 95
Pope-Hennessy, James, 53, 72
Powell, Anthony, 82, 84, 134, 137, 154, 156, 166, 173, 175
Powell, L.F., 125
Powell, Violet, 134, 154, 156
Priestley, J.B., 15, 17, 53, 68, 79, 84, 134
Pritchett, V.S., 26
Pryce-Jones, Alan, 30
Purohit, Mr, 114, 118, 119

Quennell, Peter, 134
Quickswood, Lord, 23, 148

Rae, John, 157
Ramsay, A.B., 27
Ramsey, Archbishop, 11, 13, 15
Rayner Wood, A.C., 68, 176
Reichmann, Hans & Eva, 157, 159, 183
Reilly, Sir Patrick & Lady, 53
Rendall, Montague, 62
Richardson, Ralph, 53, 173
Roberts, S.C., 46, 121, 122, 183
Roger, *see* Fulford
*Roll of Honour*, 120, 122
Rose, *see* Bourne
Rossetti, D.G., 99, 106, 125
Rothenstein, John, 46
Routh, Dick, 5, 7, 102
Ruskin, John, 103
Russell, Bertrand, 107, 109, 141
Ruth, *see* Simon

Saintsbury, George, 102
Sargent, Malcolm, 4, 7, 31, 49, 108, 112, 117, 118, 165, 166, 168

Sassoon, Siegfried, 40, 41, 42, 82, 83, 114, 120, 183
Scott, C.P., 115
Scott, Sir Walter, 9, 10, 89
Seward, Anna, 20
Shakespeare, 21, 23, 26, 85, 104, 155, 161
Shaw, Bernard, 20, 97–98, 135
Shawe-Taylor, Desmond, 18
Sheba, Queen of, 19
Sheppard, David, 34
Shirer, W.L., 16, 20
Siddons, Mrs, 20
Siegfried, *see* Sassoon
Silk, Dennis, 183
Simcox, Edith, 78
Simon, Ruth, *passim*
*Sir Richard Roos*, 1, 2
Sitwell, Sir George, 152, 174
Sitwell, Osbert, 174
Skittles, 71, 72
Smith, F.E., 117
Snow, C.P., 137, 172, 175, 179
Somervell, Donald, 8
Sparrow, John, 14, 41, 66, 91, 154, 156, 157, 166, 173
Spence, Basil, 60
Spooner, R.H., 115, 116
Steegmuller, Francis, 49, 101, 120, 123, 126
Steen, Marguerite, 178
Sterling, John, 10–11
Stevenson, R.L., 105, 179
Stewart, J.I.M., 92
Stewart Cox, Mary, 109
Stoeber, Elias, 177
Stone, Laurence, 130
Stone, Reynolds, 57, 133
Sullivan, Sir Arthur, 5
Summerskill, Lady, 29
Sutherland, Graham, 119
Swift, Dean, 139
Swinburne, A.C., 85, 87, 88
Swinnerton, Frank, 173
Sykes, Christopher, 5
Syriax, Dr, 111, 116

T.S.E., *see* Eliot
Tempest, Marie, 179
Tennyson, Lord, 20, 29, 64–65, 80
Thomas, the Rev., 36
Thorndike, Sybil, 63
Tim, *see* Nugent
Tommy, *see* Lascelles

Trumper, Victor, 76
Tuppy, *see* Headlam
Turner, Charles Tennyson, 3
Turner, Reggie, 111
Twain, Mark, 122
Tynan, Kenneth, 47
Tyrwhitt, Admiral, 152

*Ulysses*, 145

Van Oss, Oliver, 12, 14, 22, 96, 97, 99
*Vice Versa*, 127
Victoria, Queen, 10

Wagner, Richard, 26, 141
Wain, John, 7, 9
Walpole, Horace, 123, 127
Walpole, Robin, 153, 154
Ward, A.W., 102
Waring, Sir Holburt, 88
Warre, Edmond, 14
Watts-Dunton, T., 87, 88
Waugh, Evelyn, 84, 126
Wavell, General, 70
Webb, Beatrice, 26

Webster, John, 18, 19, 21, 23
Wedgwood, Veronica, 180, 181
*Weir of Hermiston*, 105, 107
Wellington, first Duke of, 70, 72
Wellington, seventh Duke of, 72, 183
Wells, C.M., 33
Wells, H.G., 70, 89, 135, 144, 146, 147, 148, 173
Wesker, Arnold, 47, 48
Wheeler-Bennett, J.W., 180
Whiston, the Rev Robert, 95, 97, 106
White, Terence de Vere, 92
Whitworth, A.W., 61
Wilde, Oscar, *passim*
Williams, Sir Griffith, 29
Wilson, D.A., 58
Wilson, John Dover, 79
Wodehouse, P.G., 54, 84, 122, 125
Wolsey, Cardinal, 132
*Women in Love*, 139
Woolf, Leonard, 134
Woolf, Virginia, 70, 100

Yeats, W.B., 94
Young, Andrew, 53